CHRISTIAN HYMNS

FOR

PUBLIC AND PRIVATE WORSHIP.

A

COLLECTION COMPILED BY A COMMITTEE

OF THE

CHESHIRE PASTORAL ASSOCIATION

FIFTY-FIRST EDITION.

BOSTON:
CROSBY, NICHOLS, AND COMPANY,
117 WASHINGTON STREET.
1859.

PREFACE.

The following Collection of Hymns has been compiled by a Committee of the Cheshire Pastoral Association. The work was undertaken to meet the wants of several societies within its own limits, and may not, therefore, have a very extended circulation beyond them; for many compilations already engage public attention and patronage. Our object has been to make a selection embracing a large number and variety of hymns, adapted to all the purposes of public and private worship, and one which at the same time might be furnished at a low price.

We have sought to give it a lyrical character, and thus adapt it to the choir as well as to the pulpit. In pursuance of this idea, a greater variety of metres than usual has been introduced. By selecting also a large amount of introductory and closing hymns for worship, and by paying special regard to the Christian ordinances, to funeral and mourning occasions, to social and domestic worship, and to philanthropic, national, annual, and missionary celebrations, we have endeavoured to provide for wants which have not hitherto been sufficiently considered. Above all, we have made it our chief aim to give an earnest Scriptural tone to the work, by gathering together in one all the noblest strains of devotional poetry from whatever quarter and denomination, provided the sentiments were not inconsistent with our own faith. But if there should appear, here and there, the glimpse of a discarded doctrine, or the remnant of an antiquated creed, let it be remembered how difficult and ungracious a task it is to fetter the free wing of a rapt imagination and enkindled heart, though reason may sometimes pause and judgment condemn.

We have culled from a most extensive field of both the later and the earlier poets, and have introduced not a few hymns of merit, which have appeared in no previous compilation. Slight alterations have occasionally been made, but we have preferred to restore rather than to change. While we have wished to assemble the holy minstrels of every name and church in a loving brotherhood of harmony and devotion, that should make us forget, if possible, while singing the praises of God, the jars and discords of the great Christian family, we have, nevertheless, welcomed with a peculiar delight "the goodly fellowship" of our own sweet singers. We are indebted to the names of Adams, Barbauld, Bowring, Bryant, Bulfinch, Flint, Follen, Frothingham, Furness, Gilman, Moore, Norton, Peabody, Pierpont, and Ware for some of the finest hymns in the English language.

To those friends, who have kindly afforded us their aid in making this compilation, we would here express our thankful acknowledgments.

In the title of the book, we embody our leading idea and purpose in this enterprise, which have been to provide a collection, not of Jewish psalms or elegant songs, but essentially Christian hymns, pitched, so to say, after the grand master-tone of our faith, whatever intermingling subordinate notes they might have of joy or sorrow, encouragement or warning, praise or confession. We have striven that the high doctrines, duties, and promises of our holy religion might shine forth from these pages in their noon-day distinctness, and arrayed in all the charms of taste and melody, that the great Master might be honored with the love of his disciples, and the greater Father worshipped with the fervent adoration, praise, and thanksgiving of his children.

L. W. L.
W. A. W.
C. C.
A. A. L.

January 29, 1845.

GENERAL INDEX OF SUBJECTS.

TABLE OF FIRST LINES.

PARTICULAR INDEX OF SUBJECTS.

TABLE OF METRES.

INDEX OF AUTHORS AND SOURCES.

CHRISTIAN HYMNS.

INTRODUCTION OF WORSHIP, AND THE SABBATH.

1. 6 & 4s. M. ANONYMOUS.

Solemn Invocation.

1 COME, thou Almighty King!
Help us thy name to sing;
Help us to praise!
Father all-glorious,
O'er all victorious,
Come and reign over us,
Ancient of Days!

2 Come, thou all-gracious Lord!
By heaven and earth adored,
Our prayer attend!
Come, and thy children bless;
Give thy good word success;
Make thine own holiness
On us descend!

3 Never from us depart;
Rule thou in every heart,
Hence, evermore!

Thy sovereign majesty
May we in glory see,
And to eternity
Love and adore.

2. 8 & 7s. M. Wesley's Coll.

Divine Love.

1 LOVE divine, all love excelling,
Joy of heaven to earth come down!
Fix in us thy humble dwelling,
All thy faithful mercies crown.
Father! thou art all compassion,
Pure, unbounded love thou art;
Visit us with thy salvation,
Enter every longing heart.

2 Breathe, O, breathe thy loving spirit
Into every troubled breast;
Let us all in thee inherit,
Let us find thy promised rest.
Come, almighty to deliver,
Let us all thy life receive,
Graciously come down, and never,
Never more thy temples leave.

3. L. M. Tate & Brady

All exhorted to Adoration and Praise.

1 WITH one consent, let all the earth
To God their cheerful voices raise;
Glad homage pay, with hallowed mirth,
And sing before him songs of praise; —

2 Assured that he is God alone,
From whom both we and all proceed, —
We whom he chooses for his own,
The flock which he delights to feed.

3 O, enter, then, his temple gate;
Thence to his courts devoutly press;
And still your grateful hymns repeat,
And still his name with praises bless:

4 For he 's the Lord, supremely good;
His mercy is for ever sure;
His truth, which always firmly stood,
To endless ages shall endure.

4. C. M. MRS. FOLLEN.

Love of Sabbath Service.

1 HOW sweet, upon this sacred day,
The best of all the seven,
To cast our earthly thoughts away,
And think of God and heaven!

2 How sweet to be allowed to pray
Our sins may be forgiven!
With filial confidence to say,
"Father, who art in heaven!"

3 How sweet the words of peace to hear
From him to whom 't is given
To wake the penitential tear,
And lead the way to heaven!

4 And if to make our sins depart
In vain the will has striven,
He who regards the inmost heart
Will send his grace from heaven.

5 Then hail, thou sacred, blessèd day,
The best of all the seven,
When hearts unite their vows to pay
Of gratitude to Heaven!

5. S. M. WATTS.

Exhortation to Praise.

1 COME, sound his praise abroad,
And hymns of glory sing:

Jehovah is the sovereign God,
  The universal King.

2 Come, worship at his throne ;
  Come, bow before the Lord ;
We are his work and not our own ;
  He formed us by his word.

3 To-day attend his voice,
  Nor dare provoke his rod ;
Come, like the people of his choice,
  And own your gracious God.

6. L. M. 6 L. HEBER

Seeking Refuge.

1 FORTH from the dark and stormy sky,
Lord, to thine altar's shade we fly ;
Forth from the world, its hope and fear,
Father, we seek thy shelter here :
Weary and weak, thy grace we pray ;
Turn not, O Lord, thy guests away.

2 Long have we roamed in want and pain ;
Long have we sought thy rest in vain ;
Wildered in doubt, in darkness lost,
Long have our souls been tempest-tost .
Low at thy feet our sins we lay ;
Turn not, O Lord, thy guests away.

7. L. M. RAFFLES

The Hour of Prayer.

1 BLEST hour, when mortal man retires
  To hold communion with his God,
To send to heaven his warm desires,
  And listen to the sacred word.

2 Blest hour, when earthly cares resign
  Their empire o'er his anxious breast,
While, all around, the calm divine
  Proclaims the holy day of rest.

3 Blest hour, when God himself draws nigh,
Well pleased his people's voice to hear,
To hush the penitential sigh,
And wipe away the mourner's tear.

4 Blest hour! for where the Lord resorts
Foretastes of future bliss are given,
And mortals find his earthly courts
The house of God, the gate of heaven.

8. S. M. E. TAYLOR

Invitation to the House of God.

1 COME to the house of prayer,
O thou afflicted, come;
The God of peace shall meet thee there,
He makes that house his home.

2 Come to the house of praise,
Ye who are happy now;
In sweet accord your voices raise,
In kindred homage bow.

3 Ye aged, hither come,
For ye have felt his love;
Soon shall your trembling tongues be dumb,
Your lips forget to move.

4 Ye young, before his throne,
Come, bow; your voices raise;
Let not your hearts his praise disown
Who gives the power to praise.

5 Thou, whose benignant eye
In mercy looks on all,
Who seest the tear of misery,
And hear'st the mourner's call,—

6 Up to thy dwelling-place
Bear our frail spirits on,
Till they outstrip time's tardy pace.
And heaven on earth be won.

9. C. M. H. M. Williams

Habitual Devotion.

1 WHILE thee I seek, protecting Power,
Be my vain wishes stilled;
And may this consecrated hour
With better hopes be filled.

2 Thy love the power of thought bestowed;
To thee my thoughts would soar;
Thy mercy o'er my life has flowed;
That mercy I adore.

3 In each event of life, how clear
Thy ruling hand I see!
Each blessing to my soul more dear,
Because conferred by thee.

4 In every joy that crowns my days,
In every pain I bear,
My heart shall find delight in praise,
Or seek relief in prayer.

5 When gladness wings my favored hour,
Thy love my thoughts shall fill;
Resigned, when storms of sorrow lower,
My soul shall meet thy will.

6 My lifted eye, without a tear,
The gathering storm shall see;
My steadfast heart shall know no fear;
That heart shall rest on thee.

10. L. M. E. Taylor

The Lord's Day.

1 O FATHER, though the anxious fear
May cloud to-morrow's doubtful way,
Nor fear nor doubt shall enter here;
All shall be thine at least to-day.

2 We will not bring divided hearts
To worship at thy sacred shrine;

But each unholy thought departs,
And leaves the temple wholly thine.

3 O Father, God below, above!
Man's noblest work is praising thee;
Thy spirit o'er our hearts shall move,
And tune them all to harmony.

11. C. M. BARBAULD.

The Sabbath of the Soul.

1 SLEEP, sleep to-day, tormenting cares,
Of earth and folly born;
Ye shall not dim the light that streams
From this celestial morn.

2 To-morrow will be time enough
To feel your harsh control;
Ye shall not violate this day,
The Sabbath of my soul.

3 Sleep, sleep for ever, guilty thoughts;
Let fires of vengeance die;
And, purged from sin, may I behold
A God of purity!

12. S. M. BULFINCH

Sabbath Worship.

1 HAIL to the Sabbath day!
The day divinely given,
When men to God their homage pay,
And earth draws near to heaven.

2 Lord, in this sacred hour
Within thy courts we bend,
And bless thy love, and own thy power,
Our Father and our Friend.

3 But thou art not alone
In courts by mortals trod;

Nor only is the day thine own
When man draws near to God.

4 Thy temple is the arch
Of yon unmeasured sky ;
Thy Sabbath, the stupendous march
Of grand eternity.

5 Lord, may that holier day
Dawn on thy servants' sight ;
And purer worship may we pay
In heaven's unclouded light.

13. H. M. COTTERILL

The Resurrection celebrated.

1 AWAKE, ye saints, awake,
And hail the sacred day ;
In loftiest songs of praise
Your joyful homage pay ;
Come bless the day | The type of heaven's
That God hath blest, | Eternal rest.

2 On this auspicious morn
The Lord of life arose,
And burst the bars of death,
And vanquished all our foes ;
And now he pleads | And reaps the fruit
Our cause above, | Of all his love.

3 All hail, triumphant Lord !
Heaven with hosannas rings ;
And earth, in humbler strains,
Thy praise responsive sings ;
Worthy the Lamb, | Through endless years
That once was slain, | To live and reign.

14. L. M. BARBAULD.

The Sacrifice of the Heart.

1 WHEN, as returns this solemn day,
Man comes to meet his Maker, God.

What rites, what honors, shall he pay ?
How spread his sovereign name abroad ?

2 From marble domes and gilded spires
Shall curling clouds of incense rise,
And gems, and gold, and garlands, deck
The costly pomp of sacrifice ?

3 Vain, sinful man ! creation's Lord
Thy golden offerings well may spare ,
But give thy heart, and thou shalt find
Here dwells a God who heareth prayer.

4 O, grant us, in this solemn hour,
From earth and sin's allurements free,
To feel thy love, to own thy power,
And raise each raptured thought to thee !

15. 7s. M. 6 L. NEWTON.

The Sabbath in the Sanctuary.

1 SAFELY through another week
God has brought us on our way ;
Let us now a blessing seek,
Waiting in his courts to-day, —
Day of all the week the best,
Emblem of eternal rest.

2 While we seek supplies of grace,
Through the dear Redeemer's name,
Show thy reconciling face,
Take away our sin and shame ;
From our worldly cares set free,
May we rest, this day, in thee.

3 Here we come thy name to praise ;
Let us feel thy presence near ;
May thy glory meet our eyes,
While we in thy house appear ;
Here afford us, Lord, a taste
Of our everlasting feast.

4 May the gospel's joyful sound
Conquer sinners, comfort saints,
Make the fruits of grace abound,
Bring relief from all complaints :
Thus let all our Sabbaths prove,
Till we join the church above.

16. L. M. WATTS.

Praise to our Creator.

1 YE nations round the earth, rejoice
Before the Lord, your sovereign King
Serve him with cheerful heart and voice ;
With all your tongues his glory sing.

2 The Lord is God ; 't is he alone
Doth life, and breath, and being give ;
We are his work, and not our own,
The sheep that on his pastures live.

3 Enter his gates with songs of joy ;
With praises to his courts repair ;
And make it your divine employ
To pay your thanks and honors there

4 The Lord is good ; the Lord is kind ;
Great is his grace, his mercy sure ;
And all the race of man shall find
His truth from age to age endure.

17. S. M. WATTS

The Sabbath welcomed.

1 WELCOME, sweet day of rest,
That saw the Lord arise ;
Welcome to this reviving breast
And these rejoicing eyes.

2 The King himself comes near,
And feasts his saints to-day ;
Here we may sit, and see him here,
And love, and praise, and pray.

3 One day amid the place
Where Christ, my Lord, has been
Is sweeter than ten thousand days
Of pleasure and of sin.

4 My willing soul would stay
In such a frame as this,
Till called to rise and soar away
To everlasting bliss.

18. S. P. M. WATTS

Delight in the House of God.

1 HOW pleased and blest was I
To hear the people cry,
"Come, let us seek our God to-day!"
Yes, with a cheerful zeal,
We haste to Zion's hill,
And there our vows and honors pay.

2 Zion, thrice happy place,
Adorned with wondrous grace,
And walls of strength embrace thee round,
In thee our tribes appear,
To pray, and praise, and hear
The sacred gospel's joyful sound.

3 May peace attend thy gate,
And joy within thee wait,
To bless the soul of every guest;
The man who seeks thy peace,
And wishes thine increase,
A thousand blessings on him rest.

19. L. M. WATTS.

The Sovereign Jehovah.

1 BEFORE Jehovah's awful throne,
Ye nations bow with sacred joy;
Know that the Lord is God alone;
He can create and he destroy.

2 His sovereign power, without our aid,
Made us of clay, and formed us men ;
And when, like wandering sheep, we strayed,
He brought us to his fold again.

3 We are his people ; we his care ;
Our souls, and all our mortal frame :
What lasting honors shall we rear,
Almighty Maker, to thy name ?

4 We 'll crowd thy gates, with thankful songs,
High as the heaven our voices raise ;
And Earth, with her ten thousand tongues,
Shall fill thy courts with sounding praise.

5 Wide as the world is thy command ;
Vast as eternity thy love ;
Firm as a rock thy truth shall stand,
When rolling years shall cease to move.

20. C. M. BARBAULD

The Lord's Day Morning.

1 AGAIN the Lord of life and light
Awakes the kindling ray,
Unseals the eyelids of the morn,
And pours increasing day.

2 O, what a night was that which wrapt
The heathen world in gloom !
O, what a sun, which broke, this day
Triumphant from the tomb !

3 This day be grateful homage paid,
And loud hosannas sung ;
Let gladness dwell in every heart,
And praise on every tongue.

4 Ten thousand differing lips shall join
To hail this welcome morn ;
Which scatters blessings from its wings
To nations yet unborn.

21. 7s. M. MONTGOMERY.

Prayer for a Blessing on Public Worship.

1 TO thy temple we repair ;
Lord, we love to worship there ;
While to thee our prayers ascend
Let thine ear in love attend ;

2 While thy glorious name is sung,
Tune our lips, inspire our tongue ;
Then our joyful souls shall bless
Christ, the Lord our Righteousness.

3 While thy word is heard with awe,
While we tremble at thy law,
Let thy gospel's wondrous love
Every doubt and fear remove.

4 From thy house when we return,
Let our hearts within us burn ;
Then, at evening, we may say,
"We have walked with God to-day"

22. L. M. TATE & BRADY

Public Worship.

1 O, COME, loud anthems let us sing,
Loud thanks to our Almighty King ;
For we our voices high should raise,
When our salvation's Rock we praise

2 Into his presence let us haste,
To thank him for his favors past ;
To him address, in joyful songs,
The praise that to his name belongs.

3 O, let us to his courts repair,
And bow with adoration there ;
Down on our knees devoutly all
Before the Lord, our Maker, fall !

23. L. M. SALISBURY COLL.

The House of God.

1 LO, God is here! Let us adore,
And humbly bow before his face;
Let all within us feel his power,
Let all within us seek his grace.

2 Lo, God is here! Him, day and night,
United choirs of angels sing;
To him, enthroned above all height,
Heaven's host their noblest homage bring

3 Being of beings, may our praise
Thy courts with grateful fragrance fill!
Still may we stand before thy face,
Still hear and do thy sovereign will!

24. C. M. WATTS

Longing for the House of God.

1 EARLY, my God, without delay,
I haste to seek thy face;
My thirsty spirit faints away
Without thy cheering grace.

2 So pilgrims on the scorching sand,
Beneath a burning sky,
Long for a cooling stream at hand;
And they must drink, or die.

3 Not life itself, with all its joys,
Can my best passions move,
Or raise so high my cheerful voice,
As thy forgiving love.

4 Thus, till my last, expiring day,
I'll bless my God and King;
Thus will I lift my hands to pray,
And tune my lips to sing.

25. S. M. Urwick's Coll

Pleasures of Spiritual Worship.

1 HOW sweet to bless the Lord,
And in his praises join,
With saints his goodness to record,
And sing his power divine!

2 These seasons of delight
The dawn of glory seem,
Like rays of pure, celestial light,
Which on our spirits beam.

3 O, blest assurance this;
Bright morn of heavenly day;
Sweet foretaste of eternal bliss,
That cheers the pilgrim's way.

4 Thus may our joys increase,
Our love more ardent grow,
While rich supplies of Jesus' grace
Refresh our souls below.

26. L. M. Pierpont

Worship acceptable from every Place.

1 O THOU, to whom, in ancient time,
The lyre of Hebrew bards was strung,
Whom kings adored in songs sublime,
And prophets praised with glowing tongue.

2 Not now on Zion's height alone
Thy favored worshipper may dwell,
Nor where, at sultry noon, thy Son
Sat, weary, by the patriarch's well.

3 From every place below the skies,
The grateful song, the fervent prayer,
The incense of the heart, may rise
To heaven, and find acceptance there.

4 O Thou, to whom, in ancient time,
The lyre of prophet-bards was strung,

To thee, at last, in every clime,
Shall temples rise and praise be sung.

27. 7s. M. J. Taylor.

The acceptable Worship.

1 FATHER of our feeble race,
Wise, beneficent, and kind,
Spread o'er nature's ample face
Flows thy goodness unconfined:
Musing in the silent grove,
Or the busy walks of men,
Still we trace thy wondrous love,
Claiming large returns again.

2 Lord, what offerings shall we bring,
At thine altars when we bow?
Hearts, the pure, unsullied spring
Whence the kind affections flow;
Soft compassion's feeling soul,
By the melting eye expressed;
Sympathy, at whose control
Sorrow leaves the wounded breast;—

3 Willing hands to lead the blind,
Heal the wounded, feed the poor;
Love, embracing all our kind;
Charity, with liberal store:
Teach us, O thou Heavenly King,
Thus to show our grateful mind,
Thus th' accepted offering bring,—
Love to thee and all mankind.

28. C. M. Rippon's Coll.

Worship.

1 HOLY and reverend is the name
Of our Eternal King;
"Thrice holy Lord!" the angels cry;
"Thrice holy!" let us sing.

2 The deepest reverence of the mind
Pay, O my soul, to God ;
Lift with thy hands a holy heart
To his sublime abode.

3 With sacred awe pronounce his name,
Whom words nor thoughts can reach :
A contrite heart will please him more
Than the best forms of speech.

4 Thou holy God ! preserve my soul
From all pollution free ;
The pure in heart are thy delight,
And they thy face shall see.

29. S. M. SPIRIT OF THE PSALMS.

Enjoyment in Worship.

1 SWEET is the task, O Lord,
Thy glorious acts to sing,
To praise thy name, and hear thy word,
And grateful offerings bring.

2 Sweet, at the dawning hour,
Thy boundless love to tell ;
And, when the night-wind shuts the flower,
Still on the theme to dwell.

3 Sweet, on this day of rest,
To join, in heart and voice,
With those who love and serve thee best,
And in thy name rejoice.

4 To songs of praise and joy
Be every Sabbath given,
That such may be our blest employ
Eternally in heaven.

30. C. M. BOWRING

Pure Worship.

1 THE offerings to thy throne which rise,
Of mingled praise and prayer,

Are but a worthless sacrifice
  Unless the heart is there.

2 Upon thine all-discerning ear
  Let no vain words intrude;
No tribute but the vow sincere,—
  The tribute of the good.

3 My offerings will indeed be blest,
  If sanctified by thee,—
If thy pure spirit touch my breast
  With its own purity.

4 O, may that spirit warm my heart
  To piety and love,
And to life's lowly vale impart
  Some rays from heaven above!

31. L. M. WATTS.

Delight in the Sabbath.

1 SWEET is the work, my God, my King,
To praise thy name, give thanks, and sing;
To show thy love by morning light,
And talk of all thy truth at night.

2 Sweet is the day of sacred rest;
No mortal care shall seize my breast;
O, may my heart in tune be found,
Like David's harp of solemn sound!

3 My heart shall triumph in my Lord,
And bless his works, and bless his word,
Thy works of grace, how bright they shine!
How deep thy counsels! how divine!

4 When shall I see, and hear, and know,
All I desired or wished below,
And every power find sweet employ
In an eternal world of joy?

32. C. M. WATTS.

Anticipating Worship.

1 LORD, in the morning thou shalt hear
My voice ascending high ;
To thee will I direct my prayer,
To thee lift up mine eye.

2 Thou art a God before whose sight
The wicked shall not stand ;
Sinners shall ne'er be thy delight,
Nor dwell at thy right hand.

3 But to thy house will I resort,
To taste thy mercies there ;
I will frequent thine holy court,
And worship in thy fear.

4 O, may thy spirit guide my feet
In ways of righteousness,
Make every path of duty straight
And plain before my face.

33. C. M. H. WARE, JR.

Invoking God's Aid.

1 FATHER in heaven, to thee my heart
Would lift itself in prayer ;
Drive from my soul each earthly thought,
And show thy presence there.

2 Each moment of my life renews
The mercies of my Lord,
Each moment is itself a gift
To bear me on to God.

3 O, help me break the galling chains
This world has round me thrown,
Each passion of my heart subdue,
Each darling sin disown.

4 O Father, kindle in my breast
A never-dying flame

Of holy love, of grateful trust
In thine almighty name.

34. L. M. STENNETT

Holy Enjoyment anticipated.

1 ANOTHER six days' work is done,
Another Sabbath is begun ;
Return, my soul, enjoy thy rest,
Improve the day that God hath blest.

2 O, that our thoughts and thanks may rise,
As grateful incense, to the skies,
And draw from heaven that sweet repose
Which none but he that feels it knows !

3 A heavenly calm pervades the breast,
The earnest of that glorious rest
Which for the church of God remains,
The end of cares, the end of pains.

4 With joy, great God, thy works we view,
In various scenes, both old and new ;
With praise, we think on mercies past ;
With hope, we future pleasures taste.

5 In holy duties let the day,
In holy pleasures, pass away ;
How sweet a Sabbath thus to spend,
In hope of one that ne'er shall end !

35. C. M. EDMESTON

The Lord's Day Morning.

1 WHEN the worn spirit wants repose,
And sighs her God to seek,
How sweet to hail the evening's close,
That ends the weary week !

2 How sweet to hail the early dawn,
That opens on the sight,
When first that soul-reviving morn
Sheds forth new rays of light !

3 Sweet day! thine hours too soon will cease,
Yet, while they gently roll,
Breathe, Heavenly Spirit, source of peace,
A Sabbath o'er my soul!

4 When will my pilgrimage be done,
The world's long week be o'er,
That Sabbath dawn which needs no sun,
That day, which fades no more?

36. L. M. DODDRIDGE.

The eternal Sabbath.

1 LORD of the Sabbath, hear our vows,
On this thy day, in this thy house,
And own, as grateful sacrifice,
The songs which from thy churches rise.

2 Thine earthly Sabbaths, Lord, we love;
But there 's a nobler rest above;
To that our longing souls aspire,
With earnest hope and strong desire.

3 No more fatigue, no more distress,
Nor sin, nor death, shall reach the place;
No groans to mingle with the songs
Which warble from immortal tongues; —

4 No rude alarms of raging foes;
No cares to break the long repose;
No midnight shade, no clouded sun,
But sacred, high, eternal noon.

5 O long-expected day, begin!
Dawn on these realms of woe and sin;
Fain would we leave this weary road,
And sleep in death to rest with God.

37. 7s. M. BOWRING

Lowly Praise.

1 LORD, in heaven, thy dwelling-place,
Hear the praises of our race,

And, while hearing, let thy grace
 Dews of sweet forgiveness pour;
While we know, benignant King,
That the praises which we bring
Are a worthless offering
 Till thy blessing makes it more.

2 More of truth, and more of might,
More of love, and more of light,
More of reason, and of right,
 From thy pardoning grace be given!
It can make the humblest song
Sweet, acceptable, and strong,
As the strains the angels' throng
 Pour around the throne of heaven.

38. L. M. CHRISTIAN PSALMIST

Amidst Temptation.

1 MY gracious Lord, whose changeless love
 To me nor earth nor death can part,
When shall my feet forget to rove?
 Ah, what shall fix this faithless heart?

2 Cold, weary, languid, heartless, dead,
 To thy dread courts I oft repair;
By conscience dragged, or custom led,
 I come, nor know that God is there.

3 O God, thy sovereign aid impart,
 And guard the gifts thyself hast given;
My portion thou, my treasure, art,
 And life, and happiness, and heaven.

4 Would aught with thee my wishes share,
 Though dear as life the idol be,
The idol from my breast I 'll tear,
 Resolved to seek my all from thee.

39. S. M. WATTS

Call to joyous Worship.

1 COME, we that love the Lord,
And let our joys be known ;
Join in a song with sweet accord,
And thus surround the throne.

2 The sorrows of the mind
Be banished from the place ;
Religion never was designed
To make our pleasures less.

3 The men of grace have found
Glory begun below ;
Celestial fruits on earthly ground
From faith and hope may grow.

4 Then let our songs abound,
And every tear be dry ;
We 're marching through Immanuel's ground,
To fairer worlds on high.

40. L. M. BOWRING.

Introduction to Evening Worship.

1 HOW shall we praise thee, Lord of light !
How shall we all thy love declare !
The earth is veiled in shades of night,
But heaven is open to our prayer, —
That heaven, so bright with stars and suns, —
That glorious heaven which has no bound,
Where the full tide of being runs,
And life and beauty glow around.

2 We would adore thee, God sublime,
Whose power and wisdom, love and grace,
Are greater than the round of time,
And wider than the bounds of space

O, how shall thought expression find,
All lost in thine immensity!
How shall we seek thee, glorious Mind,
Amid thy dread infinity!

3 But thou art present with us here,
As in thy glittering, high domain;
And grateful hearts and humble fear
Can never seek thy face in vain.
Help us to praise thee, Lord of light;
Help us thy boundless love declare;
And, while we crowd thy courts to-night,
Aid us, and hearken to our prayer.

41. C. M. MONTGOMERY

Preparation of the Heart.

1 LORD, teach us how to pray aright,
With reverence and with fear:
Though dust and ashes in thy sight,
We may, we must, draw near.

2 Burdened with guilt, convinced of sin,
In weakness, want, and woe,
Fightings without, and fears within,
Lord, whither shall we go?

3 God of all grace, we come to thee,
With broken, contrite hearts;
Give what thine eye delights to see,—
Truth in the inward parts.

4 Give deep humility; the sense
Of godly sorrow give;
A strong, desiring confidence,
To hear thy voice and live;—

5 Patience, to watch, and wait, and weep,
Though mercy long delay;
Courage, our fainting souls to keep,
And trust thee, though thou slay.

6 Give these, and then thy will be done;
Thus, strengthened with all might,
We, by thy spirit and thy Son,
Shall pray, and pray aright.

42. S. M. MONTGOMERY.

The Lord's Prayer.

OUR Heavenly Father, hear
The prayer we offer now:
Thy name be hallowed far and near,
To thee all nations bow.

2 Thy kingdom come; thy will
On earth be done in love,
As saints and seraphim fulfil
Thy perfect law above.

3 Our daily bread supply,
While by thy word we live;
The guilt of our iniquity
Forgive as we forgive.

4 From dark temptation's power
Our feeble hearts defend;
Deliver in the evil hour,
And guide us to the end.

5 Thine, then, for ever be
Glory and power divine;
The sceptre, throne, and majesty
Of heaven and earth are thine.

43. L. M. M. W. HALE.

The Day of Rest.

1 THIS day let grateful praise ascend
To thee, our Father and our Friend,
Thee, Author of this holy light,
Thee, throned in boundless power and might.

2 O, let the sacred hours be given
To truth, to duty, and to heaven;

While trusting faith and holy love
Rise fervent to thy throne above.

3 Grant that our earthly Sabbaths be
But dawnings of eternity,
To shadow forth the glorious rest,
The heavenly quiet, of the blest.

44. C. M. JERVIS

Homage and Devotion.

1 WITH sacred joy we lift our eyes
To those bright realms above,
That glorious temple in the skies,
Where dwells eternal love.

2 Before the gracious throne we bow
Of heaven's Almighty King;
Here we present the solemn vow,
And hymns of praise we sing.

3 O Lord, while in thy house we kneel
With trust and holy fear,
Thy mercy and thy truth reveal,
And lend a gracious ear.

4 With fervor teach our hearts to pray,
And tune our lips to sing;
Nor from thy presence cast away
The sacrifice we bring.

45. L. M. SIR J. E. SMITH

Devout Worship of God.

1 PRAISE waits in Zion, Lord, for thee;
Thy saints adore thy holy name;
Thy creatures bend th' obedient knee,
And, humbly, thy protection claim.

2 Thy hand has raised us from the dust;
The breath of life thy spirit gave;
Where, but in thee, can mortals trust?
Who, but our God, has power to save?

3 Eternal Source of truth and light,
To thee we look, on thee we call;
Lord, we are nothing in thy sight,
But thou to us art all in all.

4 Still may thy children in thy word
Their common trust and refuge see;
O, bind us to each other, Lord,
By one great tie, — the love of thee.

5 So shall our sun of hope arise,
With brighter still and brighter ray,
Till thou shalt bless our longing eyes
With beams of everlasting day.

46. 7s. M. J. TAYLOR.

Engagedness in Devotion.

1 LORD, before thy presence come,
Bow we down with holy fear;
Call our erring footsteps home,
Let us feel that thou art near.

2 Wandering thoughts and languid powers
Come not where devotion kneels;
Let the soul expand her stores,
Glowing with the joy she feels.

3 At the portals of thine house,
We resign our earth-born cares:
Nobler thoughts our souls engross,
Songs of praise and fervent prayers.

47. L. M. FROTHINGHAM.

Truth and Love.

1 O GOD, whose presence glows in all
Within, around us, and above!
Thy word we bless, thy name we call,
Whose word is truth, whose name is love.

2 That truth be with the heart believed
Of all who seek this sacred place;

With power proclaimed, in peace received,
Our spirit's light, thy spirit's grace.

3 That love its holy influence pour,
To keep us meek and make us free,
And throw its binding blessings more
Round each with all, and all with thee.

4 Send down its angel to our side, —
Send in its calm upon the breast ;
For we would know no other guide,
And we can need no other rest.

48. H. M. WATTS.

Longing for the House of God.

1 LORD of the worlds above !
How pleasant and how fair
The dwellings of thy love,
Thine earthly temples, are !
To thine abode | With warm desires
My heart aspires, | To see my God.

2 O happy souls, who pray
Where God appoints to hear !
O happy men, who pay
Their constant service there !
They praise thee still ; | Who love the way
And happy they | To Zion's hill.

3 They go from strength to strength,
Through this dark vale of tears,
Till each arrives at length,
Till each in heaven appears :
O glorious seat, | Shall thither bring
When God, our King, | Our willing feet.

49. 8 & 7s. M. J. TAYLOR.

The Fount of Blessing.

1 FAR from mortal cares retreating,
Sordid hopes, and vain desires,

Here, our willing footsteps meeting,
  Every heart to heaven aspires.

2 From the fount of glory beaming,
  Light celestial cheers our eyes,
Mercy from above proclaiming,
  Peace and pardon from the skies.

3 Who may share this great salvation ?
  Every pure and humble mind,
Every kindred, tongue, and nation,
  From the stains of guilt refined.

4 Blessings all around bestowing,
  God withholds his care from none,
Grace and mercy ever flowing
  From the fountain of his throne.

50. C. M. MONTGOMERY.

Introduction to Evening Worship.

1 ON the first Christian Sabbath eve,
  When his disciples met
O'er his lost fellowship to grieve,
  Nor knew the Scripture yet, —

2 Lo ! in their midst his form was seen,
  The form in which he died ;
Their Master's marred and wounded mien, —
  His hands, his feet, his side.

3 Then were they glad their Lord to know,
  And hailed him yet with fear ; —
Jesus, again thy presence show :
  Meet thy disciples here.

4 Be in our midst ; let faith rejoice
  Our risen Lord to view,
And make our spirits hear thy voice
  Say, " Peace be unto you ! "

5 And while with thee, in social hours.
  We commune through thy word,

May our hearts burn, and all our powers
Confess, "It is the Lord."

51. L. M. WATTS

Blessedness of worshipping God in his Temple.

1 HOW pleasant, how divinely fair,
O Lord of hosts, thy dwellings are!
With long desire my spirit faints
To meet th' assemblies of thy saints.

2 Blest are the saints, who dwell on high,
Around thy throne, above the sky;
Thy brightest glories shine above,
And all their work is praise and love.

3 Blest are the souls who find a place
Within the temple of thy grace;
There they behold thy gentler rays,
And seek thy face, and learn thy praise.

4 Blest are the men whose hearts are set
To find the way to Zion's gate;
God is their strength; and, through the road,
They lean upon their helper, God.

5 Cheerful they walk, with growing strength,
Till all shall meet in heaven at length;
Till all before thy face appear,
And join in nobler worship there.

52. C. M. PRESBYTERIAN COLL.

Prayer for special Favor.

1 WITHIN thy house, O Lord, our God,
In glory now appear;
Make this a place of thine abode,
And shed thy blessings here.

2 When we thy mercy-seat surround,
Thy spirit, Lord, impart;
And let thy gospel's joyful sound
With power reach every heart.

3 Here let the blind their sight obtain ;
Here give the mourners rest ;
Let Jesus here triumphant reign,
Enthroned in every breast.

4 Here let the voice of sacred joy
And humble prayer arise,
Till higher strains our tongues employ
In realms beyond the skies.

53. 7s. M. BOWRING

Humble Worship.

1 WHEN before thy throne we kneel,
Filled with awe and holy fear,
Teach us, O our God, to feel
All thy sacred presence near.

2 Check each proud and wandering thought
When on thy great name we call ;
Man is naught, is less than naught ;
Thou, our God, art all in all.

3 Weak, imperfect creatures, we
In this vale of darkness dwell,
Yet presume to look to thee
'Midst thy light ineffable.

4 O, receive the praise that dares
Seek thy heaven-exalted throne ;
Bless our offerings, hear our prayers,
Infinite and Holy One !

54. C. P. M. MERRI :K

The Sabbath and the Sanctuary.

1 THE festal morn, my God, is come,
That calls me to thy sacred dome,
Thy presence to adore :
My feet the summons shall attend,
With willing steps thy courts ascend,
And tread the hallowed floor.

2 With holy joy I hail the day,
That warns my thirsting soul away;
What transports fill my breast!
For, lo! my great Redeemer's power
Unfolds the everlasting door,
And leads me to his rest!

3 Hither, from earth's remotest end,
Lo! the redeemed of God ascend,
Their tribute hither bring;
Here, crowned with everlasting joy,
In hymns of praise their tongues employ,
And hail th' immortal King.

55. L. M. New York Coll.

Sabbath Day.

1 WE bless thee for this sacred day,
Thou who hast every blessing given,
Which sends the dreams of earth away,
And yields a glimpse of opening heaven.

2 Lord, in this day of holy rest,
We would improve the calm repose;
And, in thy service truly blest,
Forget the world, its joys and woes.

3 Lord, may thy truth upon the heart
Now fall and dwell as heavenly dew,
And flowers of grace in freshness start
Where once the weeds of error grew.

4 May prayer now lift her sacred wings,
Contented with that aim alone
Which bears her to the King of kings,
And rests her at his sheltering throne.

56. L. M. H. Ware, Jr

Supplication.

1 GREAT God, the followers of thy Son,
We bow before thy mercy-seat,

To worship thee, the Holy One,
And pour our wishes at thy feet.

2 O, grant thy blessing here to-day!
O, give thy people joy and peace!
The tokens of thy love display,
And favor that shall never cease.

3 We seek the truth which Jesus brought;
His path of light we long to tread;
Here be his holy doctrines taught,
And here their purest influence shed.

4 May faith and hope and love abound;
Our sins and errors be forgiven;
And we, in thy great day, be found
Children of God, and heirs of heaven.

57. C. M. ANONYMOUS

A Sabbath Morning.

1 HOW sweet, how calm, this Sabbath morn!
How pure the air that breathes,
And soft the sounds upon it borne,
And light its vapor wreaths!

2 It seems as if the Christian's prayer,
For peace and joy and love,
Were answered by the very air
That wafts its strain above.

3 Let each unholy passion cease,
Each evil thought be crushed,
Each anxious care that mars thy peace
In Faith and Love be hushed.

CLOSE OF WORSHIP.

58. 7s. M. H K. WHITE

Praise to God.

1 CHRISTIANS, brethren, ere we part,
Every voice and every heart
Join, and to our Father raise
One last hymn of grateful praise.

2 Though we here should meet no more,
Yet there is a brighter shore;
There, released from toil and pain,
There we all may meet again.

3 Now to Him who reigns in heaven
Be eternal glory given!
Grateful for thy love divine,
O, may all our hearts be thine!

59. L. M. WATTS

Ascription.

1 FROM all that dwell below the skies
Let the Creator's praise arise;
Let the Redeemer's name be sung,
Through every land, by every tongue.

2 Eternal are thy mercies, Lord;
Eternal truth attends thy word:
Thy praise shall sound from shore to shore,
Till suns shall rise and set no more.

60. 8 & 7s., or 8, 7, & 4s. M. BURDER.

Dismission.

1 LORD, dismiss us with thy blessing;
Fill our hearts with joy and peace;
Let us each, thy peace possessing,
Triumph in redeeming grace:

O, refresh us,
Travelling through this wilderness.

2 Thanks we give, and adoration,
For the gospel's joyful sound ;
May the fruits of thy salvation
In our hearts and lives abound :
May thy presence
With us evermore be found.

61. S. M. WATTS

The Spread of Truth.

1 THY name, almighty Lord,
Shall sound through distant lands :
Great is thy grace, and sure thy word ;
Thy truth for ever stands.

2 Far be thine honor spread,
And long thy praise endure,
Till morning light and evening shade
Shall be exchanged no more.

62. 8 & 7s. M. NEWTON.

Prayer for a Blessing.

1 MAY the grace of Christ, our Saviour,
And the Father's boundless love,
With the Holy Spirit's favor,
Rest upon us from above.

2 Thus may we abide in union
With each other and the Lord,
And possess, in sweet communion,
Joys which earth cannot afford.

63. 7s. M. COWPER.

Hymn of Benediction.

1 NOW may he who from the dead
Brought the Shepherd of the sheep,
Jesus Christ, our King and Head,
All our souls in safety keep.

2 May he teach us to fulfil
What is pleasing in his sight,
Perfect us in all his will,
And preserve us day and night!

64. 7s. M. Anonymous

A Blessing implored.

1 THANKS for mercies past receive;
Pardon of our sins renew;
Teach us, henceforth, how to live
With eternity in view.

2 Bless thy word to old and young;
Grant us, Lord, thy peace and love;
And, when life's short race is run,
Take us to thy house above.

65. C. M. Watts.

Salvation.

1 SALVATION! O, the joyful sound!
'T is pleasure to our ears,
A sovereign balm for every wound,
A cordial for our fears.

2 Buried in sorrow and in sin,
At death's dark door we lay;
But we arise, by grace divine,
To see a heavenly day.

3 Salvation! let the echo fly
The spacious earth around,
While all the armies of the sky
Conspire to raise the sound.

66. L. M. Edmeston

The Close of the Sabbath.

1 SWEET is the light of Sabbath eve,
And soft the sunbeams lingering there,
For these blest hours the world I leave,
Wafted on wings of faith and prayer.

2 The time how lovely and how still ;
  Peace shines and smiles on all below, —
The plain, the stream, the wood, the hill, —
  All fair with evening's setting glow.

3 Season of rest ! the tranquil soul
  Feels the sweet calm and melts to love, —
And while these sacred moments roll,
  Faith sees a smiling heaven above.

4 Nor will our days of toil be long ;
  Our pilgrimage will soon be trod ;
And we shall join the ceaseless song,
  The endless Sabbath of our God.

67. 8 & 7s. M. FAWCETT

Glory to God.

1 PRAISE to thee, thou great Creator !
  Praise to thee from every tongue !
Join, my soul, with every creature,
  Join the universal song.

2 For ten thousand blessings given,
  For the hope of future joy,
Sound his praise through earth and heaven,
  Sound Jehovah's praise on high !

68. 7s. M. SALISBURY COLL

Prayer for a Blessing.

1 GLORIOUS in thy saints appear ;
Plant thy heavenly kingdom here ;
Light and life to all impart ;
Shine on each believing heart ;—

2 And, in every grace complete,
Make us, Lord, for glory meet ;
Till we stand before thy sight,
Partners with the saints in light.

69. C. M. WATTS.

Triumphant Praise.

1 O, FOR a shout of sacred joy
To God, the sovereign King!
Let every land their tongues employ,
And hymns of triumph sing.

2 While angels shout and praise their King,
Let mortals learn their strains;
Let all the earth his honors sing;
O'er all the earth he reigns.

3 Speak forth his praise with awe profound;
Let knowledge guide the song;
Nor mock him with a solemn sound
Upon a thoughtless tongue.

70. S. M. KELLY.

Rejoicing at the Resurrection of Christ.

1 "THE Lord is risen indeed!"
Attending angels hear;
Up to the courts of heaven, with speed,
The joyful tidings bear.

2 Then wake your golden lyres,
And strike each cheerful chord;
Join, all ye bright celestial choirs,
To sing our risen Lord.

71. L. M. WATTS

The faithful Shepherd.

1 THOUGH I walk through the gloomy vale,
Where death and all its terrors are,
My heart and hope shall never fail,
For God my Shepherd's with me there.

2 Amid the darkness and the deeps,
Thou art my comfort, thou my stay;
Thy staff supports my feeble steps,
Thy rod directs my doubtful way.

72. 7s. M. S. F. Smith

Sabbath Evening.

1 SOFTLY fades the twilight ray
Of the holy Sabbath day;
Gently as life's setting sun,
When the Christian's course is run.

2 Night her solemn mantle spreads
O'er the earth as daylight fades;
All things tell of calm repose
At the holy Sabbath's close.

3 Peace is on the world abroad;
'T is the holy peace of God,—
Symbol of the peace within,
When the spirit rests from sin.

4 Still the Spirit lingers near,
Where the evening worshipper
Seeks communion with the skies,
Pressing onward to the prize.

5 Saviour, may our Sabbaths be
Days of peace and joy in thee,
Till in heaven our souls repose,
Where the Sabbath ne'er shall close.

73. C. M. Cappe's Sel.

Prayer for Divine Direction.

1 ETERNAL Source of life and light!
Supremely good and wise!
To thee we bring our grateful vows,
To thee lift up our eyes.

2 Our dark and erring minds illume
With truth's celestial rays;
Inspire our hearts with sacred love,
And tune our lips to praise.

3 Safely conduct us, by thy grace,
Through life's perplexing road;

And place us, when that journey 's o'er
At thy right hand, O God !

74. 7 & 6s. M. ANONYMOUS

Praise for Salvation.

1 TO thee be praise for ever,
Thou glorious King of kings !
Thy wondrous love and favor
Each ransomed spirit sings.

2 We 'll celebrate thy glory,
With all thy saints above,
And shout the joyful story
Of thy redeeming love.

75. S. M. WATTS

Greatness of God's Mercy.

1 MY soul, repeat His praise
Whose mercies are so great,
Whose anger is so slow to rise,
So ready to abate.

2 His power subdues our sins,
And his forgiving love,
Far as the east is from the west,
Doth all our guilt remove.

3 High as the heavens are raised
Above the ground we tread,
So far the riches of his grace
Our highest thoughts exceed.

76. C. M. WATTS

Praise to God from all Nations.

1 O, ALL ye nations, praise the Lord,
Each with a different tongue ;
In every language learn his word,
And let his name be sung.

2 His mercy reigns through every land ,
Proclaim his grace abroad ;

For ever firm his truth shall stand;
Praise ye the faithful God.

77. S. M. DODDRIDGE

The watchful Servant.

1 YE servants of the Lord,
Each in his office wait;
With joy obey his heavenly word,
And watch before his gate.

2 Let all your lamps be bright,
And trim the golden flame;
Gird up your loins, as in his sight,
For holy is his name.

78. C. M. CHRISTIAN PSALMIST.

The Good Seed.

1 ALMIGHTY God, thy word is cast
Like seed into the ground;
Now let the dew of heaven descend,
And righteous fruits abound.

2 Let not the foe of Christ and man
This holy seed remove;
But give it root in every heart,
To bring forth fruits of love.

79. 7 & 6s. M. (Peculiar.) RIPPON'S COLL

The Soul aspiring to Heaven.

1 RISE, my soul, and stretch thy wings,
Thy better portion trace;
Rise from transitory things
Towards heaven, thy native place.
Sun, and moon, and stars decay;
Time shall soon this earth remove;
Rise, my soul, and haste away
To seats prepared above.

2 Rivers to the ocean run,
Nor stay in all their course ;
Fire, ascending, seeks the sun ;
Both speed them to their source.
So a soul that 's born of God
Pants to view his glorious face ;
Upward tends to his abode,
To rest in his embrace.

80. C. M. MONTGOMERY.

After Divine Service.

1 AGAIN our ears have heard the voice
At which the dead shall live ;
O, may the sound our hearts rejoice,
And strength immortal give !

2 And have we heard the word with joy ?
And have we felt its power ?
To keep it be our blest employ,
Till life's extremest hour.

81. C. M. C. WESLEY

Self-Consecration.

1 ETERNAL Father, God of love,
To thee our hearts we raise ;
Thy all-sustaining power we prove,
And gladly sing thy praise.

2 Thine, wholly thine, O, let us be ;
Our sacrifice receive ;
Made, and preserved, and saved by thee,
To thee ourselves we give.

82. 8 & 7s. M. BICKERSTETH

Closing Hymn.

1 ISRAEL'S Shepherd, guide me, feed me,
Through my pilgrimage below,
And beside the waters lead me,
Where thy flock rejoicing go.

2 Lord, thy guardian presence ever,
Meekly kneeling, I implore;
I have found thee, and would never,
Never wander from thee more.

83. L. M. HEBER

Close of Service.

1 LORD, now we part in thy blest name,
In which we here together came;
Grant us our few remaining days
To work thy will and spread thy praise.

2 Teach us in life and death to bless
The Lord, our strength and righteousness;
And grant us all to meet above;
Then shall we better sing thy love.

84. C. M. WATTS.

A blessed Gospel.

1 BLEST are the souls that hear and know
The gospel's joyful sound;
Peace shall attend the paths they go,
And light their steps surround.

2 Their joy shall bear their spirits up,
Through their Redeemer's name;
His righteousness exalts their hope,
Nor dares the world condemn.

3 The Lord, our glory and defence,
Strength and salvation gives:
Christian, thy King for ever reigns,
Thy God for ever lives.

85. S. M. CAMPBELL'S COLL

Filial Confidence.

1 BLEST Shepherd, I am thine;
Still keep me in thy fear;
Now fill my heart with grace divine;
Bring thy salvation near.

2 Among thy little flock
I need the Shepherd's care;
Pour waters from the smitten Rock,
And pastures green prepare.

86. C M. WATTS

Praise for Christ.

1 NOW the full glories of the Lamb
Adorn the heavenly plains;
Bright seraphs chant Immanuel's name,
And try their choicest strains.

2 O, may I bear some humble part
In that immortal song;
Wonder and joy shall tune my heart,
And love command my tongue.

87. C. M. CAMPBELL'S COLL.

Watch and Pray.

1 THE Saviour bids us watch and pray,
For soon the hour will come
That calls us from the earth away,
To our eternal home.

2 O, Saviour, we would watch and pray,
And hear thy sacred voice,
And walk, as thou hast marked the way,
To heaven's eternal joys.

88. 7s. M. NEWTON

Parting of Christians.

1 FOR a season called to part,
Let us now ourselves commend
To the gracious eye and heart
Of our ever-present Friend.

2 Father, hear our humble prayer:
Tender Shepherd of thy sheep,
Let thy mercy and thy care
All our souls in safety keep.

3 In thy strength may we be strong;
Sweeten every cross and pain;
And our wasting lives prolong,
Till we meet on earth again

89. S. M. WATTS.

Man's Frailty, God's Compassion.

1 OUR days are as the grass,
Or like the morning flower;
When blasting winds sweep o'er the field,
It withers in an hour.

2 But thy compassions, Lord,
To endless years endure,
And children's children ever find
Thy words of promise sure.

90. L. P. M. TATE & BRADY.

Exhortation to universal Praise.

1 YE saints and servants of the Lord,
The triumphs of his name record;
His sacred name for ever bless:
Where'er the circling sun displays
His rising beams or setting rays,
Due praise to his great name address.

2 God, through the world, extends his sway!
The regions of eternal day
But shadows of his glory are:
To him whose majesty excels,
Who made the heaven wherein he dwells,
Let no created power compare.

91. H. M. CONDER.

Universal Praise.

JEHOVAH'S praise sublime
Through the wide earth be sung;

Ye realms of every clime!
Ye tribes of every tongue! —
His infinite compassion bless,
His ever-during faithfulness.

92. 7s. M. MONTGOMERY

Praise from all Lands.

1 ALL ye nations, praise the Lord;
All ye lands, your voices raise;
Heaven and earth, with loud accord,
Praise the Lord, for ever praise.

2 For his truth and mercy stand,
Past, and present, and to be,
Like the years of his right hand,
Like his own eternity.

3 Praise him, ye who know his love;
Praise him from the depths beneath;
Praise him in the heights above;
Praise your Maker, all that breathe.

93. 7s. M. S. F ADAMS.

Dews and Tears.

1 GENTLY fall the dews of eve,
Raising still the languid flowers;
Sweetly flow the tears that grieve
O'er a mourner's stricken hours.

2 Blessed tears and dews that yet
Lift us nearer unto heaven!
Let us still his praise repeat,
Who in mercy all hath given.

94. S. M. WESLEY'S COLL

Prayer for Strength and Guidance.

1 GOD of almighty love,
By whose sufficient grace
I lift my heart to things above,
And humbly seek thy face.

2 Through Jesus Christ the just,
My faint desires receive,
And let me in thy goodness trust
And to thy glory live.

95. H. M. NEWTON.

For a Blessing.

1 TO thee our wants are known,
From thee are all our powers ;
Accept what is thine own,
And pardon what is ours :
Our praises, Lord, and prayers, receive,
And to thy words a blessing give.

2 O, grant that each of us
Now met before thee here
May meet together thus,
When thou and thine appear :
To thy blest presence may we come
And dwell in an eternal home.

96. 7s. M. SPIRIT OF THE PSALMS

The Heir of Heaven.

1 WHO, O Lord, when life is o'er,
Shall to heaven's blest mansions soar ;
Who, an ever-welcome guest,
In thy holy place shall rest ?

2 He, whose heart thy love has warmed ;
He, whose will to thine conformed,
Bids his life unsullied run ;
He, whose words and thoughts are one ; —

3 He, who shuns the sinner's road,
Loving those who love their God ;
Who, with hope, and faith unfeigned,
Treads the path by thee ordained.

97. 7 & 5s. M. ANONYMOUS

Death of the Virtuous.

1 MARK the virtuous man and see
Peace and joy his steps attend,
All his path is purity,
Happy is his end.

2 Come and see his dying bed ;
Calm his latest moments roll ;
Angels hover round his bed ;
Heaven receives his soul.

98. L. M. 6 L. T. MOORE.

The Song of Angels.

1 ARRAYED in clouds of golden light,
More bright than heaven's resplendent bow,
Jehovah's angel comes by night
To bless the sleeping world below ;
How soft the music of his tongue,
How sweet the hallowed strains he sung.

2 Good-will henceforth to man be given,
The light of glory beams on earth ;
Let angels tune the harps of heaven,
And saints below rejoice with mirth :
On Bethlehem's plains the shepherds sing,
And Judah's children hail their King.

99. C. M. STEELE

Penitential Joy.

1 O, WHILE I breathe to thee, my Lord,
The penitential sigh,
Confirm thy kind, forgiving word,
With pity in thine eye.

2 Then shall the mourner at thy feet
Rejoice to seek thy face ;
And grateful own how kind, how sweet,
Is thy forgiving grace.

100. 7s. M. KELLY

A Blessing desired.

1 FATHER, bless thy word to all;
Quick and powerful let it prove:
O, may sinners hear thy call;
Let thy people grow in love.

2 Thine own gracious message bless;
Follow it with power divine;
Give the gospel great success;
Thine the work, the glory thine.

3 Father, bid the world rejoice;
Send, O, send thy truth abroad;
Let the nations hear thy voice,—
Hear it, and return to God.

101. L. M. WATTS

The Joy and Blessing of Worship.

1 LORD, how delightful 't is to see
A whole assembly worship thee;
At once they sing, at once they pray;
They hear of heaven and learn the way

2 O, write upon my memory, Lord,
The text and doctrines of thy word;
That I may break thy laws no more,
But love thee better than before.

102. 8 & 7s. M. AN NYMOUS

Ascription.

1 GRACIOUS Source of every blessing!
Guard our breasts from anxious fears;
Let us each, thy care possessing,
Sink into the vale of years.

2 All our hopes on thee reclining,
Peace companion of our way:
May our sun, in smiles declining,
Rise in everlasting day.

103. 8 & 7s. M. S. F. Adams

Close of Worship.

1 PART in peace! is day before us?
Praise His name for life and light;
Are the shadows lengthening o'er us?
Bless His care who guards the night.

2 Part in peace! with deep thanksgiving,
Rendering, as we homeward tread,
Gracious service to the living,
Tranquil memory to the dead.

3 Part in peace! such are the praises
God, our Maker, loveth best;
Such the worship that upraises
Human hearts to heavenly rest.

104. S. M. Mason.

Blessedness of the Pure in Heart.

1 BLEST are the pure in heart,
For they shall see our God;
The secret of the Lord is theirs;
Their soul is his abode.

2 Still to the lowly soul
He doth himself impart,
And for his temple and his throne
Selects the pure in heart.

105. L. M. Collyer.

Pleading for Mercy.

1 FATHER of mercies, God of love,
O, hear a humble suppliant's cry;
Bend from thy lofty throne above,
Thy glorious throne of majesty.

2 O, deign to listen to my voice,—
One pardoning word can make me whole,—
Come, bid my drooping heart rejoice,
And soothe the anguish of my soul.

ADORATION, PRAISE, AND THANKSGIVING.

106. 7s. M. SALISBURY COLL

Adoration.

1 HOLY, holy, holy Lord!
Be thy glorious name adored!
Lord, thy mercies never fail;
Hail, celestial goodness, hail!

2 Though unworthy, Lord, thine ear,
Deign our humble songs to hear;
Purer praise we hope to bring,
When around thy throne we sing.

3 There no tongue shall silent be;
All shall join in harmony;
That, through heaven's capacious round,
Praise to thee may ever sound.

4 Lord, thy mercies never fail;
Hail, celestial goodness, hail!
Holy, holy, holy Lord,
Be thy glorious name adored!

107. L. M. TATE & BRADY.

Praise to the great Jehovah.

1 BE thou, O God, exalted high;
And, as thy glory fills the sky,
So let it be on earth displayed,
Till thou art here, as there, obeyed.

2 O God, my heart is fixed; 't is bent
Its thankful tribute to present;
And, with my heart, my voice I'll raise
To thee, my God, in songs of praise.

3 Thy praises, Lord, I will resound
To all the listening nations round;

Thy mercy highest heaven transcends;
Thy truth beyond the clouds extends.

4 Be thou, O God, exalted high;
And, as thy glory fills the sky,
So let it be on earth displayed,
Till thou art here, as there, obeyed.

108. 10 & 11s. M. GRANT

God glorious.

1 O, WORSHIP the King, all glorious above,
And gratefully sing his wonderful love,
Our Shield and Defender, the Ancient of Days,
Pavilioned in splendor, and girded with praise.

2 O, tell of his might, and sing of his grace,
Whose robe is the light, whose canopy, space;
His chariots of wrath the deep thunder-clouds form,
And dark is his path on the wings of the storm.

3 Thy bountiful care what tongue can recite?
It breathes in the air, it shines in the light,
It streams from the hills, it descends to the plain,
And sweetly distils in the dew and the rain.

4 Frail children of dust, and feeble as frail,
In thee do we trust, nor find thee to fail;
Thy mercies how tender! how firm to the end!
Our Maker, Defender, Preserver, and Friend.

5 Father Almighty, how faithful thy love!
While angels delight to hymn thee above,
The humbler creation, though feeble their lays,
With true adoration shall lisp to thy praise.

109. C. M. PATRICK.

Te Deum.

1 O GOD, we praise thee, and confess
That thou the only Lord
And everlasting Father art,
By all the earth adored.

2 To thee all angels cry aloud ;
To thee the powers on high,
Both cherubim and seraphim,
Continually do cry, —

3 " O holy, holy, holy Lord,
Whom heavenly hosts obey,
The world is with the glory filled
Of thy majestic sway.

4 The apostles' glorious company,
And prophets crowned with light
With all the martyrs' noble host,
Thy constant praise recite.

5 The holy church throughout the world,
O Lord, confesses thee,
That thou eternal Father art,
Of boundless majesty.

110. H. M. TATE & BRADY

Universal Praise.

1 YE boundless realms of joy,
Exalt your Maker's fame ;
His praise your song employ
Above the starry frame ;
Your voices raise, | And seraphim,
Ye cherubim, | To sing his praise.

2 Thou moon, that rul'st the night,
And sun, that guid'st the day,
Ye glittering stars of light,
To him your homage pay ;
His praise declare, | And clouds that move
Ye heavens above, | In liquid air.

3 Let them adore the Lord,
And praise his holy name,
By whose almighty word
They all from nothing came ;

And all shall last | His firm decree
From changes free ; | Stands ever fast.

4 United zeal be shown
His wondrous fame to raise,
Whose glorious name alone
Deserves our endless praise ;
Earth's utmost ends | His glorious sway
His power obey ; | The sky transcends.

111. 8 & 7s. M. ANCIENT HYMNS

Thrice Holy.

1 BRIGHT the vision that delighted
Once the sight of Judah's seer ;
Sweet the countless tongues united
To entrance the prophet's ear.
Round the Lord in glory seated,
Cherubim and seraphim
Filled his temple, and repeated
Each to each th' alternate hymn :—

2 "Lord, thy glory fills the heaven ;
Earth is with its fulness stored ;
Unto thee be glory given,
Holy, holy, holy Lord ! "
Heaven is still with glory ringing ;
Earth takes up the angels' cry,
"Holy, holy, holy," singing,
"Lord of hosts, the Lord most high ! "

3 Ever thus in God's high praises,
Brethren, let our tongues unite,
Whilst our thoughts his greatness raises,
And our love his gifts excite.
With his seraph train before him,
With his holy church below,
Thus conspire we to adore him,
Bid we thus our anthem flow :—

4 "Lord, thy glory fills the heaven;
Earth is with its fulness stored;
Unto thee be glory given,
Holy, holy, holy Lord!
Thus thy glorious name confessing,
We adopt thy angels' cry,
'Holy, holy, holy,' blessing
Thee, the Lord of hosts most high!"

112. L. M. MRS. OPIE.

Praise of God peculiarly due from Man

1 THERE seems a voice in every gale,
A tongue in every opening flower,
Which tells, O Lord! the wondrous tale
Of thy indulgence, love, and power.

2 The birds that rise on soaring wing
Appear to hymn their Maker's praise,
And all the mingling sounds of spring
To thee a general pæan raise.

3 And shall my voice, great God, alone
Be mute 'midst Nature's loud acclaim?
No; let my heart with answering tone
Breathe forth in praise thy holy name.

4 And Nature's debt is small to mine;
Thou bad'st her being bounded be,
But—matchless proof of love divine—
Thou gav'st immortal life to me.

113. L. P. M. WATTS

Universal Praise.

1 LET all the earth their voices raise,
To sing a lofty psalm of praise,
And bless the great Jehovah's name;
His glory let the heathen know,
His wonders to the nations show,
And all his works of grace proclaim.

2 He framed the globe, he spread the sky,
And all the shining worlds on high;
He reigns complete in glory there:
His beams are majesty and light,
His glories how divinely bright!
His temple how divinely fair!

3 Let heaven be glad, let earth rejoice,
Let ocean lift its roaring voice,
Proclaiming loud, "Jehovah reigns!"
For joy let fertile valleys sing,
And tuneful groves their tribute bring
To Him whose power the world sustains.

4 Come the great day, the glorious hour,
When earth shall own his sovereign power,
And barbarous nations fear his name;
Then shall the universe confess
The beauty of his holiness,
And in his courts his grace proclaim.

114. L. M. ROSCOE

Song of Adoration.

1 LET one loud song of praise arise
To God, whose goodness ceaseless flows,
Who dwells enthroned above the skies,
And life and breath on all bestows.

2 Let all of good this bosom fires
To him, sole good, give praises due;
Let all the truth himself inspires
Unite to sing him only true.

3 In ardent adoration joined,
Obedient to thy holy will,
Let all our faculties, combined,
Thy just commands, O God, fulfil.

4 O, may the solemn-breathing sound
Like incense rise before thy throne,

Where thou, whose glory knows no bound,
  Great Cause of all things, dwell'st alone!

115. L. M. BLACKLOCK.

Majesty and Dominion of God.

1 COME, O my soul, in sacred lays
Attempt thy great Creator's praise:
But, O, what tongue can speak his fame?
What verse can reach the lofty theme?

2 Enthroned amid the radiant spheres,
He glory like a garment wears;
To form a robe of light divine,
Ten thousand suns around him shine.

3 In all our Maker's grand designs,
Almighty power, with wisdom, shines;
His works, through all this wondrous frame,
Declare the glory of his name.

4 Raised on devotion's lofty wing,
Do thou, my soul, his glories sing;
And let his praise employ thy tongue
Till listening worlds shall join the song.

116. S. M. MONTGOMERY.

Praise for Mercies.

1 O, BLESS the Lord, my soul;
  His grace to thee proclaim;
And all that is within me, join
  To bless his holy name.

2 O, bless the Lord, my soul;
  His mercies bear in mind;
Forget not all his benefits;
  The Lord to thee is kind.

3 He will not always chide;
  He will with patience wait;
His wrath is ever slow to rise,
  And ready to abate.

4 The Lord forgives thy sins,
    Prolongs thy feeble breath ;
  He healeth thine infirmities,
    And ransoms thee from death.

5 He clothes thee with his love,
    Upholds thee with his truth,
  And like the eagle he renews
    The vigor of thy youth.

6 Then bless his holy name
    Whose grace hath made thee whole,
  Whose loving-kindness crowns thy days ;
    O, bless the Lord, my soul.

117. 7s. M. SANDYS.

Harmony of Praise.

1 THOU who dwell'st enthroned above !
  Thou, in whom we live and move !
  Thou who art most great, most high !
  God from all eternity !

2 O, how sweet, how excellent
  'T is when tongues and hearts consent,
  Grateful hearts, and joyful tongues,
  Hymning thee in tuneful songs !

3 When the morning paints the skies,
  When the stars of evening rise,
  We thy praises will record,
  Sovereign Ruler, mighty Lord !

4 Decks the spring with flowers the field ?
  Harvest rich doth autumn yield ?
  Giver of all good below !
  Lord, from thee these blessings flow.

5 Sovereign Ruler ! mighty Lord !
  We thy praises will record ;
  Giver of these blessings ! we
  Pour the grateful song to thee.

118. 11 & 8s. M. CHURCH PSALMODY

The Lord is Great.

1 THE Lord is great; ye hosts of heaven, adore him,
And ye who tread this earthly ball;
In holy songs rejoice aloud before him,
And shout his praise who made you all.

2 The Lord is great; his majesty how glorious!
Resound his praise from shore to shore;
O'er sin, and death, and hell, now made victorious,
He rules and reigns for evermore.

3 The Lord is great; his mercy how abounding!
Ye angels, strike your golden chords;
O, praise our God, with voice and harp resounding,
The King of kings and Lord of lords.

119. C. M. ROWE

Praise from all Nature.

1 BEGIN the high celestial strain,
My raptured soul, and sing
A sacred hymn of grateful praise
To heaven's almighty King.

2 Ye curling fountains, as ye roll
Your silver waves along,
Repeat to all your verdant shores
The subject of the song.

3 Bear it, ye breezes, on your wings
To distant climes away,
And round the wide-extended world
The lofty theme convey.

4 Take up the burden of his name,
Ye clouds, as ye arise,
To deck with gold the opening morn,
Or shade the evening skies.

5 Long let it warble round the spheres,
And echo through the sky;

Let angels, with immortal skill,
Improve the harmony ;—

6 While we, with sacred rapture fired,
The blest Creator sing,
And chant our consecrated lays
To heaven's eternal King.

120. L. M. Wa·ts

Praise for Divine Protection.

1 WITH all my powers of heart and tongue
I 'll praise my Maker in my song ;
Angels shall hear the notes I raise,
Approve the song, and join the praise.

2 To God I cried, when troubles rose ;
He heard me, and subdued my foes ;
He did my rising fears control,
And strength diffused through all my soul.

3 Amid a thousand snares I stand,
Upheld and guarded by thy hand ;
Thy words my fainting soul revive,
And keep my dying faith alive.

4 I 'll sing thy truth and mercy, Lord ;
I 'll sing the wonders of thy word ;
Not all thy works and names below
So much thy power and glory show.

121. C. P. M. Ogilvie.

Praise from all Creatures.

1 BEGIN, my soul, th' exalted lay ;
Let each enraptured thought obey,
And praise th' almighty name ;
Lo ! heaven, and earth, and seas, and skies,
In one melodious concert rise,
To swell th' inspiring theme.

2 Thou heaven of heavens, his vast abode,
Ye clouds, proclaim your Maker, God;
Ye thunders, speak his power;
Lo! on the lightning's fiery wing,
In triumph rides th' Eternal King;
Th' astonished worlds adore.

3 Ye deeps, with roaring billows, rise
To join the thunders of the skies;
Praise Him who bids you roll;
His praise in softer notes declare,
Each whispering breeze of yielding air,
And breathe it to the soul.

4 Wake, all ye soaring tribes, and sing;
Ye feathered warblers of the spring,
Harmonious anthems raise
To Him who shaped your finer mould,
Who decked your glittering wings with gold,
And tuned your voice to praise.

5 Let man — by nobler passions swayed, —
Let man — in God's own image made —
His breath in praise employ,
Spread wide his Maker's name around,
Till heaven shall echo back the sound,
In songs of holy joy.

122. S. M. MONTGOMERY.

Exhortation to Praise.

1 ARISE, and bless the Lord,
Ye people of his choice;
Arise, and bless the Lord your God,
With heart, and soul, and voice.

2 O, for the living flame
From his own altar brought,
To touch our lips, our souls inspire,
And wing to heaven our thought!

3 God is our strength and song,
And his salvation ours ;
Then be his love in Christ proclaimed
With all our ransomed powers.

4 Arise, and bless the Lord ;
The Lord your God adore ;
Arise and bless his glorious name,
Henceforth, for evermore.

123. L. M. Bowring.

Perpetual Praise.

1 WHEN, wakened by thy voice of power,
The hour of morning beams in light,
My voice shall sing that morning hour,
And thee, who mad'st that hour so bright.

2 The morning strengthens into noon ;
Earth's fairest beauties shine more fair ;
And noon and morning shall attune
My grateful heart to praise and prayer.

3 When 'neath the evening western gate
The sun's retiring rays are hid,
My joy shall be to meditate,
E'en as the pious patriarch did.

4 As twilight wears a darker hue,
And gathering night creation dims,
The twilight and the midnight, too,
Shall have their harmonies and hymns.

5 So shall sweet thoughts, and thoughts sublime,
My constant inspirations be ;
And every shifting scene of time
Reflect, my God, a light from thee.

124. C. M. Sternhold

Majesty of God.

1 THE Lord descended from above,
And bowed the heavens most high,

And underneath his feet he cast
The darkness of the sky.

2 On cherubim and seraphim
Full royally he rode,
And on the wings of mighty winds
Came flying all abroad.

3 He sat serene upon the floods,
Their fury to restrain ;
And he, as sovereign Lord and King,
For evermore shall reign.

125. C. M. ANONYMOUS

Goodness of God seen in his Works.

1 HAIL, great Creator, wise and good ;
To thee our songs we raise ;
Nature, through all her various scenes,
Invites us to thy praise.

2 At morning, noon, and evening mild,
Fresh wonders strike our view ;
And, while we gaze, our hearts exult,
With transports ever new.

3 Thy glory beams in every star
Which gilds the gloom of night,
And decks the smiling face of morn
With rays of cheerful light.

4 The lofty hill, the humble lawn,
With countless beauties shine ;
The silent grove, the solemn shade,
Proclaim thy power divine.

5 Great nature's God, still may these scenes
Our serious hours engage ;
Still may our grateful hearts consult
Thy works' instructive page.

6 And while, in all thy wondrous ways,
Thy varied love we see,

O, may our hearts, great God, be led,
Through all thy works, to thee.

126. C. M. WARDLAW

Praise to God.

1 LIFT up to God the voice of praise,
Whose breath our souls inspired;
Loud, and more loud, the anthems raise,
With grateful ardor fired.

2 Lift up to God the voice of praise,
Whose goodness, passing thought,
Loads every moment, as it flies,
With benefits unsought.

3 Lift up to God the voice of praise,
From whom salvation flows,
Who sent his Son our souls to save
From sin and all its woes.

4 Lift up to God the voice of praise,
For hope's transporting ray,
Which lights, through darkest shades of death,
To realms of endless day.

127. C. M. 6 L. CONDER

On the Sea-shore.

1 BEYOND, beyond that boundless sea,
Above that dome of sky,
Farther than thought itself can flee,
Thy dwelling is on high;
Yet dear the awful thought to me,
That thou, my God, art nigh.

2 We hear thy voice when thunders roll
Through the wide fields of air;
The waves obey thy dread control;
Yet still thou art not there:
Where shall I find Him, O my soul,
Who yet is everywhere?

3 O, not in circling depth, or height,
But in the conscious breast,
Present to faith, though veiled from sight,
There does his spirit rest:
O, come, thou Presence Infinite,
And make thy creature blest.

128. C. P. M. HENRY MOORE

The Love of God.

1 MY God! thy boundless love I praise;
How bright on high its glories blaze!
How sweetly bloom below!
It streams from thine eternal throne;
Through heaven its joys for ever run,
And o'er the earth they flow.

2 'T is love that paints the purple morn,
And bids the clouds, in air upborne,
Their genial drops distil;
In every vernal beam it glows,
And breathes in every gale that blows,
And glides in every rill.

3 But in thy word I see it shine
With grace and glories more divine,
Proclaiming sins forgiven;
There, Faith, bright cherub, points the way
To realms of everlasting day,
And opens all her heaven.

4 Then let the love, that makes me blest,
With cheerful praise inspire my breast,
And ardent gratitude;
And all my thoughts and passions tend
To thee, my Father and my Friend,
My soul's eternal good.

129. C. M. TATE & BRADY.

Praising God in all Changes.

1 THROUGH all the changing scenes of life,
In trouble and in joy,
The praises of my God shall still
My heart and tongue employ.

2 Of his deliverance I will boast,
Till all who are distressed
From my example comfort take,
And charm their griefs to rest.

3 The hosts of God encamp around
The dwellings of the just;
Deliverance he affords to all
Who on his succour trust.

4 O, make but trial of his love,—
Experience will decide
How blest they are, and only they,
Who in his faith confide.

5 Fear him, ye saints, and you will then
Have nothing else to fear:
Make you his service your delight,—
He 'll make your wants his care.

130. H. M. SACRED LYRICS

Perpetual Praise.

1 TO thee, great Source of light!
My thankful voice I 'll raise;
And all my powers unite
To celebrate thy praise;
And, till my voice is lost in death,
May praise employ my every breath.

2 And when this feeble tongue
Lies silent in the dust,
My soul shall dwell among
The spirits of the just;

Then, with the shining hosts above,
In nobler strains I 'll sing thy love.

131. L. M. WATTS

The Glory of God in his Works and in his Word.

1 THE heavens declare thy glory, Lord;
In every star thy wisdom shines;
But when our eyes behold thy word,
We read thy name in fairer lines.

2 The rolling sun, the changing light,
And nights, and days, thy power confess;
But that blest volume thou hast writ
Reveals thy justice and thy grace.

3 Sun, moon, and stars convey thy praise
Around the earth, and never stand;
So, when thy truth began its race,
It touched and glanced on every land.

4 Nor shall thy spreading gospel rest
Till through the world thy truth has run,
Till Christ has all the nations blest
That see the light or feel the sun.

5 Great Sun of Righteousness, arise!
O, bless the world with heavenly light!
Thy gospel makes the simple wise;
Thy laws are pure, thy judgments right.

6 Thy noblest wonders here we view,
In souls renewed and sins forgiven;
Lord, cleanse my sins, my soul renew,
And make thy word my guide to heaven

132. 8 & 7s. M. DUBLIN COLL.

Praise the Lord.

1 PRAISE the Lord; ye heavens adore him;
Praise him, angels, in the height,
Sun and moon, rejoice before him;
Praise him, all ye stars of light.

2 Praise the Lord, for he hath spoken;
Worlds his mighty voice obeyed;
Laws, which never can be broken,
For their guidance he hath made.

3 Praise the Lord, for he is glorious;
Never shall his promise fail;
God hath made his saints victorious;
Sin and death shall not prevail.

4 Praise the God of our salvation;
Hosts on high his power proclaim;
Heaven and earth, and all creation,
Praise and magnify his name.

133. 6 & 4s. M. SACRED LYRICS.

Praise in the Courts of the Lord.

1 PRAISE ye Jehovah's name;
Praise through his courts proclaim;
Rise and adore;
High o'er the heavens above
Sound his great acts of love,
While his rich grace we prove,
Vast as his power.

2 Now let the trumpet raise
Triumphant sounds of praise,
Wide as his fame;
There let the harp be found;
Organs, with solemn sound,
Roll your deep notes around,
Filled with his name.

3 While his high praise ye sing,
Shake every sounding string:
Sweet the accord!
He vital breath bestows:
Let every breath that flows
His noblest fame disclose:
Praise ye the Lord.

134. H. M. WATTS.

Perfections of God.

1 THE Lord Jehovah reigns ;
His throne is built on high ;
The garments he assumes
Are light and majesty :
His glories shine | No mortal eye
With beams so bright | Can bear the sight.

2 The thunders of his hand
Keep the wide world in awe,
His power and justice stand
To guard his holy law :
And where his love | His truth confirms
Resolves to bless, | And seals the grace.

3 And can this mighty King
Of glory condescend ?
And will he write his name
My Father and my Friend ?
I love his name, | Join all my powers
I love his word : | And praise the Lord.

135. C. H. M. ANONYMOUS

The surpassing Glory of God.

1 SINCE o'er thy footstool here below
Such radiant gems are strown,
O, what magnificence must glow,
Great God, about thy throne !
So brilliant here these drops of light –
There the full ocean rolls — how bright !

2 If night's blue curtain of the sky —
With thousand stars inwrought,
Hung like a royal canopy
With glittering diamonds fraught —
Be, Lord, thy temple's outer veil,
What splendor at the shrine must dwell !

3 The dazzling sun at noonday hour —
 Forth from his flaming vase
Flinging o'er earth the golden shower
 Till vale and mountain blaze —
But shows, O Lord, one beam of thine :
What, then, the day where thou dost shine !

4 O, how shall these dim eyes endure
 That noon of living rays !
Or how our spirits, so impure,
 Upon thy glory gaze !
Anoint, O Lord, anoint our sight,
And fit us for that world of light.

136. C. M. WATTS.

Power and Majesty of God.

1 WITH reverence let the saints appear,
 And bow before the Lord ;
His high commands with reverence hear,
 And tremble at his word.

2 How terrible thy glories be !
 How bright thine armies shine !
Where is the power that vies with thee ?
 Or truth compared with thine ?

3 The northern pole, and southern, rest
 On thy supporting hand ;
Darkness and day from east to west
 Move round at thy command.

4 Thy words the raging winds control,
 And rule the boisterous deep ;
Thou mak'st the sleeping billows roll,
 The rolling billows sleep.

5 Justice and judgment are thy throne,
 Yet wondrous is thy grace ;
While truth and mercy, joined in one,
 Invite us near thy face.

137. H. M. WATTS.

Exhortation to Praise.

1 YE tribes of Adam, join
With heaven, and earth, and seas,
And offer notes divine
To your Creator's praise ;
Ye holy throng | In worlds of light
Of angels bright, | Begin the song.

2 The shining worlds above
In glorious order stand,
Or in swift courses move,
By his supreme command :
He spake the word, | From nothing came
And all their frame | To praise the Lord

3 Let all the nations fear
The God that rules above ;
He brings his people near,
And makes them taste his love ;
While earth and sky | His saints shall raise
Attempt his praise, | His honors high.

138. L. M. WATTS

Praise from all Creatures.

1 NATURE, with all her powers, shall sing
Her great Creator and her King ;
Nor air, nor earth, nor skies, nor seas,
Deny the tribute of their praise.

2 Ye seraphs, who sit near his throne,
Begin to make his glories known ;
Tune high your harps, and spread the sound
Throughout creation's utmost bound.

3 O, may our ardent zeal employ
Our loftiest thoughts and loudest songs ;
Let there be sung, with warmest joy,
Hosanna from ten thousand tongues.

4 Yet, mighty God, our feeble frame
Attempts in vain to reach thy name;
The highest notes that angels raise
Fall far below thy glorious praise.

139. L. M. 6 l. T. Moore

God the Life and Light of the World.

1 THOU art, O God, the life and light
Of all this wondrous world we see;
Its glow by day, its smile by night,
Are but reflections caught from thee.
Where'er we turn, thy glories shine,
And all things fair and bright are thine.

2 When day, with farewell beam, delays
Among the opening clouds of even,
And we can almost think we gaze
Through golden vistas into heaven,
Those hues that make the sun's decline
So soft, so radiant, Lord, are thine.

3 When night, with wings of starry gloom,
O'ershadows all the earth and skies,
Like some dark, beauteous bird, whose plume
Is sparkling with unnumbered eyes,
That sacred gloom, those fires divine,
So grand, so countless, Lord, are thine.

4 When youthful spring around us breathes,
Thy spirit warms her fragrant sigh;
And every flower the summer wreaths
Is born beneath thy kindling eye:
Where'er we turn, thy glories shine,
And all things fair and bright are thine.

140. C. M. Frisbie

The Lord's Prayer.

1 O THOU, enthroned in worlds above,
Our Father and our Friend,

Lo ! at the footstool of thy love
  Thy children humbly bend.

2 All reverence to thy name be given,
  Thy kingdom wide displayed :
And, as thy will is done in heaven,
  Be it on earth obeyed.

3 Our table may thy bounty spread,
  From thine exhaustless store,
From day to day with daily bread,
  Nor would we ask for more.

4 That pardon we to others give,
  Do thou to us extend ;
From all temptation, O, relieve,
  From every ill defend.

5 And now to thee belong, Most High,
  The kingdom, glory, power,
Through the broad earth and spacious sky,
  Till time shall be no more.

141. L. M. STEELE

The Voice of Nature.

1 THERE is a God, all nature speaks,
  Through earth, and air, and seas, and skies,
See, from the clouds his glory breaks,
  When the first beams of morning rise !

2 The rising sun, serenely bright,
  O'er the wide world's extended frame
Inscribes, in characters of light,
  His mighty Maker's glorious name.

3 Diffusing life, his influence spreads,
  And health and plenty smile around ;
And fruitful fields and verdant meads
  Are with a thousand blessings crowned.

4 Ye curious minds, who roam abroad,
  And trace creation's wonders o'er !

Confess the footsteps of the God,
   And bow before him and adore.

142. C. M. WATTS

Praise to God.

1 LET them neglect thy glory, Lord,
   Who never knew thy grace;
But our loud songs shall still record
   The wonders of thy praise.

2 We raise our shouts, O God, to thee,
   And send them to thy throne;
All glory to the Father be,
   The undivided One.

3 Hosanna! let the earth and skies
   Repeat the joyful sound;
Rocks, hills, and vales reflect the voice
   In one eternal round.

143. C. M. HEGINBOTHAM

Praise at all Times.

1 MY soul shall praise thee, O my God,
   Through all my mortal days,
And in eternity prolong
   Thy vast, thy boundless praise.

2 In every smiling, happy hour,
   Be this my sweet employ;
Thy praise refines my earthly bliss,
   And heightens all my joy.

3 When anxious grief and gloomy care
   Afflict my throbbing breast,
My tongue shall learn to speak thy praise,
   And lull each pain to rest.

4 Nor shall my tongue alone proclaim
   The honors of my God;
My life, with all its active powers,
   Shall spread thy praise abroad.

5 And when these lips shall cease to move,
When death shall close these eyes,
My soul shall then to nobler heights
Of joy and transport rise.

6 My powers shall then, in lofty strains,
Their grateful tribute pay ;
The theme demands an angel's tongue,
An everlasting day.

144. S. M. WATTS

Universal Praise.

1 LET every creature join
To praise th' eternal God ;
Ye heavenly hosts, the song begin,
And sound his name abroad.

2 Thou sun with golden beams,
And moon with paler rays,
Ye starry lights, ye twinkling flames,
Shine to your Maker's praise.

3 He built those worlds above,
And fixed their wondrous frame ;
By his command they stand or move
And ever speak his name.

4 By all his works above
His honors be expressed ;
But saints that taste his saving love
Should sing his praises best.

145. S. M. STEELE.

God our constant Benefactor.

1 MY Maker and my King,
To thee my all I owe :
Thy sovereign bounty is the spring
Whence all my blessings flow.

2 Thou ever good and kind,
A thousand reasons move,

A thousand obligations bind,
My heart to grateful love.

3 The creature of thy hand,
On thee alone I live :
My God, thy benefits demand
More praise than tongue can give.

4 O, let thy grace inspire
My soul with strength divine ;
Let all my powers to thee aspire,
And all my days be thine.

146. L. M. DODDRIDGE.

God's Mercies above all Return.

1 IN glad amazement, Lord, I stand,
Amidst the bounties of thy hand :
How numberless those bounties are !
How rich, how various, and how fair !

2 But, O, what poor returns I make !
What lifeless thanks I pay thee back !
Lord, I confess, with humble shame,
My offerings scarce deserve the name.

3 Fain would my laboring heart devise
To bring some nobler sacrifice ;
It sinks beneath the mighty load,
"What shall I render to my God ?"

4 To him I consecrate my praise,
And vow the remnant of my days ;
Yet what, at best, can I pretend
Worthy such gifts from such a Friend !

5 In deep abasement, Lord, I see
My emptiness and poverty :
Enrich my soul with grace divine,
And make me worthier to be thine.

6 Give me, at length, an angel's tongue,
That heaven may echo with my song :

The theme, too great for time, shall be
The joy of long eternity.

147. L. M. DYER.

Praise from the Works of God.

1 GREATEST of beings! Source of life,
Sovereign of air, and earth, and sea!
All nature feels thy power, and all
A silent homage pays to thee.

2 Waked by thy hand, the morning sun
Pours forth to thee its earlier rays,
And spreads thy glories as it climbs;
While raptured worlds look up and praise.

3 The moon to the deep shades of night
Speaks the mild lustre of thy name;
While all the stars that cheer the scene
Thee, the great Lord of light, proclaim.

4 And groves, and vales, and rocks, and hills,
And every flower, and every tree,
Ten thousand creatures warm with life,
Have each a grateful song for thee.

5 But man was formed to rise to heaven:
And, blest with reason's clearer light,
He views his Maker through his works,
And glows with rapture at the sight.

6 Nor can the thousand songs that rise,
Whether from air, or earth, or sea,
So well repeat Jehovah's praise,
Or raise such sacred harmony.

148. 10 & 11s. M. PARK

Thanksgiving and Praise.

MY soul, praise the Lord, speak good of his name!
His mercies record, his bounties proclaim:
To God, their creator, let all creatures raise
The song of thanksgiving, the chorus of praise!

2 Though hid from man's sight, God sits on his throne,
Yet here by his works their author is known:
The world shines a mirror its Maker to show,
And heaven views its image reflected below.

3 By knowledge supreme, by wisdom divine,
God governs this earth with gracious design;
O'er beast, bird, and insect, his providence reigns,
Whose will first created, whose love still sustains.

4 And man, his last work, with reason endued,
Who, falling through sin, by grace is renewed;
To God, his creator, let man ever raise
The song of thanksgiving, the chorus of praise!

149. L. M. MRS. FOLLEN

Goodness of God.

1 GOD, thou art good! each perfumed flower,
The waving field, the dark green wood,
The insect fluttering for an hour, —
All things proclaim that God is good.

2 I hear it in each breath of wind;
The hills that have for ages stood,
And clouds with gold and silver lined,
All still repeat that God is good.

3 Each little rill, that many a year
Has the same verdant path pursued,
And every bird, in accents clear,
Joins in the song that God is good.

4 The countless hosts of twinkling stars,
That sing his praise with light renewed;
The rising sun each day declares,
In rays of glory, God is good.

5 The moon, that walks in brightness, says
That God is good! and man, endued
With power to speak his Maker's praise,
Should still repeat that God is good.

150. L. M. DODDRIDGE.

Song of Gratitude and Praise.

1 GOD of my life, through all my days
I 'll tune the grateful notes of praise ;
The song shall wake with opening light,
And warble to the silent night.

2 When anxious care would break my rest,
And grief would tear my throbbing breast,
The notes of praise, ascending high,
Shall check the murmur and the sigh.

3 When death o'er nature shall prevail,
And all the powers of language fail,
Joy through my swimming eyes shall break,
And mean the thanks I cannot speak.

4 But, O, when that last conflict 's o'er,
And I am chained to earth no more,
With what glad accents shall I rise,
To join the music of the skies !

5 Then shall I learn th' exalted strains
That echo through the heavenly plains,
And emulate, with joy unknown,
The glowing seraphs round thy throne

PERFECTIONS AND PROVIDENCE OF GOD.

151. L. M. KIPPIS.

God incomprehensible.

1 GREAT God ! in vain man's narrow view
Attempts to look thy nature through ;
Our laboring powers with reverence own
Thy glories never can be known.

2 Not the high seraph's mighty thought,
Who countless years his God has sought,
Such wondrous height or depth can find,
Or fully trace thy boundless mind.

3 And yet thy kindness deigns to show
Enough for mortal minds to know;
While wisdom, goodness, power divine,
Through all thy works and conduct shine.

4 O, may our souls with rapture trace
Thy works of nature and of grace;
Explore thy sacred truth, and still
Press on to know and do thy will.

152. S. P. M. WATTS.

The Majesty of God.

1 THE Lord Jehovah reigns,
And royal state maintains,
His head with awful glories crowned,
Arrayed in robes of light,
Begirt with sovereign might,
And rays of majesty around.

2 Upheld by thy commands,
The world securely stands,
And skies and stars obey thy word;
Thy throne was fixed on high
Ere stars adorned the sky;
Eternal is thy kingdom, Lord.

3 Thy promises are true;
Thy grace is ever new;
There fixed, thy church shall ne'er remove,
Thy saints, with holy fear,
Shall in thy courts appear,
And sing thine everlasting love.

153. C. M. WATTS.

God the Creator.

1 ETERNAL Wisdom, thee we praise ;
Thee all thy creatures sing ;
While with thy name rocks, hills, and seas,
And heaven's high palace, ring.

2 Thy hand, how wide it spread the sky !
How glorious to behold !
Tinged with a blue of heavenly dye,
And decked with sparkling gold.

3 Thy glories blaze all nature round,
And strike the gazing sight,
Through skies, and seas, and solid ground,
With terror and delight.

4 Almighty power, and equal skill,
Shine through the worlds abroad,
Our souls with vast amazement fill,
And speak the builder, God.

5 But still, the wonders of thy grace
Our warmer passions move ;
Here we behold our Saviour's face,
And here adore his love.

154. C. M. ANONYMOUS.

Is there a God?

1 IS there a God ? Yon rising sun
In answer meet replies,
Writes it in flame upon the earth,
Proclaims it round the skies.

2 Is there a God ? Hark ! from on high
His thunder shakes the poles ;
I hear his voice in every wind,
In every wave that rolls.

3 Is there a God ? With sacred fear,
I upward turn my eyes ;

"There is!" each glittering lamp of light. —
"There is!" my soul replies.

4 If such convictions to my mind
His works aloud impart,
O, let the wisdom of his word
Inscribe them on my heart.

155. C. M. TATE & BRADY

God unchangeable.

1 THROUGH endless years thou art the same,
O thou eternal God;
Each future age shall know thy name,
And tell thy works abroad.

2 The strong foundations of the earth
Of old by thee were laid;
By thee the beauteous arch of heaven,
With matchless skill, was made.

3 Soon shall this goodly frame of things,
Created by thy hand,
Be, like a vesture, laid aside,
And changed at thy command.

4 But thy perfections, all divine,
Eternal as thy days,
Through everlasting ages shine,
With undiminished rays.

156. L. M. SPIRIT OF THE PSALMS

Omnipresence of God.

1 FATHER of spirits, nature's God!
Our inmost thoughts are known to thee;
Thou, Lord, canst hear each idle word,
And every private action see.

2 Could we, on morning's swiftest wings,
Pursue our flight through trackless air,
Or dive beneath deep ocean's springs,
Thy presence still would meet us there.

3 In vain may guilt attempt to fly,
Concealed beneath the pall of night;
One glance from thy all-piercing eye
Can kindle darkness into light.

4 Search thou our hearts, and there destroy
Each evil thought, each secret sin,
And fit us for those realms of joy,
Where naught impure shall enter in.

157. L. M. WATTS.

Omniscience and Omnipresence of God.

1 LORD, thou hast searched and seen me through;
Thine eye commands, with piercing view,
My rising and my resting hours,
My heart and flesh, with all their powers.

2 My thoughts, before they are my own,
Are to my God distinctly known;
He knows the words I mean to speak,
Ere from my opening lips they break.

3 Within thy circling power I stand;
On every side I find thy hand;
Awake, asleep, at home, abroad,
I am surrounded still with God.

4 Amazing knowledge, vast and great!
What large extent! what lofty height!
My soul, with all the powers I boast,
Is in the boundless prospect lost.

5 O, may these thoughts possess my breast,
Where'er I rove, where'er I rest,
Nor let my weaker passions dare
Consent to sin, for God is there.

158. L. M. NEEDHAM

Wisdom and Knowledge of God.

1 AWAKE, my tongue; thy tribute bring
To Him who gave thee power to sing;

Praise Him who has all praise above,
The source of wisdom and of love.

2 How vast his knowledge ! how profound !
A depth where all our thoughts are drowned !
The stars he numbers, and their names
He gives to all their heavenly flames.

3 Through each bright world above, behold
Ten thousand thousand charms unfold ;
Earth, air, and mighty seas combine
To speak his wisdom all divine.

4 But in redemption, O, what grace !
Its wonders, O, what thought can trace !
Here wisdom shines for ever bright ;
Praise him, my soul, with sweet delight.

159. C. M. H. K. WHITE

Almighty Power and Majesty of God.

1 THE Lord our God is clothed with might,
The winds obey his will ;
He speaks, and in the heavenly height
The rolling sun stands still.

2 Rebel, ye waves, and o'er the land
With threatening aspect roar ;
The Lord uplifts his awful hand,
And chains you to the shore.

3 Ye winds of night, your force combine ;
Without his high behest,
Ye shall not, in the mountain-pine,
Disturb the sparrow's nest.

4 His voice sublime is heard afar ;
In distant peals it dies ;
He binds the whirlwinds to his car,
And sweeps the howling skies.

5 Ye nations bend ; in reverence bend ;
Ye monarchs, wait his nod,

And bid the choral song ascend
To celebrate our God.

160. C. M. Cowper.

Purposes of God developed by his Providence.

1 GOD moves in a mysterious way,
His wonders to perform ;
He plants his footsteps in the sea,
And rides upon the storm.

2 Ye fearful saints, fresh courage take
The clouds ye so much dread
Are big with mercy, and shall break
With blessings on your head.

3 Judge not the Lord by feeble sense,
But trust him for his grace ;
Behind a frowning providence
He hides a smiling face.

4 His purposes will ripen fast,
Unfolding every hour ;
The bud may have a bitter taste,
But sweet will be the flower.

5 Blind unbelief is sure to err,
And scan his work in vain ;
God is his own interpreter,
And he will make it plain.

161. L. M. Spirit of the Psalms.

Eternity of God.

1 ERE mountains reared their forms sublime,
Or heaven and earth in order stood,
Before the birth of ancient time,
From everlasting thou art God.

2 A thousand ages, in their flight,
With thee are as a fleeting day ;
Past, present, future, to thy sight
At once their various scenes display.

3 But our brief life 's a shadowy dream,
A passing thought, that soon is o'er,
That fades with morning's earliest beam,
And fills the musing mind no more.

4 To us, O Lord, the wisdom give
Each passing moment so to spend,
That we at length with thee may live,
Where life and bliss shall never end.

162. C. M. WATTS.

Foreknowledge and Providence of God.

1 LET the whole race of creatures lie
Abased before the Lord!
Whate'er his powerful hand has formed,
He governs with a word.

2 Ten thousand ages ere the skies
Were into motion brought,
All the long years and worlds to come
Stood present to his thought.

3 There 's not a sparrow, nor a worm,
O'erlooked in his decrees:
He raises monarchs to a throne,
Or sinks, with equal ease.

4 If light attend the course we go,
'T is he provides the rays;
And 't is his hand that hides the sun,
If darkness cloud our days.

5 Trusting thy wisdom, God of love!
We would not wish to know
What, in the book of thy decrees,
Awaits us here below.

6 Be this alone our fervent prayer;
Whate'er our lot shall be, —
Or joys, or sorrows, — may they form
Our souls for heaven and thee!

163. C. M. WATTS.

God is everywhere.

1 IN all my vast concerns with thee,
In vain my soul would try
To shun thy presence, Lord, or flee
The notice of thine eye.

2 Thine all-surrounding sight surveys
My rising and my rest ;
My public walks, my private ways,
And secrets of my breast.

3 My thoughts lie open to the Lord,
Before they 're formed within ;
And, ere my lips pronounce the word,
He knows the sense I mean.

4 O, wondrous knowledge, deep and high !
Where can a creature hide ?
Within thy circling arms I lie,
Beset on every side.

5 So let thy grace surround me still,
And like a bulwark prove,
To guard my soul from every ill,
Secured by sovereign love.

164. L. M. WATTS

Perfections and Providence of God.

1 HIGH in the heavens, Eternal God !
Thy goodness in full glory shines ;
Thy truth shall break through every cloud
That veils and darkens thy designs.

2 For ever firm thy justice stands,
As mountains their foundations keep ;
Wise are the wonders of thy hands ;
Thy judgments are a mighty deep.

3 Thy providence is kind and large ;
Both man and beast thy bounty share;

The whole creation is thy charge,
But saints are thy peculiar care.

4 My God ! how excellent thy grace,
Whence all our hope and comfort springs !
The sons of Adam in distress
Fly to the shadow of thy wings.

5 Life, like a fountain, rich and free,
Springs from the presence of my Lord ;
And in thy light our souls shall see
The glories promised in thy word.

165. L. M. 6 L. MONTGOMERY.

God good and omniscient.

1 HOW precious are thy thoughts of peace,
O God ! to me, — how great the sum !
New every morn, they never cease ;
They were, they are, and yet shall come,
In number and in compass more
Than ocean's sand, or ocean's shore.

2 Search me, O God ! and know my heart ;
Try me, my secret soul survey ;
And warn thy servant to depart
From every false and evil way :
So shall thy truth my guidance be,
In life and immortality.

166. C. M. FAWCETT

The Ways of God inscrutable.

1 THY way, O God ! is in the sea ;
Thy paths I cannot trace,
Nor comprehend the mystery
Of thine unbounded grace.

2 Here the dark veils of flesh and sense
My captive soul surround ;
Mysterious deeps of providence
My inward thoughts confound.

3 As, through a glass, I dimly see
The wonders of thy love,
How little do I know of thee,
Or of the joys above !

4 Though but in part I know thy will,
I bless thee for the sight :
When will thy love the whole reveal
In glory's clearer light ?

5 In rapture shall I then survey
Thy providence and grace ;
And spend an everlasting day
In wonder, love, and praise.

167. 8 & 7s. M. BOWRING

God is Love.

1 GOD is love ; his mercy brightens
All the path in which we rove ;
Bliss he wakes and woe he lightens ;
God is wisdom, God is love.

2 Chance and change are busy ever ;
Man decays, and ages move ;
But his mercy waneth never ;
God is wisdom, God is love.

3 E'en the hour that darkest seemeth
Will his changeless goodness prove ;
From the gloom his brightness streameth ;
God is wisdom, God is love.

4 He with earthly cares entwineth
Hope and comfort from above :
Everywhere his glory shineth ;
God is wisdom, God is love.

168. C. M. GIBBONS

Goodness of God.

1 THY goodness, Lord, our souls confess ;
Thy goodness we adore ; —

A spring whose blessings never fail;
A sea without a shore.

2 Sun, moon, and stars thy love declare
In every golden ray;
Love draws the curtains of the night,
And love brings back the day.

3 Thy bounty every season crowns
With all the bliss it yields,
With joyful clusters loads the vines,
With strengthening grain the fields.

4 But chiefly thy compassion, Lord,
Is in the gospel seen;
There, like a sun, thy mercy shines,
Without a cloud between.

5 There pardon, peace, and holy joy,
Through Jesus' name, are given;
He on the cross was lifted high,
That we might reign in heaven.

169. S. M. WATTS.

Praising God for Mercies.

1 O, BLESS the Lord, my soul!
Let all within me join,
And aid my tongue to bless his name,
Whose favors are divine.

2 O, bless the Lord, my soul,
Nor let his mercies lie
Forgotten in unthankfulness,
And without praises die.

3 'T is he forgives thy sins,
'T is he relieves thy pain,
'T is he that heals thy sicknesses,
And makes thee young again.

4 He crowns thy life with love,
When ransomed from the grave:

He that redeemed my soul from death
Hath sovereign power to save.

5 He fills the poor with good;
He gives the sufferers rest:
The Lord hath judgments for the proud,
And justice for th' oppressed.

6 His wondrous works and ways
He made by Moses known;
But sent the world his truth and grace
By his belovéd Son.

170. H. M. J. Young.

God's wondrous Love.

1 O, FOR a shout of joy
Loud as the theme we sing!
To this divine employ
Your hearts and voices bring;
Sound, sound, through all the earth abroad,
The love, th' eternal love, of God.

2 Unnumbered myriads stand,
Of seraphs bright and fair,
Or bow at his right hand,
And pay their homage there;
But strive in vain, with loudest chord,
To sound the wondrous love of God.

3 Though earth and hell assail,
And doubts and fears arise,
The weakest shall prevail,
And grasp the heavenly prize,
And through an endless age record,
The love, th' unchanging love, of God.

171. C. M. Burder.

God is Love.

1 COME, ye that know and fear the Lord,
And lift your souls above;

Let every heart and voice accord,
  To sing, that God is love.

2 Behold, his loving-kindness waits
  For those who from him rove,
And calls of mercy reach their hearts,
  To teach them God is love.

3 O, may we all, while here below,
  This best of blessings prove:
Till warmer hearts, in brighter worlds,
  Shall shout that God is love.

172. S. M. DODDRIDGE.

God's Care a Remedy for ours.

1 HOW gentle God's commands!
  How kind his precepts are!
Come, cast your burdens on the Lord,
  And trust his constant care.

2 His bounty will provide,
  His saints securely dwell;
That hand which bears creation up
  Shall guard his children well.

3 Why should this anxious load
  Press down your weary mind:
O, seek your Heavenly Father's throne,
  And peace and comfort find.

4 His goodness stands approved,
  Unchanged from day to day;
I 'll drop my burden at his feet,
  And bear a song away.

173. C. M. MONTGOMERY

The Earth full of the Goodness of God.

1 GOD, in the high and holy place,
  Looks down upon the spheres;
Yet, in his providence and grace,
  To every eye appears.

2 He bows the heavens; the mountains stand,
A highway for our God;
He walks amidst the desert-land;
'T is Eden where he trod.

3 The forests in his strength rejoice;
Hark! on the evening breeze,
As once of old, Jehovah's voice
Is heard among the trees.

4 In every stream his bounty flows,
Diffusing joy and wealth;
In every breeze his spirit blows, —
The breath of life and health.

5 His blessings fall in plenteous showers
Upon the lap of earth,
That teems with foliage, fruits, and flowers,
And rings with infant mirth.

6 If God hath made this world so fair,
Where sin and death abound,
How beautiful beyond compare
Will paradise be found!

174. C. M. WATTS

God's Goodness.

1 SWEET is the memory of thy grace,
My God, my Heavenly King!
Let age to age thy righteousness
In songs of glory sing.

2 God reigns on high, but ne'er confines
His goodness to the skies;
Through all the earth his bounty shines,
And every want supplies.

3 How kind are thy compassions, Lord!
How slow thine anger moves!
But soon he sends his pardoning word,
To cheer the souls he loves.

4 Sweet is the memory of thy grace,
My God, my Heavenly King!
Let age to age thy righteousness
In songs of glory sing.

175. C. M. BROWNE

Universal Goodness of God.

1 LORD! thou art good; all nature shows
Its mighty author kind;
Thy bounty through creation flows,
Full, free, and unconfined.

2 The whole, and every part, proclaims
Thine infinite good-will;
It shines in stars, and flows in streams,
And blooms on every hill.

3 We view it o'er the spreading main,
And heavens which spread more wide;
It drops in gentle showers of rain,
And rolls in every tide.

4 Long hath it been diffused abroad,
Through ages past and gone;
Nor ever can exhausted be,
But still keeps flowing on.

5 Through the vast whole it pours supplies,
Spreads joy through every part:
O, may such love attract my eyes,
And captivate my heart!

6 My highest admiration raise,
My best affections move!
Employ my tongue in songs of praise,
And fill my heart with love!

176. 7s. M. MILTON.

Perfections and Providence of God.

1 LET us with a joyful mind
Praise the Lord, for he is kind,

For his mercies shall endure,
Ever faithful, ever sure.

2 Let us sound his name abroad,
For of gods he is the God,
Who by wisdom did create
Heaven's expanse and all its state ;

3 Did the solid earth ordain
How to rise above the main :
Who, by his commanding might,
Filled the new-made world with light ;

4 Caused the golden-tresséd sun
All the day his course to run ;
And the moon to shine by night,
'Mid her spangled sisters bright.

5 All his creatures God doth feed,
His full hand supplies their need ;
Let us therefore warble forth
His high majesty and worth.

6 He his mansion hath on high,
'Bove the reach of mortal eye ;
And his mercies shall endure,
Ever faithful, ever sure.

177. C. M. TATE & BRADY

God's Condescension.

1 O THOU, to whom all creatures bow
Within this earthly frame,
Through all the world how great art thou !
How glorious is thy name !

2 When heaven, thy glorious work on high,
Employs my wondering sight, —
The moon, that nightly rules the sky,
With stars of feebler light, —

3 Lord, what is man, that he is blessed
With thy peculiar care !

Why on his offspring is conferred
Of love so large a share ?

4 O Thou, to whom all creatures bow
Within this earthly frame,
Through all the world how great art thou !
How glorious is thy name !

178. C. P. M. Exeter Coll

Providential Goodness of God.

1 GREAT Source of unexhausted good,
Who giv'st us health, and friends, and food,
And peace, and calm content,
Like fragrant incense, to the skies
Let songs of grateful praises rise,
For all thy blessings lent.

2 Through all the dangers of the day,
Thy providence attends our way,
To guard us and to guide ;
Thy grace directs our wandering will,
And warns us, lest seducing ill
Allure our souls aside.

3 Thy smiles, with a reviving light,
Cheer the long, darksome hours of night,
And gild the thickest gloom ;
Thy watchful love around our bed
Doth softly, like a curtain, spread,
And guard the peaceful room.

4 To thee our lives, our all, we owe,
Our peace and sweetest joys below,
And brightest hopes above ;
Then let our lives, and all that 's ours,
Our souls, and all our active powers,
Be sacred to thy love.

179. S. M. CHRISTIAN PSALMIST

God working in the Soul.

1 'T IS God, the Spirit, leads
In paths before unknown :
The work to be performed is ours ;
The strength is all his own.

2 Assisted by his grace,
We still pursue our way,
And hope at last to reach the prize,
Secure in endless day.

3 'T is he that works to will,
'T is he that works to do,
His is the power by which we act,
His be the glory too.

180. L. M. DODDRIDGE.

Providential Bounties improved.

1 FATHER of lights ! we sing thy name
Who kindlest up the lamp of day ;
Wide as he spreads his golden flame,
His beams thy power and love display.

2 Fountain of good ! from thee proceed
The copious drops of genial rain,
Which, o'er the hill and through the mead,
Revive the grass, and swell the grain.

3 Through the wide world thy bounties spread ;
Yet millions of our guilty race,
Though by thy daily bounty fed,
Affront thy law, and spurn thy grace.

4 Not so may our forgetful hearts
O'erlook the tokens of thy care ;
But what thy liberal hand imparts
Still own in praise, still ask in prayer.

5 So shall our suns more grateful shine,
And showers in sweeter drops shall fall,

When all our hearts and lives are thine,
And thou, O God! enjoyed in all.

181. L. M. WESLEY'S COLL

Deliverances acknowledged

1 GOD of my life, whose gracious power
Through varied deaths my soul hath led,
Or turned aside the fatal hour,
Or lifted up my sinking head, —

2 In all my ways thy hand I own,
Thy ruling providence I see;
Assist me still my course to run,
And still direct my paths to thee.

3 Whither, O, whither should I fly,
But to my loving Father's breast,
Secure within thine arms to lie,
And safe beneath thy wings to rest?

4 I have no skill the snare to shun;
But thou, O God, my wisdom art:
I ever into ruin run;
But thou art greater than my heart.

5 Foolish, and impotent, and blind,
Lead me a way I have not known;
Bring me where I my heaven may find, —
The heaven of loving thee alone.

182. L. M. ADDISON

The Heavens declare the Glory of God.

1 THE spacious firmament on high,
With all the blue ethereal sky,
And spangled heavens, a shining frame,
Their great Original proclaim.
Th' unwearied sun, from day to day,
Doth his Creator's power display;
And publishes to every land
The work of an almighty hand

2 Soon as the evening shades prevail,
The moon takes up the wondrous tale,
And nightly to the listening earth
Repeats the story of her birth;
Whilst all the stars which round her burn,
And all the planets in their turn,
Confirm the tidings as they roll,
And spread the truth from pole to pole.

3 What though, in solemn silence, all
Move round this dark terrestrial ball;
What though no real voice nor sound
Amidst their radiant orbs be found;
In reason's ear they all rejoice,
And utter forth a glorious voice;
For ever singing, as they shine, —
"The hand that made us is divine."

183. 6s. M. DRUMMOND

Unity of God.

1 THE God who reigns alone
O'er earth, and sea, and sky,
Let man with praises own,
And sound his honors high.

2 Him all in heaven above,
Him all on earth below,
Th' exhaustless Source of love,
The great Creator, know.

3 He formed the living frame,
He gave the reasoning mind;
Then only he may claim
The worship of mankind.

4 So taught his only Son,
Blest messenger of grace!
Th' Eternal is but one,
No second holds his place.

184. S. M. WATTS

God our Shepherd.

1 THE Lord my Shepherd is;
I shall be well supplied;
Since he is mine, and I am his,
What can I want beside?

2 He leads me to the place
Where heavenly pasture grows,
Where living waters gently pass,
And full salvation flows.

3 If e'er I go astray,
He doth my soul reclaim,
And guides me, in his own right way,
For his most holy name.

4 While he affords his aid,
I cannot yield to fear;
Though I should walk through death's dark shade,
My Shepherd 's with me there.

185. L. M. 6 L. ADDISON.

God our Shepherd.

1 THE Lord my pasture shall prepare,
And feed me with a shepherd's care;
His presence shall my wants supply,
And guard me with a watchful eye:
My noonday walks he shall attend,
And all my midnight hours defend.

2 When in the sultry glebe I faint,
Or on the thirsty mountain pant,
To fertile vales and dewy meads
My weary, wandering steps he leads,
Where peaceful rivers, soft and slow,
Amid the verdant landscape flow.

3 Though in a bare and rugged way,
Through devious, lonely wilds I stray,

Thy bounty shall my pains beguile ;
The barren wilderness shall smile,
With sudden greens and herbage crowned,
And streams shall murmur all around.

4 Though in the paths of death I tread,
With gloomy horrors overspread,
My steadfast heart shall fear no ill ;
For thou, O Lord ! art with me still ;
Thy friendly crook shall give me aid,
And guide me through the dreadful shade.

186. 7s. M. WESLEYAN.

God a Refuge.

1 FATHER, Refuge of my soul,
Let me to thy bosom fly,
While the nearer waters roll,
While the tempest still is high :
Hide me, O my Father, hide,
Till the storm of life is past ;
Safe into the haven guide ;
O, receive my soul at last !

2 Other refuge have I none ;
Helpless hangs my soul on thee ;
Leave, O, leave me not alone !
Still support and comfort me.
All my trust on thee is stayed,
All my help from thee I bring ;
Cover my defenceless head
With the shadow of thy wing.

3 Thou, O God, art all I want ;
Boundless love, through Christ, I find :
Raise the fallen, cheer the faint,
Heal the sick, and lead the blind.
Thou of life the fountain art ;
Freely let me take of thee ;
Reign, O Lord, within my heart ;
Reign to all eternity.

187. H. M. WATTS

God's Mercies of Creation and Redemption.

1 GIVE thanks to God most high,
The universal Lord ;
The sovereign King of kings ;
And be his grace adored.
His power and grace | And let his name
Are still the same ; | Have endless praise.

2 How mighty is his hand !
What wonders hath he done !
He formed the earth and seas,
And spread the heavens alone.
Thy mercy, Lord, | And ever sure
Shall still endure ; | Abides thy word.

3 He sent his only Son
To save us from our woe,
From darkness, sin, and death,
And every hurtful foe.
His power and grace | And let his name
Are still the same ; | Have endless praise.

4 Give thanks aloud to God,
To God the Heavenly King ;
And let the spacious earth
His works and glories sing.
Thy mercy, Lord, | And ever sure
Shall still endure ; | Abides thy word.

188. C. M. DODDRIDGE.

God our All.

1 HOW firm the saint's foundation stands !
His hopes can ne'er remove,
Sustained by God's almighty hand,
And sheltered in his love.

2 God is the treasure of his soul,
A source of sacred joy,

Which no afflictions can control,
Nor death itself destroy.

3 Lord, may we feel thy cheering beams,
And taste thy saints' repose ;
We will not mourn the perished streams,
While such a fountain flows.

189. L. M. 6 L. BOWRING.

God's merciful Providence.

1 O, LET my trembling soul be still,
While darkness veils this mortal eye,
And wait thy wise, thy holy will,
Wrapped yet in fears and mystery :
I cannot, Lord, thy purpose see ;
Yet all is well, since ruled by thee.

2 When, mounted on thy clouded car,
Thou send'st thy darker spirits down,
I can discern thy light afar,
Thy light sweet beaming through thy frown .
And, should I faint a moment, then
I think of thee, and smile again.

3 So, trusting in thy love, I tread
The narrow path of duty on :
What though some cherished joys are fled ?
What though some flattering dreams are gone
Yet purer, brighter joys remain :
Why should my spirit, then, complain ?

190. C. M. WATTS.

God, as seen in Nature.

1 I SING th' almighty power of God,
That made the mountains rise,
That spread the flowing seas abroad,
And built the lofty skies.

2 I sing the wisdom that ordained
The sun to rule the day ;

The moon shines full at his command,
  And all the stars obey.

3 I sing the goodness of the Lord,
  That filled the earth with food;
He formed the creatures with his word,
  And then pronounced them good.

4 Lord! how thy wonders are displayed,
  Where'er I turn mine eye!
If I survey the ground I tread,
  Or gaze upon the sky!

5 There 's not a plant or flower below,
  But makes thy glories known;
And clouds arise, and tempests blow,
  By order from thy throne.

6 Creatures that borrow life from thee
  Are subject to thy care;
There 's not a place where we can flee,
  But God is present there.

191. S. M. STEELE.

God our Father.

1 MY Father! cheering name!
  O, may I call thee mine?
Give me the humble hope to claim
  A portion so divine.

2 This can my fears control,
  And bid my sorrows fly:
What real harm can reach my soul
  Beneath my Father's eye?

3 Whate'er thy will denies,
  I calmly would resign;
For thou art just, and good, and wise:
  O, bend my will to thine!

4 Whate'er thy will ordains,
  O, give me strength to bear;

Still let me know a father reigns,
And trust a father's care.

5 Thy ways are little known
To my weak, erring sight;
Yet shall my soul, believing, own
That all thy ways are right.

6 My Father! — blissful name!
Above expression dear!
If thou accept my humble claim,
I bid adieu to fear.

192. C. M. WATTS.

The Works of God recounted to Posterity.

1 LET children hear the mighty deeds
Which God performed of old,
Which in our younger years we saw,
And which our fathers told.

2 He bids us make his glories known,
His works of power and grace;
And we 'll convey his wonders down
Through every rising race.

3 Our lips shall tell them to our sons,
And they again to theirs,
That generations yet unborn
May teach them to their heirs.

4 Thus shall they learn, in God alone
Their hope securely stands,
That they may ne'er forget his works,
But practise his commands.

193. L. M. FLINT'S COLL.

The Divine Glories celebrated.

1 TO thee, O Lord, with humble fear,
The heavenly hosts their voices raise;
E'en mortals share thy bounties here;
Let mortals, too, attempt thy praise.

2 Of all things thou the parent art,
Of all things thou alone the end ;
On thee still fix our wandering heart,
To thee let all our actions tend.

3 Thou, Lord, art light ; thy native ray
No shade, no variation knows ;
To our dark souls thy light display,
The glory of thy face disclose.

4 Thou, Lord, art love ; the fountain thou
Whence mercy unexhausted flows ;
On barren hearts, O, shed it now,
And make the desert bear the rose !

5 So shall our every power to thee
In love and holy service rise ;
Yea, body, soul, and spirit be
Thy ever-living sacrifice.

194. L. M. Mrs Gilman

God our Father.

1 IS there a lone and dreary hour,
When worldly pleasures lose their power ?
My Father ! let me turn to thee,
And set each thought of darkness free.

2 Is there a time of rushing grief,
Which scorns the prospect of relief ?
My Father ! break the cheerless gloom,
And bid my heart its calm resume.

3 Is there an hour of peace and joy,
When hope is all my soul's employ ?
My Father ! still my hopes will roam,
Until they rest with thee, their home.

4 The noontide blaze, the midnight scene,
The dawn, or twilight's sweet serene,
The glow of life, the dying hour,
Shall own my Father's grace and power.

THE SCRIPTURES.

195. L. P. M. WATTS

Delight and Instruction from the Bible.

1 I LOVE the volume of thy word ;
What light and joy those leaves afford
To souls benighted and distressed !
Thy precepts guide my doubtful way ;
Thy fear forbids my feet to stray ;
Thy promise leads my heart to rest.

2 Thy threatenings wake my slumbering eyes,
And warn me where my danger lies ;
But 't is thy blessèd gospel, Lord,
That makes my guilty conscience clean,
Converts my soul, subdues my sin,
And gives a free, but large, reward.

3 Who knows the errors of his thoughts ?
My God, forgive my secret faults,
And from presumptuous sins restrain ;
Accept my poor attempts of praise,
That I have read thy book of grace,
And book of nature, not in vain.

196. L. M. WATTS

Strength and Peace from the Divine Word.

1 THERE is a stream whose gentle flow
Supplies the city of our God ;
Life, love, and joy still gliding through,
And watering our divine abode.

2 That sacred stream, thy holy word,
Supports our faith, our fear controls ;
Sweet peace thy promises afford,
And give new strength to fainting souls.

197. C. M. COWPER

Light and Glory of the Word.

1 THE Spirit breathes upon the word,
And brings the truth to sight;
Precepts and promises afford
A sanctifying light.

2 A glory gilds the sacred page,
Majestic like the sun:
It gives a light to every age;
It gives, but borrows none.

3 The hand that gave it still supplies
The gracious light and heat:
His truths upon the nations rise;
They rise, but never set.

4 Let everlasting thanks be thine
For such a bright display,
As makes a world of darkness shine
With beams of heavenly day.

5 My soul rejoices to pursue
The steps of Him I love,
Till glory break upon my view
In brighter worlds above.

198. L. M. 6 L. SPIRIT OF THE PSALMS

Praise to God for his Word.

1 JOIN, all ye servants of the Lord,
To praise him for his sacred word, —
That word, like manna, sent from heaven,
To all who seek it freely given;
Its promises our fears remove,
And fill our hearts with joy and love.

2 It tells us, though oppressed with cares,
The God of mercy hears our prayers;
Though steep and rough th' appointed way,
His mighty arm shall be our stay;

Though deadly foes assail our peace,
His power shall bid their malice cease.

3 It tells who first inspired our breath,
And who redeemed our souls from death;
It tells of grace, — grace freely given, —
And shows the path to God and heaven:
O, bless we, then, our gracious Lord,
For all the treasures of his word.

199. L. M. BOWRING.

Progress of Gospel Truth.

1 UPON the gospel's sacred page
The gathered beams of ages shine;
And, as it hastens, every age
But makes its brightness more divine.

2 On mightier wing, in loftier flight,
From year to year does knowledge soar;
And, as it soars, the gospel light
Adds to its influence more and more.

3 Truth, strengthened by the strength of thought,
Pours inexhaustible supplies,
Whence sagest teachers may be taught,
And wisdom's self become more wise.

4 More glorious still as centuries roll,
New regions blessed, new powers unfurled,
Expanding with th' expanding soul,
Its waters shall o'erflow the world; —

5 Flow to restore, but not destroy;
As when the cloudless lamp of day
Pours out its floods of light and joy,
And sweeps each lingering mist away.

200. C. M. WATTS.

Excellency of the Scriptures.

1 LET all the heathen writers join
To form one perfect book;

Great God, if once compared with thine,
How mean their writings look !

2 Not the most perfect rules they gave
Could show one sin forgiven,
Nor lead a step beyond the grave ;
But thine conduct to heaven.

3 I 've seen an end of what we call
Perfection here below, —
How short the powers of nature fall,
And can no farther go.

4 Our faith, and love, and every grace,
Fall far below thy word ;
But perfect truth and righteousness
Dwell only with the Lord.

201. C. M. Episcopal Coll

Sufficiency of the Scriptures.

1 GREAT God, with wonder and with praise
On all thy works I look ;
But still thy wisdom, power, and grace
Shine brightest in thy book.

2 Here are my choicest treasures hid ;
Here my best comfort lies ;
Here my desires are satisfied ;
And here my hopes arise.

3 Lord, make me understand thy law ;
Show what my faults have been ;
And from thy gospel let me draw
The pardon of my sin.

202. L. M. Exeter Coll.

Divine Love displayed in the Blessings of the Gospel.

1 TO thee my heart, Eternal King !
Would now its thankful tribute bring ,
To thee its humble homage raise,
In songs of ardent, grateful praise.

2 All nature shows thy boundless love,
In worlds below and worlds above ;
But in thy blessed word I trace
The richer glories of thy grace.

3 There what delightful truths are given ;
There Jesus shows the way to heaven ,
His name salutes my listening ear,
Revives my heart, and checks my fear.

4 There Jesus bids our sorrows cease,
And gives the laboring conscience peace ;
Raises our grateful feelings high,
And points to mansions in the sky.

5 For love like this, O, may our song
Through endless years thy praise prolong ;
And distant climes thy name adore,
Till time and nature are no more !

203. S. M. BEDDOME.

Superiority of the Scriptures.

1 O LORD, thy perfect word
Directs our steps aright ;
Nor can all other books afford
Such profit or delight.

2 Celestial light it sheds,
To cheer this vale below ;
To distant lands its glory spreads,
And streams of mercy flow.

3 True wisdom it imparts ;
Commands our hope and fear ;
O, may we hide it in our hearts,
And feel its influence there.

204. C. M. WESLEY'S COLL.

Prayer for a Blessing on the Word.

1 FATHER of all, in whom, alone,
We live, and move, and breathe,

One bright, celestial ray send down,
 And cheer thy sons beneath.

2 While in thy word we search for thee,
 O, fill our souls with awe;
Thy light impart, that we may see
 The wonders of thy law.

3 Now let our darkness comprehend
 The light that shines so clear;
Now thy revealing Spirit send,
 And give us ears to hear.

4 Before us make thy goodness pass,
 Which here, by faith, we know;
Let us in Jesus see thy face,
 And die to all below.

205. C. M. MONTGOMERY

Perfection of the Law and Testimony.

1 THY law is perfect, Lord of light,
 Thy testimonies sure;
The statutes of thy realm are right,
 And thy commandment pure.

2 Let these, O God, my soul convert,
 And make thy servant wise:
Let these be gladness to my heart,
 The dayspring to mine eyes.

3 By these may I be warned betimes;
 Who knows the guile within?
Lord, save me from presumptuous crimes,
 Cleanse me from secret sin.

4 So may the words my lips express,
 The thoughts that throng my mind,
O Lord, my strength and righteousness,
 With thee acceptance find.

206. C. M. Spirit of the Psalms.

The Study of God's Word.

1 HAPPY the children of the Lord,
Who, walking in his sight,
Make all the precepts of his word
Their study and delight.

2 That precious wealth shall be their dower,
Which cannot know decay,
Which moth nor rust shall e'er devour,
Nor spoiler take away.

3 For them that heavenly light shall spread,
Whose cheering rays illume
The darkest hours of life, and shed
A glory round the tomb.

4 Their works of piety and love,
Performed through Christ their Lord,
For ever registered above,
Shall meet a sure reward.

207. C. M. Heber.

The Seed of the Word.

1 O GOD, by whom the seed is given,
By whom the harvest blest;
Whose word, like manna showered from heaven,
Is planted in our breast;

2 Preserve it from the passing feet
And plunderers of the air;
The sultry sun's intenser heat,
And weeds of worldly care!

3 Though buried deep, or thinly strown,
Do thou thy grace supply:
The hope in earthly furrows sown
Shall ripen in the sky.

208. L. M. BEDDOME.

The Scriptures our Light and Guide.

1 WHEN Israel through the desert passed,
A fiery pillar went before,
To guide them through the dreary waste,
And lessen the fatigues they bore.

2 Such is thy glorious word, O God ;
'T is for our light and guidance given ;
It sheds a lustre all abroad,
And points the path to bliss and heaven.

3 It fills the soul with sweet delight,
And quickens its inactive powers ;
It sets our wandering footsteps right,
Displays thy love and kindles ours.

4 Its promises rejoice our hearts ;
Its doctrines are divinely true ;
Knowledge and pleasure it imparts ;
It comforts and instructs us too.

5 Ye favored lands, who have this word !
Ye saints, who feel its saving power !
Unite your tongues to praise the Lord,
And his distinguished grace adore.

209. C. M. C. WESLEY

Heavenly Bread.

1 WHAT is the chaff, the word of man,
When set against the wheat ?
Can it a dying soul sustain,
Like that immortal meat ?

2 Thy word, O God, with heavenly bread
The children doth supply ;
And those who by thy word are fed,
Their souls shall never die.

210. L. M. DODDRIDGE.

Divine Teachings and their happy Consequences.

1 BRIGHT Source of intellectual rays,
Father of spirits and of grace,
O, dart, with energy unknown
Celestial beamings from thy throne.

2 Thy sacred book we would survey,
Enlightened with that heavenly day,
And ask thy Spirit, with the word,
To teach our souls to know the Lord.

3 So shall our children learn the road
That leads them to their fathers' God;
And, formed by lessons so divine,
Shall infant minds with knowledge shine.

4 So shall the haughtiest soul submit,
With children placed at Jesus' feet;
The rising swell of pride shall cease,
And thy sweet voice be heard in peace.

211. C. M. STENNETT.

The Riches of God's Word.

1 LET worldly men from shore to shore
Their chosen good pursue;
Thy word, O Lord, we value more
Than treasures of Peru.

2 Here mines of knowledge, love, and joy
Are opened to our sight;
The purest gold without alloy,
And gems divinely bright.

3 The counsels of redeeming grace
These sacred leaves unfold;
And here the Saviour's lovely face
Our raptured eyes behold.

4 Here light descending from above
Directs our doubtful feet;

Here promises of heavenly love
  Our ardent wishes meet.

5 Our numerous griefs are here redressed,
  And all our wants supplied ;
Naught we can ask to make us blest
  Is in this book denied.

212. S. M. WATTS

Power of God's Word.

1 BEHOLD, the morning sun
  Begins his glorious way ;
His beams through all the nations run,
  And life and light convey.

2 But where the gospel comes,
  It spreads diviner light ;
It calls dead sinners from their tombs,
  And gives the blind their sight.

3 How perfect is thy word !
  And all thy judgments just !
For ever sure thy promise, Lord,
  And we securely trust.

4 My gracious God, how plain
  Are thy directions given !
O, may I never read in vain,
  But find the path to heaven.

213. C. M. WATTS

Love of the Scriptures.

1 O, HOW I love thy holy law !
  'T is daily my delight ;
And thence my meditations draw
  Divine advice by night.

2 I wake before the dawn of day,
  To meditate thy word ;
My soul with longing melts away,
  To hear thy gospel, Lord.

3 Thy heavenly words my heart engage,
And well employ my tongue,
And, through my weary pilgrimage,
Yield me a heavenly song.

4 When nature sinks, and spirits droop,
Thy promises of grace
Are pillars to support my hope,
And there I write thy praise.

214. C. M. STEELE.

The Bible suited to our Wants.

1 FATHER of mercies, in thy word
What endless glory shines!
For ever be thy name adored,
For these celestial lines.

2 'T is here the tree of knowledge grows,
And yields a free repast;
Here purer sweets than nature knows
Invite the longing taste.

3 'T is here the Saviour's welcome voice
Spreads heavenly peace around,
And life, and everlasting joys,
Attend the blissful sound.

4 O, may these heavenly pages be
My study and delight;
And still new beauties may I see,
And still increasing light.

215. S. M. SCOTT.

Searching the Scriptures.

1 IMPOSTURE shrinks from light,
And dreads the curious eye;
But sacred truths the test invite,
They bid us search and try.

2 O, may we still maintain
A meek, inquiring mind;

Assured we shall not search in vain,
But hidden treasures find.

3 With understanding blest,
Created to be free,
Our faith on man we dare not rest,
Subject to none but thee.

4 Lord, give the light we need ;
With soundest knowledge fill ;
From noxious error guard our creed,
From prejudice our will.

5 The truth thou shalt impart
May we with firmness own,
Abhorring each evasive art,
And fearing thee alone.

216. C. M. FAWCETT.

Value of the Scriptures.

1 HOW precious is the book divine,
By inspiration given !
Bright as a lamp its doctrines shine
To guide our souls to heaven.

2 It sweetly cheers our drooping hearts
In this dark vale of tears ;
Life, light, and joy it still imparts,
And quells our rising fears.

3 This lamp, through all the dreary night
Of life, shall guide our way,
Till we behold the glorious light
Of an eternal day.

JESUS CHRIST, HIS CHARACTER AND OFFICES.

217. 8 & 7s. M. CAWOOD.

Song of the Angels of Bethlehem.

1 HARK! what mean those holy voices,
Sweetly sounding through the skies?
Lo! th' angelic host rejoices;
Heavenly hallelujahs rise.

2 Listen to the wondrous story,
Which they chant in hymns of joy:
"Glory in the highest, glory!
Glory be to God most high!

3 "Peace on earth, good-will from heaven,
Reaching far as man is found:
Souls redeemed and sins forgiven:—
Loud our golden harps shall sound.

4 "Christ is born, the great Anointed;
Heaven and earth his praises sing!
O, receive whom God appointed,
For your Prophet, Priest, and King."

5 Let us learn the wondrous story
Of our great Redeemer's birth;
Spread the brightness of his glory,
Till it cover all the earth.

218. C. M. PATRICK.

Nativity of Christ.

1 WHILE shepherds watched their flocks by night,
All seated on the ground,
The angel of the Lord came down,
And glory shone around.

2 "Fear not," said he, — for mighty dread
Had seized their troubled mind;

"Glad tidings of great joy I bring
To you and all mankind.

3 "To you, in David's town, this day
Is born, of David's line,
The Saviour, who is Christ the Lord;
And this shall be the sign: —

4 "The heavenly babe you there shall find
To human view displayed,
All meanly wrapped in swathing bands,
And in a manger laid."

5 Thus spake the seraph, and forthwith
Appeared a shining throng
Of angels praising God, and thus
Addressed their joyful song: —

6 "All glory be to God on high,
And to the earth be peace!
Good-will henceforth, from heaven to men,
Begin and never cease."

219. C. M. E. H. Sears

Christmas Hymn.

1 CALM on the listening ear of night
Come heaven's melodious strains,
Where wild Judea stretches far
Her silver-mantled plains!

2 Celestial choirs, from courts above,
Shed sacred glories there;
And angels, with their sparkling lyres,
Make music on the air.

3 The answering hills of Palestine
Send back the glad reply;
And greet, from all their holy heights,
The dayspring from on high.

4 O'er the blue depths of Galilee
There comes a holier calm,

And Sharon waves, in solemn praise,
  Her silent groves of palm.

5 "Glory to God!" the sounding skies
  Loud with their anthems ring;—
"Peace to the earth,—good-will to men,
  From heaven's Eternal King!"

6 Light on thy hills, Jerusalem!
  The Saviour now is born!
And bright on Bethlehem's joyous plains
  Breaks the first Christmas morn.

220. 7s. M. Bowring

Report of the Watchman.

1 WATCHMAN! tell us of the night,
  What its signs of promise are.
Traveller! o'er yon mountain's height
  See that glory-beaming star.

2 Watchman! does its beauteous ray
  Aught of hope or joy foretell?
Traveller! yes; it brings the day,
  Promised day of Israel.

3 Watchman! tell us of the night;
  Higher yet that star ascends.
Traveller! blessedness and light,
  Peace and truth, its course portends.

4 Watchman! will its beams alone
  Gild the spot that gave them birth?
Traveller! ages are its own;
  See, it bursts o'er all the earth.

5 Watchman! tell us of the night,
  For the morning seems to dawn.
Traveller! darkness takes its flight;
  Doubt and terror are withdrawn.

6 Watchman! let thy wanderings cease;
  Hie thee to thy quiet home.

Traveller ! lo ! the Prince of Peace,
Lo ! the Son of God, is come.

221. C. M. SPIRIT OF THE PSALMS.

The guiding Star.

1 BRIGHT was the guiding star, that led,
With mild, benignant ray,
The Gentiles to the lowly bed
Where our Redeemer lay.

2 But, lo ! a brighter, clearer light
Now points to his abode ;
It shines through sin and sorrow's night,
To guide us to our Lord.

3 O, haste to follow where it leads ;
The gracious call obey,
Be rugged wilds, or flowery meads,
The Christian's destined way.

4 O, gladly tread the narrow path,
While light and grace are given ;
Who meekly follow Christ on earth
Shall reign with him in heaven.

222. 7s. M. SPIRIT OF THE PSALMS

Birth of Christ.

1 HAIL, all hail the joyful morn !
Tell it forth from earth to heaven,
That to us a child is born,
That to us a son is given.

2 Angels, bending from the sky,
Chanted at the wondrous birth ;
"Glory be to God on high,
Peace, — good-will to man on earth."

3 Join we then our feeble lays
To the chorus of the sky ;
And, in songs of grateful praise,
Glory give to God on high.

223. C. M. S. W. Livermore

The Coming of Christ.

1 GLORY to God, and peace on earth,
Was once by angels sung;
Glad tidings of a Saviour's birth
Through plains of Bethlehem rung.

2 He came to make the feeble strong,
To heal the deaf and blind,
To give the dumb the voice of song,
And free the captive mind.

3 He came the light of life to show,
The true and living way;
Where streams of joy unceasing flow,
And lead to endless day.

4 Glory to God! the gospel's sound
Our churches echo still;
Spread it, O Lord, the world around,
And with its spirit fill.

5 Glory to God! our hearts acclaim;
O, haste the happy time,
When songs shall sound the Saviour's name
O'er every distant clime.

224. 7s. M. M. W. Hale.

Christmas.

1 WHEN in silence, o'er the deep,
Darkness kept its deathlike sleep;
Soon as God his mandate spoke,
Light in wondrous beauty broke.

2 But a beam of holier light
Gilded Bethlehem's lonely night,
When the glory of the Lord,
Mercy's sunlight, shone abroad.

3 "Peace on earth, good-will to men,"
Burst the glorious anthem then;

Angels, bending from above,
Joined that strain of holy love.

4 Floating o'er the waves of time,
Comes to us that song sublime,
Bearing to the pilgrim's ear,
Words to soothe, sustain, and cheer.

5 For creation's blessed light,
Praise to thee, thou God of might!
Seraph-strains thy name should bless
For the Sun of Righteousness!

225. C. P. M. Miss Roscoe.

Christmas Hymn.

1 O, LET your mingling voices rise,
In grateful rapture, to the skies,
And hail a Saviour's birth:
Let songs of joy the day proclaim,
When Jesus all-triumphant came
To bless the sons of earth.

2 He came to bid the weary rest,
To heal the sinner's wounded breast,
To bind the broken heart,
To spread the light of truth around,
And to the world's remotest bound
The heavenly gift impart.

3 He came our trembling souls to save
From sin, from sorrow, and the grave,
And chase our fears away;
Victorious over death and time,
To lead us to a happier clime,
Where reigns eternal day.

226. H. M. Salisbury Coll.

The Song of Angels.

1 HARK! what celestial sounds,
What music fills the air!

Soft warbling to the morn,
It strikes the ravished ear :
Now all is still ; | In tuneful notes,
Now wild it floats, | Loud, sweet, and shrill.

2 Th' angelic hosts descend,
With harmony divine :
See how from heaven they bend,
And in full chorus join :
" Fear not," say they ; | Jesus, your King,
" Great joy we bring : | Is born to-day."

3 He comes your souls to save
From death's eternal gloom ;
To realms of bliss and light
He lifts you from the tomb :
Your voices raise, | Your songs unite
With sons of light ; | Of endless praise.

4 Glory to God on high !
Ye mortals spread the sound,
And let your raptures fly
To earth's remotest bound ;
For peace on earth, | To man is given,
From God in heaven, | At Jesus' birth.

227. L. M. H. K. White

The Star of Bethlehem.

1 WHEN, marshalled on the nightly plain,
The glittering host bestud the sky,
One star alone of all the train
Can fix the sinner's wandering eye.

2 Hark ! hark ! to God the chorus breaks,
From every host, from every gem ;
But one alone the Saviour speaks, —
It is the Star of Bethlehem !

3 Once on the raging seas I rode ;
The storm was loud, the night was dark ;

The ocean yawned, and rudely blowed
  The wind that tossed my foundering bark.

4 Deep horror then my vitals froze;
  Death-struck, I ceased the tide to stem;
When suddenly a star arose, —
  It was the Star of Bethlehem.

5 It was my guide, my light, my all;
  It bade my dark forebodings cease;
And, through the storm and danger's thrall,
  It led me to the port of peace.

6 Now, safely moored, my perils o'er,
  I 'll sing, first in night's diadem,
For ever, and for evermore, —
  The Star — the Star of Bethlehem!

228. C. M. WESLEY

A Light to lighten the Gentiles.

1 THE race that long in darkness pined
  Have seen a glorious light;
The people dwell in day, who dwelt
  In death's surrounding night.

2 To hail thy rise, thou better Sun,
  The gathering nations come,
With joy, as when the reapers bear
  The harvest treasures home.

3 To us a child of hope is born,
  To us a son is given;
And him shall all the earth obey,
  And all the hosts of heaven.

4 His power increasing still shall spread,
  His reign no end shall know;
His throne shall justice guard above,
  And peace abound below.

229. L. M. WATTS.

Glory and Grace in Christ.

1 NOW to the Lord a noble song!
Awake, my soul; awake, my tongue;
Hosanna to th' eternal name,
And all his boundless love proclaim.

2 See where it shines in Jesus' face,
The brightest image of his grace;
God, in the person of his Son,
Has all his mightiest works outdone.

3 The spacious earth and spreading flood
Proclaim the wise and powerful God;
And thy rich glories from afar
Sparkle in every rolling star.

4 But in his looks a glory stands, —
The noblest labor of thine hands;
The pleasing lustre of his eyes
Outshines the wonders of the skies.

5 Grace! 't is a sweet, a charming theme;
My thoughts rejoice at Jesus' name;
Ye angels, dwell upon the sound;
Ye heavens, reflect it to the ground.

230. C. M. T. FLETCHER

The Baptism and Inspiration of Jesus.

1 IN Judah's rugged wilderness,
Where Jordan rolls his flood,
In manners strict, and rude in dress,
The holy Baptist stood.

2 And while upon the river's side
The people thronged to hear,
"Repent," the sacred preacher cried;
"The heavenly kingdom 's near."

3 Now Jesus to the stream descends;
His feet the waters lave,

And o'er his head, that humbly bends,
  The Baptist pours the wave ;—

4 When, lo ! a heavenly form appears,
  Descending as a dove ;
And wondrous sounds th' assembly hears,
  Proclaiming from above,—

5 "This is my well-belovéd Son ;
  On him my spirit rests ;
Now is his reign of grace begun ;
  Attend his high behests."

6 The sacred voice has reached our ear,
  And still through distant lands
Shall sound, till all his name revere,
  And honor his commands.

231. C. M. DODDRIDGE.

Christ's Message.

1 HARK ! the glad sound ! the Saviour comes !
  The Saviour promised long !
Let every heart prepare a throne,
  And every voice a song.

2 On him the Spirit, largely poured,
  Exerts its sacred fire ;
Wisdom and might, and zeal and love,
  His holy breast inspire.

3 He comes, the prisoner to release,
  In Satan's bondage held ;
The gates of brass before him burst,
  The iron fetters yield.

4 He comes, from thickest films of vice
  To clear the mental ray,
And on the eyeballs of the blind
  To pour celestial day.

5 He comes, the broken heart to bind,
  The bleeding soul to cure,

And with the treasures of his grace
T' enrich the humble poor.

6 Our glad hosannas, Prince of Peace,
Thy welcome shall proclaim,
And heaven's eternal arches ring
With thy belovéd name.

232. S. M. WATTS

Blessedness of Gospel Times.

1 HOW beauteous are their feet,
Who stand on Zion's hill!
Who bring salvation on their tongues,
And words of peace reveal!

2 How charming is their voice!
How sweet the tidings are! —
"Zion, behold thy Saviour King!
He reigns and triumphs here."

3 How happy are our ears,
That hear this joyful sound,
Which kings and prophets waited for,
And sought, but never found!

4 How blesséd are our eyes,
That see this heavenly light!
Prophets and kings desired it long,
But died without the sight.

5 The watchmen join their voice,
And tuneful notes employ;
Jerusalem breaks forth in songs,
And deserts learn the joy.

6 O God, make bare thine arm
Through all the earth abroad·
Let every nation now behold
Their Saviour and their Lord.

233. L. M. MILMAN

Christ's Entry into Jerusalem.

1 RIDE on, ride on in majesty!
Hark, all the tribes hosanna cry!
Thy humble beast pursues his road,
With palms and scattered garments strowed.

2 Ride on, ride on in majesty!
In lowly pomp ride on to die!
O Christ, thy triumphs now begin
O'er captured death and conquered sin.

3 Ride on, ride on in majesty!
The wingèd squadrons of the sky
Look down with sad and wondering eyes,
To see th' approaching sacrifice.

4 Ride on, ride on in majesty!
Thy last and fiercest strife is nigh;
The Father, on his sapphire throne,
Expects his own anointed Son!

234. C. H. M. HEMANS.

The Agony in Gethsemane.

1 HE knelt; the Saviour knelt and prayed,
When but his Father's eye
Looked, through the lonely garden's shade,
On that dread agony;
The Lord of high and heavenly birth
Was bowed with sorrow unto death.

2 The sun went down in fearful hour;
The heavens might well grow dim,
When this mortality had power
To thus o'ershadow him;
That he who came to save might know
The very depths of human woe.

3 He knew them all, — the doubt, the strife,
The faint, perplexing dread;

The mists that hang o'er parting life
All darkened round his head ;
And the Deliverer knelt to pray ;
Yet passed it not, that cup, away.

4 It passed not, though the stormy wave
Had sunk beneath his tread ;
It passed not, though to him the grave
Had yielded up its dead ;
But there was sent him, from on high,
A gift of strength, for man to die.

5 And was his mortal hour beset
With anguish and dismay ?
How may we meet our conflict yet
In the dark, narrow way ?
How, but through him that path who trod ?
" Save, or we perish, Son of God."

235. L. M. BULFINCH.

Christ the Sufferer.

1 O, SUFFERING Friend of human kind !
How, as the fatal hour drew near,
Came thronging on thy holy mind
The images of grief and fear.

2 Gethsemane's sad midnight scene,
The faithless friends, th' exulting foes,
The thorny crown, the insult keen,
The scourge, the cross, before thee rose.

3 Did not thy spirit shrink dismayed,
As the dark vision o'er it came ;
And, though in sinless strength arrayed,
Turn, shuddering, from the death of shame ?

4 Onward, like thee, through scorn and dread,
May we our Father's call obey,
Steadfast thy path of duty tread,
And rise, through death, to endless day.

236. L. M. STENNETT.

Christ suffering on the Cross.

1 ' 'T IS finished!"—so the Saviour cried,
And meekly bowed his head and died:
" 'T is finished!"—yes, the race is run,
The battle fought, the victory won.

2 " 'T is finished!"—all that Heaven foretold
By prophets in the days of old;
And truths are opened to our view,
That kings and prophets never knew.

3 " 'T is finished!"—Son of God, thy power
Hath triumphed in this awful hour;
And yet our eyes with sorrow see
That life to us was death to thee.

4 " 'T is finished!"—let the joyful sound
Be heard through all the nations round;
" 'Tis finished!"—let the triumph rise
And swell the chorus of the skies.

237. L. M. WATTS.

Christ's Dying, Rising, and Reigning.

1 HE dies! the Friend of sinners dies!
Lo! Salem's daughters weep around
A solemn darkness veils the skies;
A sudden trembling shakes the ground

2 Here 's love and grief beyond degree;
The Lord of glory dies for men!
But, lo! what sudden joys we see!
Jesus, the dead, revives again!

3 The rising Lord forsakes the tomb;
The tomb in vain forbids his rise;
Cherubic legions guard him home,
And shout him welcome to the skies.

4 Break off your tears, ye saints, and tell
How high our great Deliverer reigns;

Sing how he spoiled the hosts of hell,
And led the monster Death in chains.

5 Say, " Live for ever, wondrous King !
Born to redeem, and strong to save " ;
Then ask the monster, " Where 's thy sting ? "
And " Where thy victory, boasting grave ? "

238. 7s. M. COLLYER.

Resurrection of Christ.

1 MORNING breaks upon the tomb !
Jesus dissipates its gloom !
Day of triumph through the skies,
See the glorious Saviour rise !

2 Christians, dry your flowing tears ;
Chase those unbelieving fears ;
Look on his deserted grave ;
Doubt no more his power to save.

3 Ye who are of death afraid,
Triumph in the scattered shade ;
Drive your anxious fears away ;
See the place where Jesus lay.

4 So the rising sun appears,
Shedding radiance o'er the spheres ;
So returning beams of light
Chase the terrors of the night.

239. L. M. BUTCHER

Resurrection of Christ.

1 HOSANNA ! let us join to sing
The glories of our rising King ;
Recount his deeds of might, and tell
How Jesus triumphed when he fell.

2 Soon as the morning's early ray
Brings on the third, th' appointed day,
Behold the angel cleave the skies,
Roll back the stone, and Jesus rise

3 With strength immortal forth he comes,
And power and life from God resumes ;
The days of pain and sorrow past,
His triumph shall for ever last.

4 Hosanna ! sons of men, record
The glories of your rising Lord ;
The triumphs of the Saviour tell,
Who died, and conquered when he fell

240. S. M. HAMMOND

Song of Moses and the Lamb.

1 AWAKE, and sing the song
Of Moses and the Lamb ;
Wake every heart, and every tongue,
To praise the Saviour's name.

2 Sing, till we feel our heart
Ascending with our tongue ;
Sing, till the love of sin depart,
And grace inspire our song.

3 Sing on your heavenly way,
Ye ransomed sinners, sing ;
Sing on, rejoicing every day
In Christ, the Heavenly King.

4 Soon shall we hear him say,
" Ye blessėd children, come ! "
Soon will he call us hence away,
To our eternal home.

5 There shall our raptured tongue
His endless praise proclaim,
And sweeter voices tune the song
Of Moses and the Lamb.

241. 7s. M. CUDWORTH.

Resurrection of Christ.

1 CHRIST, the Lord, is risen to-day,
Sons of men and angels say ;

Raise your songs of triumph high ;
Sing, ye heavens, and, earth, reply.

2 Love's redeeming work is done,
Fought the fight, the battle won ;
Lo ! our Sun's eclipse is o'er ;
Lo ! he sets in blood no more.

3 Vain the stone, the watch, the seal ;
Christ hath burst the gates of hell ;
Death in vain forbids his rise ;
Christ hath opened paradise.

4 Soar we now where Christ hath led,
Following our exalted Head :
Made like him, like him we rise ;
Ours the cross, the grave, the skies.

242. C. M. DUNCAN.

The spiritual Coronation.

1 ALL hail the power of Jesus' name !
Let angels prostrate fall ;
Bring forth the royal diadem,
And crown him Lord of all.

2 Ye chosen seed of Israel's race, —
A remnant weak and small, —
Hail him, who saves you by his grace,
And crown him Lord of all.

3 Let every kindred, every tribe,
On this terrestrial ball,
To him all majesty ascribe,
And crown him Lord of all.

4 O, that, with yonder sacred throng,
We at his feet may fall ;
We 'll join the everlasting song,
And crown him Lord of all.

243. L. M. BUTCHER

Miraculous Character of Jesus Christ.

1 WHAT works of wisdom, power, and love
Do Jesus' high commission prove !
Attest his heaven-derivéd claim,
And glorify his Father's name !

2 On eyes that never saw the day,
He pours the bright, celestial ray ;
And deafened ears, by him unbound,
Catch all the harmony of sound.

3 Lameness takes up its bed and goes
Rejoicing in the strength that flows
Through every nerve ; and, free from pain,
Pours forth to God the grateful strain.

4 The shattered mind his word restores,
And tunes afresh the mental powers ;
The dead revive, to life return,
And bid affection cease to mourn.

5 Canst thou, my soul, these wonders trace,
And not admire Jehovah's grace ?
Canst thou behold thy Saviour's power,
And not the God he served adore ?

244. P. M. H. WARE, JR

Hymn for Easter.

1 LIFT your glad voices in triumph on high,
For Jesus hath risen, and man cannot die :
Vain were the terrors that gathered around him,
And short the dominion of death and the grave ;
He burst from the fetters of darkness that bound him
Resplendent in glory, to live and to save :
Loud was the chorus of angels on high, —
The Saviour hath risen, and man shall not die.

2 Glory to God in full anthems of joy,
The being he gave us death cannot destroy :

Sad were the life we must part with to-morrow,
  If tears were our birthright, and death were our end;
But Jesus hath cheered the dark valley of sorrow,
  And bade us, immortal, to heaven ascend:
    Lift, then, your voices in triumph on high,
    For Jesus hath risen, and man shall not die.

245. C. M. C. WESLEY.

Praise to the Saviour.

1 O, FOR a thousand tongues to sing
  My dear Redeemer's praise,—
The glories of my Lord and King,
  The triumphs of his grace.

2 My gracious Master and my Lord,
  Assist me to proclaim,
To spread through all the earth abroad,
  The honors of thy name.

3 Jesus! the name that calms our fears,
  That bids our sorrows cease;
'T is music in the sinner's ears;
  'T is life, and health, and peace.

4 He breaks the power of reigning sin;
  He sets the prisoner free;
He makes the guilty conscience clean;
  And all our sorrows flee.

246. 7s. M. ANCIENT HYMNS

Rejoicing in Christ.

1 SWEET thy mem'ry, Saviour blest,
In the true believer's breast;
Musing on thy precious name,
Purest joys his heart inflame.

2 By the ear or tuneful tongue
Naught so sweet is heard or sung;
Naught the mind can dwell upon
Sweet as God's belovéd Son.

3 Thou the contrite sinner's stay,
Who thy goodness can display ?
How to those who *seek* thee kind !
What, ah ! what, to those who *find* ?

4 Tongue can speak not their delight,
Nor can pen of man indite ;
None can know, but they who prove,
What it is their Lord to love.

247. S. M. WATTS

God's Mercy in Christ.

1 RAISE your triumphant songs
To an immortal tune ;
Let all the earth resound the deeds
Celestial grace has done.

2 Sing how eternal love
Its best Belovéd chose,
And bade him raise our ruined race
From their abyss of woes.

3 His hand no thunder bears,
No terror clothes his brow,
No bolts to drive our guilty souls
To fiercer flames below.

4 Now, sinners, dry your tears ;
Let hopeless sorrow cease ;
Bow to the sceptre of his love,
And take the offered peace.

248. 8 & 7s. M. BOWRING

The Cross of Christ.

1 IN the cross of Christ I glory,
Towering o'er the wrecks of time ;
All the light of sacred story
Gathers round its head sublime.

2 When the woes of life o'ertake me,
Hopes deceive, and fears annoy,

Never shall the cross forsake me ;
Lo ! it glows with peace and joy.

3 When the sun of bliss is beaming
Light and love upon my way,
From the cross the radiance streaming
Adds more lustre to the day.

4 Bane and blessing, pain and pleasure,
By the cross are sanctified ;
Peace is there that knows no measure,
Joys that through all time abide.

249. 7s. M. LANGFORD.

Redeeming Love.

1 NOW begin the heavenly theme ;
Sing aloud in Jesus' name ;
Ye who his salvation prove
Triumph in redeeming love.

2 Ye who see the Father's grace
Beaming in the Saviour's face,
As to Canaan on ye move,
Praise and bless redeeming love.

3 Mourning souls, dry up your tears ;
Banish all your guilty fears ;
Welcome, all by sin oppressed,
Welcome to his sacred rest ;

4 Hither, then, your music bring ;
Strike aloud each cheerful string ;
Mortals, join the host above, —
Join to praise redeeming love.

250. C. M. DODDRIDGE

"He is risen."

1 YE humble souls that seek the Lord,
Chase all your fears away ;
And bow with reverence down, to see
The place where Jesus lay.

2 Thus low the Lord of life was brought,—
Such wonders love can do!
Thus cold in death that bosom lay
Which throbbed and bled for you.

3 But dry your tears and tune your songs,
The Saviour lives again;
Not all the bolts and bars of death
The conqueror could detain.

4 High o'er th' angelic band he rears
His once dishonored head;
And through unnumbered years he reigns,
Who dwelt among the dead.

251. 7s. M. 6 l. C. Wesley

Sun of Righteousness.

1 CHRIST, whose glory fills the skies,
Christ, the true, the only light,
Sun of Righteousness, arise,
Triumph o'er the shades of night;
Dayspring from on high, be near;
Daystar, in my heart appear.

2 Dark and cheerless is the morn,
If thy light is hid from me;
Joyless is the day's return,
Till thy mercy's beams I see;
Till they inward light impart,
Warmth and gladness to my heart.

3 Visit, then, this soul of mine;
Pierce the gloom of sin and grief;
Fill me, radiant Sun divine;
Scatter all my unbelief;
More and more thyself display,
Shining to the perfect day.

252. C. M. EPISCOPAL. COLL.

The Way, the Truth, and the Life.

1 THOU art the Way ; to thee alone
From sin and death we flee
And he who would the Father seek
Must seek him, Lord, through thee.

2 Thou art the Truth ; thy word alone
True wisdom can impart ;
Thou, only, canst instruct the mind,
And purify the heart.

3 Thou art the Life ; the rending tomb
Proclaims thy conquering arm ;
And those who put their trust in thee
Nor death nor hell shall harm.

4 Thou art the Way, the Truth, the Life ,
Grant us to know that way,
That truth to keep, that life to win,
Which lead to endless day.

253. S. M. H. MARTINEAU.

The Coming of Christ in the Power of his Gospel.

1 LORD Jesus, come ; for here
Our path through wilds is laid ;
We watch, as for the dayspring near,
Amid the breaking shade.

2 Lord Jesus, come ; for hosts
Meet on the battle plain ;
The patriot mourns, the tyrant boasts,
And tears are shed like rain.

3 Lord Jesus, come ; for still
Vice shouts her maniac mirth ;
The famished crave in vain their fill,
While teems the fruitful earth.

4 Hark ! herald voices near,
Lead on thy happier day ;

Come, Lord, and our hosannas hear;
We wait to strow thy way.

5 Come, as in days of old,
With words of grace and power;
Gather us all within thy fold,
And never leave us more.

254. C. M. DODDRIDGE

Jesus precious to them that believe.

1 JESUS, I love thy charming name;
'T is music to my ear;
Fain would I sound it out so loud
That earth and heaven might hear.

2 Yes, thou art precious to my soul,
My transport and my trust:
Jewels to thee are gaudy toys,
And gold is sordid dust.

3 Whate'er my noblest powers can wish
In thee doth richly meet;
No light unto my eyes so dear,
No friendship half so sweet.

4 Thy grace shall dwell upon my heart,
And shed its fragrance there,—
The noblest balm of all its wounds,
The cordial of its care.

255. C. P. M. MEDLEY.

Excellency of Christ.

1 O, COULD we speak the matchless worth,
O, could we sound the glories forth,
Which in our Saviour shine,
We 'd soar, and touch the heavenly strings,
And vie with Gabriel, while he sings,
In notes almost divine.

2 We 'd sing the characters he bears,
And all the forms of love he wears,
Exalted on his throne:
In loftiest songs of sweetest praise,
We would, to everlasting days,
Make all his glories known.

3 O, the delightful day will come,
When Christ, our Lord, will bring us home,
And we shall see his face:
Then, with our Saviour, Brother, Friend,
A blest eternity we 'll spend,
Triumphant in his grace.

256. S. M. FROTHINGHAM.

Christ's Manifestation.

1 WE meditate the day
Of triumph and of rest,
When, shown of God, and shaped in clay,
The Word was manifest.

2 Lord, give it gracious sweep,
And here its errand bless,
Whose mercy sent it o'er the deep,
To glad a wilderness.

3 Ray out its starry light,
To guide our pilgrim way, —
A sign of hope to this world's night,
And brighter than its day.

4 Again thy witness-voice!
Again thy spirit-dove!
That hearts may in its trust rejoice,
And soften with its love.

5 Send round its blessèd cup
As once in Galilee;
And catch our dull affections up
To heaven, and Christ, and thee.

257. C. M. BARBAULD.

Christ's Precepts of Love.

1 BEHOLD, where, breathing love divine,
Our dying Master stands ;
His weeping followers, gathering round,
Receive his last commands.

2 From that mild Teacher's parting lips
What tender accents fell !
The gentle precept which he gave
Became its author well.

3 " Blest is the man whose softening heart
Feels all another's pain ;
To whom the supplicating eye
Was never raised in vain ; —

4 " Whose breast expands with generous warmth,
A stranger's woes to feel ;
And bleeds in pity o'er the wound
He wants the power to heal.

5 " Peace from the bosom of his Lord,
My peace to him I give ;
And when he kneels before the throne,
His trembling soul shall live.

6 " Himself, through Christ, hath mercy found, —
Free mercy from above ;
That mercy moves him to fulfil
The perfect law of love."

258. C. M. WATTS.

The Examples of Christ and the Saints.

1 GIVE me the wings of faith to rise
Within the veil and see
The saints above, how great their joys,
And bright their glories be.

2 Once they were mourners here below,
And wet their couch with tears ;

They wrestled hard, as we do now,
With sins, and doubts, and fears.

3 I ask them whence their victory came;
They, with united breath,
Ascribe their conquest to the Lamb,
Their triumph to his death.

4 Our glorious Leader claims our praise,
For his own pattern given,
While the long cloud of witnesses
Shows the same path to heaven.

259. L. M. RUSSELL.

"That ye through his Poverty might be rich."

1 O'ER the dark wave of Galilee
The gloom of twilight gathers fast,
And on the waters drearily
Descends the fitful evening blast.

2 The weary bird hath left the air,
And sunk into his sheltered nest;
The wandering beast has sought his lair,
And laid him down to welcome rest.

3 Still near the lake, with weary tread,
Lingers a form of human kind;
And on his lone, unsheltered head
Flows the chill night-damp of the wind.

4 Why seeks he not a home of rest?
Why seeks he not a pillowed bed?
Beasts have their dens, the bird its nest;
He hath not where to lay his head.

5 Such was the lot he freely chose,
To bless, to save the human race;
And through his poverty there flows
A rich, full stream of heavenly grace.

260. C. M. MONTGOMERY

Singing the Song of the Redeemed.

1 SING we the song of those who stand
Around th' eternal throne,
Of every kindred, clime, and land,
A multitude unknown.

2 Life's poor distinctions vanish here ;
To-day, the young, the old,
Our Saviour and his flock, appear
One Shepherd and one fold.

3 Toil, trial, suffering, still await
On earth the pilgrim's throng ;
Yet learn we, in our low estate,
The church triumphant's song.

4 " Worthy the Lamb, for sinners slain,"
Cry the redeemed above,
" Blessing and honor to obtain,
And everlasting love."

5 " Worthy the Lamb," on earth we sing,
" Who died our souls to save ;
Henceforth, O Death, where is thy sting ?
Thy victory, O Grave ? "

6 Then hallelujah ! power and praise
To God in Christ be given ;
May all who now this anthem raise
Renew the song in heaven !

261. C. M. WATTS.

Moses and Christ.

1 NOT to the terrors of the Lord,
The tempest, fire, and smoke ;
Not to the thunder of that word
Which God on Sinai spoke ;—

2 But we are come to Zion's hill,
The city of our God,

Where milder words declare his will,
  And spread his love abroad.

3 Behold the great, the glorious host
  Of angels, clothed in light ;
Behold the spirits of the just,
  Whose faith is turned to sight ; —

4 Behold the blest assembly there,
  Whose names are writ in heaven ;
And God, the Judge of all, declares
  Their sins to be forgiven.

5 The saints on earth, and all the dead,
  But one communion make ;
All join in Christ, their living Head,
  And of his grace partake.

6 In such society as this
  My weary soul would rest :
The man that dwells where Jesus is
  Must be for ever blest.

262. L. M. WATTS.

Christ's Kingdom among the Gentiles.

1 JESUS shall reign where'er the sun
Does his successive journeys run ;
His kingdom stretch from shore to shore,
Till moons shall wax and wane no more.

2 For him shall endless prayer be made,
And endless praises crown his head ;
His name, like sweet perfume, shall rise
With every morning sacrifice.

3 People and realms of every tongue
Dwell on his love with sweetest song ;
And infant voices shall proclaim
Their early blessings on his name.

4 Blessings abound where'er he reigns ;
The joyful prisoner bursts his chains,

The weary find eternal rest,
And all the sons of want are blest.

5 Let every creature rise and bring
Peculiar honors to our King;
Angels descend with songs again,
And earth repeat the loud Amen.

263. L. M. Mrs. Mackay

Sleeping in Jesus.

1 ASLEEP in Jesus! blesséd sleep!
From which none ever wakes to weep;
A calm and undisturbed repose,
Unbroken by the dread of foes.

2 Asleep in Jesus! peaceful rest,
Whose waking is supremely blest;
No fear, no woes, shall dim that hour,
Which manifests the Saviour's power.

3 Asleep in Jesus! time nor space
Debars this precious hiding-place;
On Indian plains, or Lapland snows,
Believers find the same repose.

4 Asleep in Jesus! far from thee
Thy kindred and their graves may be;
But thine is still a blesséd sleep,
From which none ever wakes to weep.

264. L. M. Steele.

Example of the Saviour.

1 AND is the gospel peace and love?
So let our conversation be;
The serpent blended with the dove,
Wisdom and meek simplicity.

2 Whene'er the angry passions rise,
And tempt our thoughts or tongues to strife,
On Jesus let us fix our eyes,
Bright pattern of the Christian life!

3 O, how benevolent and kind !
  How mild ! how ready to forgive !
Be this the temper of our mind,
  And his the rules by which we live.

4 To do his Heavenly Father's will
  Was his employment and delight :
Humanity and holy zeal
  Shone through his life divinely bright !

5 Dispensing good where'er he came,
  The labors of his life were love ;
If, then, we love our Saviour's name,
  Thus let us our relation prove.

265. L. M. WATTS

Example of Christ.

1 MY dear Redeemer, and my Lord,
I read my duty in thy word ;
But in thy life the law appears
Drawn out in living characters.

2 Such was thy truth, and such thy zeal,
Such deference to thy Father's will,
Such love, and meekness so divine,
I would transcribe, and make them mine.

3 Cold mountains and the midnight air
Witnessed the fervor of thy prayer,
The desert thy temptations knew,
Thy conflict, and thy victory, too

4 Be thou my pattern ; may I bear
More of thy gracious image here ;
Then God, the Judge, shall own my name
Among the followers of the Lamb.

266. S. M. DODDRIDGE.

Attraction of the Cross.

1 BEHOLD th' amazing sight,
  The Saviour lifted high !

Behold the Father's chief delight
 Expire in agony !

2 For whom, for whom, my heart,
 Were all these sorrows borne ?
Why did he feel that piercing smart,
 And meet that various scorn ?

3 For love of us he bled,
 And all in torture died ;
'T was love that bowed his fainting head,
 And oped his gushing side.

4 In sympathy of love
 Let all the earth combine ;
And, drawn by cords so gentle, prove
 The energy divine.

5 In him our hearts unite,
 Nor share his grief alone,
But from his cross pursue their flight,
 To his triumphant throne.

267. L. M. DODDRIDGE

Christ's Submission to his Father's Will.

1 "FATHER divine," the Saviour cried,
While horrors pressed on every side,
And prostrate on the ground he lay,
"Remove this bitter cup away.

2 "But if these pangs must still be borne
Or helpless man be left forlorn,
I bow my soul before thy throne,
And say, Thy will, not mine, be done."

3 Thus our submissive souls would bow,
And, taught by Jesus, lie as low ;
Our hearts, and not our lips alone,
Would say, Thy will, not ours, be done.

4 Then, though like him in dust we lie,
We 'll view the blissful moment nigh,

Which, from our portion in his pains,
Calls to the joy in which he reigns.

268. S. M. NEEDHAM.

Christ the Light of the World.

1 BEHOLD ! the Prince of Peace,
The chosen of the Lord,
God's well belovéd Son, fulfils
The sure prophetic word.

2 No royal pomp adorns
This King of Righteousness ;
Meekness and patience, truth and love,
Compose his princely dress.

3 The spirit of the Lord,
In rich abundance shed,
On this great Prophet gently lights,
And rests upon his head.

4 Jesus, the light of men !
His doctrine life imparts ;
O, may we feel its quickening power
To warm and glad our hearts.

5 Cheered by its beams, our souls
Shall run the heavenly way ;
The path which Christ has marked and trod
Will lead to endless day.

269. L. M. DODDRIDGE.

Christ the Sun of Righteousness.

1 TO thee, O God ! we homage pay,
Source of the light that rules the day !
Who, while he gilds all nature's frame,
Reflects thy rays and speaks thy name.

2 In louder strains we sing that grace
Which gives the Sun of Righteousness,
Whose nobler light salvation brings,
And scatters healing from his wings.

3 Still on our hearts may Jesus shine,
With beams of light and love divine;
Quickened by him our souls shall live,
And cheered by him shall grow and thrive.

4 O, may his glories stand confessed,
From north to south, from east to west;
Successful may his gospel run,
Wide as the circuit of the sun.

5 When shall that radiant scene arise,
When, fixed on high, in purer skies,
Christ all his lustre shall display
On all his saints through endless day!

270. 7s. M. 6 L. MONTGOMERY

Christ our Example in Suffering.

1 GO to dark Gethsemane,
Ye that feel temptation's power;
Your Redeemer's conflict see;
Watch with him one bitter hour:
Turn not from his griefs away;
Learn of Jesus Christ to pray.

2 Follow to the judgment-hall;
View the Lord of life arraigned;
O, the wormwood and the gall!
O, the pangs his soul sustained!
Shun not suffering, shame, or loss;
Learn of him to bear the cross.

3 Calv'ry's mournful mountain climb;
There, admiring at his feet,
Mark that miracle of time,
God's own sacrifice complete:
"It is finished," hear him cry;
Learn of Jesus Christ to die.

4 Early hasten to the tomb
Where they laid his breathless clay;

All is solitude and gloom :
Who has taken him away ?
Christ is risen ; he meets our eyes :
Saviour, teach us so to rise.

271. C. M. ENFIELD

Example of Christ.

1 BEHOLD, where, in a mortal form,
Appears each grace divine ;
The virtues, all in Jesus met,
With mildest radiance shine.

2 To spread the rays of heavenly light,
To give the mourner joy,
To preach glad tidings to the poor,
Was his divine employ.

3 'Midst keen reproach, and cruel scorn,
Patient and meek he stood ;
His foes, ungrateful, sought his life ;
He labored for their good.

4 In the last hour of deep distress,
Before his Father's throne,
With soul resigned, he bowed, and said,
"Thy will, not mine, be done !"

5 Be Christ our pattern and our guide ;
His image may we bear ;
O, may we tread his holy steps,
His joy and glory share !

272. 7s. M. FURNESS.

Jesus our Leader.

1 FEEBLE, helpless, how shall I
Learn to live and learn to die ?
Who, O God, my guide shall be ?
Who shall lead thy child to thee ?

2 Blesséd Father, gracious One,
Thou hast sent thy holy Son ;

He will give the light I need,
He my trembling steps will lead.

3 Through this world, uncertain, dim,
Let me ever lean on him ;
From his precepts wisdom draw,
Make his life my solemn law.

4 Thus, in deed, and thought, and word,
Led by Jesus Christ the Lord,
In my weakness, thus shall I
Learn to live and learn to die.

5 Learn to live in peace and love,
Like the perfect ones above ; —
Learn to die without a fear,
Feeling thee, my Father, near.

THE GOSPEL AND ITS INVITATIONS

273. L. M. Bowring.

The Teaching of Jesus.

1 HOW sweetly flowed the gospel sound
From lips of gentleness and grace,
When listening thousands gathered round,
And joy and gladness filled the place !

2 From heaven he came, of heaven he spoke,
To heaven he led his followers' way ;
Dark clouds of gloomy night he broke,
Unveiling an immortal day.

3 " Come, wanderers, to my Father's home ;
Come, all ye weary ones, and rest " :
Yes, sacred Teacher, we will come,
Obey thee, love thee, and be blest.

4 Decay, then, tenements of dust !
Pillars of earthly pride, decay !

A nobler mansion waits the just,
And Jesus has prepared the way.

274. L. M. BEDDOME.

Excellence of the Gospel.

1 GOD, in the gospel of his Son,
Makes his eternal counsels known;
'T is here his richest mercy shines
And truth is drawn in fairest lines.

2 Wisdom its dictates here imparts,
To form our minds, to cheer our hearts;
Its influence makes the sinner live;
It bids the drooping saint revive.

3 Our raging passions it controls,
And comfort yields to contrite souls;
It brings a better world in view,
And guides us all our journey through.

4 May this blest volume ever lie
Close to my heart, and near my eye,
Till life's last hour my soul engage,
And be my chosen heritage.

275. C. M. WATTS.

The Gospel Trumpet.

1 LET every mortal ear attend,
And every heart rejoice;
The trumpet of the gospel sounds
With an inviting voice.

2 Ho! all ye hungry, starving souls,
That feed upon the wind,
And vainly strive with earthly toys
To fill an empty mind, —

3 Eternal Wisdom has prepared
A soul-reviving feast,
And bids your longing appetites
The rich provision taste.

4 Ho ! ye that pant for living streams,
And pine away, and die, —
Here you may quench your raging thirst
With springs that never dry.

5 The happy gates of gospel grace
Stand open night and day ;
Lord, we are come to seek supplies,
And drive our wants away.

276. L. M. WATTS

Gospel Mission.

1 THUS spake the Saviour, when he sent
His ministers to preach his word :
They through the world obedient went,
And spread the gospel of their Lord :

2 " Go forth, ye heralds, in my name ;
Bid all the world my grace receive ;
The gospel jubilee proclaim,
And call them to repent and live.

3 " The joyful news to all impart,
And teach them where salvation lies ;
Bind up the broken, bleeding heart,
And wipe the tear from weeping eyes.

4 " Be wise as serpents where you go,
But harmless as the peaceful dove,
And let your heaven-taught conduct show
That you 're commissioned from above.

5 " All power is vested in my hands ;
I will protect you and defend ;
Whilst thus you follow my commands,
I 'm with you till the world shall end."

277. H. M. DODDRIDGE.

Efficacy and Success of the Gospel.

1 MARK the soft-falling snow
And the diffusive rain !

To heaven, from whence it fell,
It turns not back again ;
But waters earth | And calls forth all
Through every pore, | Her secret store.

2 Arrayed in beauteous green,
The hills and valleys shine,
And man and beast are fed
By Providence divine :
The harvest bows | The copious seed
Its golden ears, | Of future years.

3 " So," saith the God of grace,
" My gospel shall descend,
Almighty to effect
The purpose I intend ;
Millions of souls | And bear it down
Shall feel its power, | To millions more."

278. L. M. WATTS

Excellency of the Christian Religion.

1 LET everlasting glories crown
Thy head, my Saviour and my Lord ;
Thy hands have brought salvation down,
And stored the blessings in thy word.

2 In vain the trembling conscience seeks
Some solid ground to rest upon ;
With long despair the spirit breaks,
Till we apply to Christ alone.

3 How well thy blessèd truths agree !
How wise and holy thy commands !
Thy promises, how firm they be !
How firm our hope and comfort stands !

4 Should all the forms that men devise
Assault my faith with treacherous art,
I 'd call them vanity and lies,
And bind the gospel to my heart.

279. 7s. M. 6 L. HAWES

Come and welcome.

1 FROM the cross uplifted high,
Where the Saviour deigns to die,
What melodious sounds we hear,
Bursting on the ravished ear ! —
" Love's redeeming work is done ;
Come and welcome, sinner, come.

2 " Spread for thee the festal board,
See, with richest dainties stored ;
To thy Father's bosom pressed,
Yet again a child confessed,
Never from his house to roam,
Come and welcome, sinner, come.

3 " Soon the days of life shall end ;
Lo ! I come, your Saviour, Friend,
Safe your spirits to convey
To the realms of endless day,
Up to my eternal home ;
Come and welcome, sinner, come."

280. 7s. M. BARBAULD

The Invitations of the Gospel.

1 COME ! said Jesus' sacred voice,
Come, and make my paths your choice :
I will guide you to your home ;
Weary pilgrim, hither come !

2 Thou, who, houseless, sole, forlorn,
Long hast borne the proud world's scorn,
Long hast roamed the barren waste,
Weary pilgrim, hither haste !

3 Ye, who, tossed on beds of pain,
Seek for ease, but seek in vain :
Ye, whose swollen and sleepless eyes
Watch to see the morning rise :

4 Ye, by fiercer anguish torn,
In remorse for guilt who mourn ;
Here repose your heavy care !
Conscience wounded, who can bear ?

5 Sinner, come ! for here is found
Balm that flows for every wound ;
Peace that ever shall endure ;
Rest eternal, sacred, sure.

281. C. M. MONTGOMERY

Mutual Invitation.

1 COME, let us join our souls to God
In everlasting bands,
And seize the blessings he bestows
With eager hearts and hands.

2 Come, let us to his temple haste,
And seek his favor there,
Before his footstool humbly bow,
And offer fervent prayer.

3 Come, let us share, without delay,
The blessings of his grace ;
Nor shall the years of distant life
Their mem'ry e'er efface.

4 O, may our children ever haste
To seek their fathers' God,
Nor e'er forsake the happy path
Their fathers' feet have trod.

282. L. M. DODDRIDGE

Religion the one Thing needful.

1 WHY do we waste in trifling cares
The lives divine compassion spares,
While, in the various range of thought,
The one thing needful is forgot ?

2 Our Father calls us from above,
Our Saviour pleads his dying love,

Awakened conscience gives us pain;
Shall all these pleas unite in vain?

3 Not so our dying eyes will view
The objects which we now pursue;
Not so eternity appear,
When the decisive hour is near.

4 Then wake, my soul, thy way prepare,
And lose in this each meaner care;
With steady step that path be trod,
Which through the grave conducts to God.

283. S. M. EPISCOPAL COLL.

Gospel Invitations.

1 THE Spirit, in our hearts,
Is whispering, "Sinner, come!"
The Bride, the church of Christ, proclaims
To all his children, "Come!"

2 Let him that heareth say
To all about him, "Come!"
Let him that thirsts for righteousness,
To Christ, the fountain, come!

3 Yes, whosoever will,
O, let him freely come,
And freely drink the stream of life;
'T is Jesus bids him come.

4 Lo, Jesus, who invites,
Declares, "I quickly come":
Lord, even so! I wait thine hour:
Jesus, my Saviour, come!

284. 7s. M. EPISCOPAL COLL.

The Sinner entreated to awake.

1 SINNER, rouse thee from thy sleep;
Wake, and o'er thy folly weep;
Raise thy spirit, dark and dead;
Jesus waits his light to shed.

2 Wake from sleep; arise from death;
See the bright and living path;
Watchful, tread that path; be wise;
Leave thy folly; seek the skies.

3 Leave thy folly; cease from crime;
From this hour redeem thy time;
Life secure without delay;
Evil is thy mortal day.

4 O, then, rouse thee from thy sleep;
Wake, and o'er thy folly weep;
Jesus calls from death and night;
Jesus waits to shed his light.

285. S. M. SELECT HYMN

Now the Day of Grace.

1 NOW is the day of grace;
Now to the Father come;
The Lord is calling, "Seek my face,
And I will guide you home."

2 The Saviour bids you speed;
O, wherefore then delay?
He calls in love; he sees your need;
He bids you come to-day.

3 To-day the prize is won;
The promise is to save;
Then, O, be wise; to-morrow's sun
May shine upon your grave.

286. S. M. DODDRIDGE

A timely Improvement of Life.

1 THE swift-declining day,
How fast its moments fly!
While evening's broad and gloomy shade
Gains on the western sky.

2 Ye mortals! mark its pace;
Improve the hours of light;

And know, your Maker can command
An instantaneous night.

3 His word blots out the sun
In its meridian blaze ;
And cuts from sanguine, vigorous youth
The remnant of its days.

4 On the dark mountain's brow
Your feet shall quickly slide,
And from its airy summit dash
Your momentary pride.

5 What most demands your care,
O, be it still pursued !
Lest, slighted once, the season fair
Should never be renewed.

6 Then shall new lustre break
Through horror's darkest gloom,
And lead you to unchanging light,
In a celestial home.

287. 7 & 6s. M. Mo[illegible]RY

Blessings of Christ's Kingdom.

1 HAIL to the Lord's Anointed,
Great David's greater Son !
Hail ! in the time appointed
His reign on earth begun !
He comes to break oppression,
To set the captive free,
To take away transgression,
And rule in equity.

2 He comes, with succour speedy,
To those who suffer wrong ;
To help the poor and needy,
And bid the weak be strong ;
To give them songs for sighing,
Their darkness turn to light,
Whose souls, condemned and dying,
Were precious in his sight.

3 He shall descend like showers
Upon the fruitful earth,
And love and joy, like flowers,
Spring in his path to birth ;
Before him, on the mountains,
Shall peace, the herald, go ;
And righteousness, in fountains,
From hill to valley flow.

4 For him shall prayer unceasing
And daily vows ascend,
His kingdom still increasing, —
A kingdom without end :
The tide of time shall never
His covenant remove ;
His name shall stand for ever ;
That name to us is love.

288. L. M. 6 L. ANONYMOUS

The Gospel gives Peace and Rest.

1 PEACE, troubled soul, whose plaintive moan
Hath taught these rocks the notes of woe ;
Cease thy complaints, suppress thy groan,
And let thy tears forget to flow :
Behold the precious balm is found,
Which lulls thy pain, which heals thy wound.

2 Come, freely come, by sin oppressed,
Unburden here the weighty load,
Here find thy refuge and thy rest,
And trust the mercy of thy God :
Thy God 's thy Father, — glorious word !
For ever love and praise the Lord.

3 As spring the winter, day the night,
Peace sorrow's gloom shall chase away,
And smiling joy, a seraph bright,
Shall tend thy steps and near thee stay ;
Whilst glory weaves th' immortal crown,
And waits to claim thee for her own.

SPIRITUAL INFLUENCES.

289. H. M. CAMPBELL'S COLL

Pleading the Promise of the Spirit.

1 O THOU that hearest prayer,
Attend our humble cry,
And let thy servants share
Thy blessing from on high:
We plead the promise of thy word,
Grant us thy holy spirit, Lord.

2 If earthly parents hear
Their children when they cry,—
If they, with love sincere,
Their varied wants supply,—
Much more wilt thou thy love display,
And answer when thy children pray.

3 Our Heavenly Father, thou;
We, children of thy grace:
O, let thy spirit now
Descend and fill the place:
So shall we feel the heavenly flame,
And all unite to praise thy name.

4 O, may that sacred fire,
Descending from above,
Our languid hearts inspire
With fervent zeal and love:
Enlighten our beclouded eyes,
And teach our grovelling souls to rise.

5 And send thy spirit down
On all the nations, Lord,
With great success to crown
The preaching of thy word,
Till heathen lands shall own thy sway,
And cast their idol gods away.

290. 8, 6, & 4s. M. Spirit of the Psalms.

The Holy Spirit the Comforter.

1 OUR blest Redeemer, ere he breathed
His tender, last farewell,
A Guide, a Comforter, bequeathed
With us to dwell.

2 He came in tongues of living flame,
To teach, convince, subdue ;
All powerful as the wind he came,
As viewless too.

3 He came sweet influence to impart,
A gracious, willing guest,
While he can find one humble heart
Wherein to rest.

4 And his that gentle voice we hear,
Soft as the breeze of even,
That checks each fault, that calms each fear,
And speaks of heaven.

5 And every virtue we possess,
And every victory won,
And every thought of holiness,
Are his alone.

6 Spirit of purity and grace,
Our weakness, pitying, see ;
O, make our hearts thy dwelling-place,
And worthier thee.

291. L. M. Burder's Coll.

Quickening Spirit.

1 COME, Holy Spirit, calm my mind,
And fit me to approach my God ;
Remove each vain, each worldly thought,
And lead me to thy blest abode.

2 Hast thou imparted to my soul
A living spark of holy fire ?

O, kindle now the sacred flame,
And make me burn with pure desire.

3 A brighter faith and hope impart,
And let me now my Saviour see ;
O, soothe and cheer my burdened heart,
And bid my spirit rest in thee.

292. C. M. WATTS

For Fervency of Devotion.

1 COME, Holy Spirit, heavenly Dove,
With all thy quickening powers,
Kindle a flame of sacred love
In these cold hearts of ours.

2 In vain we tune our formal songs,
In vain we strive to rise ;
Hosannas languish on our tongues,
And our devotion dies.

3 Come, Holy Spirit, heavenly Dove,
With all thy quickening powers ;
Come, shed abroad a Saviour's love,
And that shall kindle ours.

293. C. M. PRATT'S COLL.

Reviving Spirit.

1 ETERNAL Spirit, God of truth,
Our contrite hearts inspire ;
Revive the flame of heavenly love,
And feed the pure desire.

2 'T is thine to soothe the sorrowing mind,
With guilt and fear oppressed ;
'T is thine to bid the dying live,
And give the weary rest.

3 Subdue the power of every sin,
Whate'er that sin may be,
That we, with humble, holy heart,
May worship only thee.

294. S. M. HART

Sanctifying Influence.

1 COME, Holy Spirit, come ;
Let thy bright beams arise ;
Dispel the sorrow from our minds,
The darkness from our eyes.

2 Convince us all of sin ;
Lead us to thine abode,
And to our wondering view reveal
Thy mercies, O our God !

3 Revive our drooping faith,
Our doubts and fears remove,
And kindle in our breasts the flame
Of never-dying love.

4 'T is thine to cleanse the heart,
To sanctify the soul,
To pour fresh life in every part
And new-create the whole.

5 Dwell, Spirit, in our hearts ;
Our minds from bondage free ;
Then shall we know, and praise, and love,
And rise at length to thee.

295. 7s. M. BATHURST.

The teaching Spirit.

1 HOLY Spirit, from on high,
Bend o'er us a pitying eye ;
Now refresh the drooping heart,
Bid the power of sin depart.

2 Light up every dark recess
Of our heart's ungodliness ;
Show us every devious way
Where our steps have gone astray.

3 Teach us, with repentant grief,
Humbly to implore relief ;

Then the Saviour's love reveal,
And our broken spirits heal.

4 May we daily grow in grace,
And pursue the heavenly race,
Trained in wisdom, led by love,
Till we reach our rest above.

296. L. M. BROWNE.

Our Guide.

1 Come, gracious Spirit, heavenly Dove,
With light and comfort from above;
Be thou our guardian, thou our guide;
O'er every thought and step preside.

2 To us the light of truth display,
And make us know and choose thy way,
Plant holy fear in every heart,
That we from God may ne'er depart.

3 Lead us to holiness, — the road
Which we must take to dwell with God,
Lead us to Christ, — the living way, —
Nor let us from his pastures stray; —

4 Lead us to God, — our final rest, —
To be with him for ever blest;
Lead us to heaven, its bliss to share, —
Fulness of joy for ever there.

297. L. M. BEDDOME.

Teachings of the Spirit.

1 COME, blessèd Spirit, heavenly Light,
Whose power and grace are unconfined,
Dispel the gloomy shades of night,
The thicker darkness of the mind.

2 To mine illumined eyes display
The glorious truth thy words reveal;
Cause me to run the heavenly way;
Make me delight to do thy will.

3 Thine inward teachings make me know
The wonders of redeeming love,
The vanity of things below,
And excellence of things above.

4 While through these dubious paths I stray,
Spread, like the sun, thy beams abroad;
O, show the dangers of the way,
And guide my feeble steps to God!

298. C. M. BREVIARY.

Holy Aspirations.

1 THE Saviour now is gone before
To yon blest realms of light:
O, thither may our spirits soar,
And wing their upward flight.

2 Lord, make us to those joys aspire,
That spring from love to thee,
That pass the carnal heart's desire,
And faith alone can see.

3 To guide us to thy glories, Lord,
To lift us to the sky,
O, may thy spirit still be poured
Upon us from on high.

299. 7s. M. STOCKER

Influences of the Spirit.

1 GRACIOUS Spirit! Love divine!
Let thy light within me shine;
All my guilty fears remove;
Fill me with thy heavenly love.

2 Life and peace to me impart;
Seal salvation on my heart;
Dwell thyself within my breast,
Earnest of immortal rest.

3 Let me never from thee stray;
Keep me in the narrow way;

Fill my soul with joy divine ;
Keep me, Lord, for ever thine.

300. C. M. DODDRIDGE.

The Spirit desired.

1 GREAT Father of our feeble race,
Behold, thy servants wait ;
With longing eyes and lifted hands,
We flock around thy gate.

2 O, shed abroad that royal gift,
Thy spirit, from above,
To bless our eyes with sacred light,
And fire our hearts with love.

3 Blest earnest of eternal joy,
Declare our sins forgiven,
And bear, with energy divine,
Our raptured thoughts to heaven.

4 Diffuse, O God, refreshing showers,
That earth its fruit may yield,
And change this barren wilderness
To Carmel's flowery field.

301. 8 & 7s. M. HASTINGS.

Guidance implored.

1 GENTLY, Lord ! O, gently lead us,
Through this lonely vale of tears ;
Through the changes thou 'st decreed us,
Till our last great change appears :
When temptations darts assail us,
When in devious paths we stray,
Let thy goodness never fail us,—
Lead us in thy perfect way.

2 In the hour of pain and anguish,
In the hour when death draws near,
Suffer not our hearts to languish,—
Suffer not our souls to fear :

And, when mortal life is ended,
May we wake among the blest,
And, by all the saints attended,
Ever on thy bosom rest.

302. 10s. M. Dr. Johnson

Imploring Divine Light.

1 O THOU, whose power o'er moving worlds presides
Whose voice created, and whose wisdom guides,
On darkling man in pure effulgence shine,
And cheer the clouded mind with light divine.

2 'T is thine alone to calm the pious breast
With silent confidence and holy rest:
From thee, great God, we spring; to thee we tend.
Path, Motive, Guide, Original, and End.

303. L. M. Doddridge

Living Waters.

1 BLEST Spirit, Source of grace divine,
What soul-refreshing streams are thine!
O, bring these healing waters nigh,
Or we must droop, and fall, and die.

2 No traveller through desert lands,
'Midst scorching suns and burning sands,
More eager longs for cooling rain,
Or pants the current to obtain.

3 Our longing souls aloud would sing;
Spring up, celestial fountain, spring;
To a redundant river flow,
And cheer this thirsty land below.

4 May this blest torrent, near my side,
Through all the desert swiftly glide;
Then, in Immanuel's land above,
Spread to a sea of joy and love!

304. S. M. WESLEYAN

For a holy Heart.

1 GREAT Source of life and light,
Thy heavenly grace impart,
And by thy holy spirit write
Thy law upon my heart:
My soul would cleave to thee;
Let naught my purpose move;
O, let my faith more steadfast be,
And more intense my love!

2 Imbue my constant mind
With deep humility,
And let an ardent zeal be joined
With perfect charity;
That grace to me impart,
With meekness to reprove,
To hate the sin with all my heart,
And still the sinner love.

3 Long as my trials last,
Long as the cross I bear,
O, let my soul on thee be cast
In confidence and prayer!
Conduct me to the shore
Of everlasting peace,
Where storm and tempest rise no more,
Where sin and sorrow cease.

305. L. M. 6 L. WESLEY'S COLL

For the Direction of God's Spirit.

1 LEADER of Israel's host, and Guide
Of all who seek the land above,
Beneath thy shadow we abide,
The cloud of thy protecting love;
Our strength thy grace, our rule thy word,
Our end the glory of the Lord.

2 By thine unerring spirit led,
We shall not in the desert stray;
We shall not full direction need,
Nor miss our providential way;
As far from danger as from fear,
While Love, almighty Love, is near.

306. C. M. Spirit of the Psalms.

The Peace-giving Spirit.

1 SPIRIT of peace, celestial Dove!
How excellent thy praise!
No richer gift than Christian love
Thy gracious power displays.

2 Sweet as the dew on herb and flower
That silently distils,
At evening's soft and balmy hour,
On Zion's fruitful hills, —

3 So with mild influence from above
Shall promised grace descend;
Till universal peace and love
O'er all the earth extend.

307. L. M. Companion Hymn Book.

The Soul thirsting for God.

1 FOUNTAIN of all-sufficient bliss
To men below, to saints above,
Fulness of joy in thee there is,
Fulness of light, fulness of love.

2 Enter, and fill my waiting mind;
Give me that peace, that calm repose,
Which self-complacence cannot find,
Which self-abasement only knows.

3 To thee my inmost soul aspires;
To thee I plight my solemn vows;
Keep me from all impure desires,
And all my best affections rouse.

4 Fit me to join thy saints on high,
Who brightly shine, in bliss complete;
Who view thy glorious majesty,
And cast their crowns before thy feet.

308. C. M. BULFINCH

Peace in the Storm.

1 LORD, in whose might the Saviour trod
The dark and stormy wave,
And trusted in his Father's arm,
Omnipotent to save; —

2 When thickly round our footsteps rise
The floods and storms of life,
Send thou thy spirit down to still
The dark and fearful strife.

3 Strong in our trust, on thee reposed,
The ocean path we 'll dare,
Though waves around us rage and foam,
Since thou art present there.

309. C. M. STEELE

Succour implored in spiritual Conflicts.

1 O GRACIOUS God, in whom I live,
My feeble efforts aid;
Help me to watch, and pray, and strive,
Though trembling and afraid.

2 Increase my faith, increase my hope,
When foes and fears prevail;
O, bear my fainting spirit up,
Or soon my strength will fail.

3 Whene'er temptations lure my heart,
Or draw my feet aside,
My God, thy powerful aid impart,
My Guardian and my Guide.

4 O, keep me in thy heavenly way,
And bid the tempter flee;

And let me never, never stray
From happiness and thee.

310. L. M. MORAVIAN

For Guardianship and Guidance.

1 O THOU, to whose all-searching sight
The darkness shineth as the light,
Search, prove my heart ; it pants for thee ;
O, burst these bonds, and set it free !

2 If in this darksome wild I stray,
Be thou my light, be thou my way ;
No foes, no violence, I fear,
No fraud, while thou, my God, art near.

3 When rising floods my soul o'erflow,
When sinks my heart in waves of woe,
O God, thy timely aid impart,
And raise my head and cheer my heart.

4 If rough and thorny be the way,
My strength proportion to my day ;
Till toil, and grief, and pain, shall cease,
Where all is calm, and joy, and peace.

311. C. M. WATTS

Prayer for quickening Grace.

1 MY soul lies cleaving to the dust ;
Lord, give me life divine ;
From vain desires, and every lust,
Turn off these eyes of mine.

2 I need the influence of thy grace
To speed me in thy way,
Lest I should loiter in my race,
Or turn my feet astray.

3 Are not thy mercies sovereign still,
And thou a faithful God ?
Wilt thou not grant me warmer zeal
To run the heavenly road ?

4 Does not my heart thy precepts love,
And long to see thy face?
And yet how slow my spirits move
Without enlivening grace!

5 Then shall I love thy gospel more,
And ne'er forget thy word,
When I have felt its quickening power
To draw me near the Lord.

312. L. M. DRYDEN.

Divine Light and Guidance implored.

1 O SOURCE of uncreated light,
By whom the worlds were raised from night,
Come, visit every pious mind;
Come, pour thy joys on human kind.

2 Plenteous in grace, descend from high,
Rich in thy matchless energy:
From sin and sorrow set us free,
And make us temples worthy thee.

3 Cleanse and refine our earthly parts,
Inflame and sanctify our hearts,
Our frailties help, our vice control,
Submit the senses to the soul.

4 Thrice holy Fount! thrice holy Fire!
Our hearts with heavenly love inspire;
Make us eternal truths receive,
Aid us to live as we believe.

5 Chase from our path each noxious foe,
And peace, the fruit of love, bestow;
And, lest our feet should step astray,
Protect and guide us in our way.

313. C. M. SALISBURY COLL

Divine Aid implored.

1 THINE influence, mighty God! is felt
Through nature's ample round;

In heaven, on earth, through air and skies,
Thy energy is found.

2 Thy sacred influence, Lord! we need
To form our hearts anew;
O, cleanse our souls from every sin,
And thy salvation show!

3 Father of light! thine aid impart
To guide our doubtful way;
Thy truth shall scatter every cloud,
And make a glorious day.

4 Supported by thy heavenly grace,
We 'll do and bear thy will;
That grace shall make each burden light,
And every murmur still.

5 Cheered by thy smiles, we 'll fearless tread
The gloomy path of death;
And, with the hopes of endless bliss,
To thee resign our breath.

314. C. M. SMART.

Heavenly Wisdom implored through the Perils of Life.

1 FATHER of light! conduct my feet
Through life's dark, dangerous road;
Let each advancing step still bring
Me nearer to my God.

2 Let heaven-eyed prudence be my guide,
And, when I go astray,
Recall my feet from folly's path
To wisdom's better way.

3 Teach me in every various scene
To keep my end in sight;
And, while I tread life's mazy track,
Let wisdom guide me right.

4 That heavenly wisdom from above
Abundantly impart;

And let it guard, and guide, and warm,
  And penetrate my heart;
5 Till it shall lead me to thyself,
  Fountain of bliss and love!
And all my darkness be dispersed
  In endless light above.

315. C. M. SPIRIT OF THE PSALMS.

God our Portion on Earth and in Heaven.

1 WHOM have we, Lord, in heaven but thee,
  And whom on earth beside?
Where else for succour can we flee,
  Or in whose strength confide?

2 Thou art our portion here below,
  Our promised bliss above;
Ne'er may our souls an object know
  So precious as thy love.

3 Thou, Lord, wilt be our guide through life,
  And help and strength supply;
Sustain us in death's fearful strife,
  And welcome us on high.

316. L. M. BULFINCH.

The Voice of God in the Heart.

1 HATH not thy heart within thee burned
  At evening's calm and holy hour,
As if its inmost depths discerned
  The presence of a loftier power?

2 Hast thou not heard 'mid forest glades,
  While ancient rivers murmured by,
A voice from forth th' eternal shades,
  That spake a present Deity?

3 And as, upon the sacred page,
  Thine eye in rapt attention turned
O'er records of a holier age,
  Hath not thy heart within thee burned?

4 It was the voice of God that spake
In silence to thy silent heart ;
And bade each worthier thought awake,
And every dream of earth depart.

5 Voice of our God, O, yet be near !
In low, sweet accents whisper peace ;
Direct us on our pathway here,
Then bid in heaven our wanderings cease.

317. L. M. WESLEYAN

The Light from above.

1 ETERNAL God, thou Light divine,
Fountain of unexhausted love,
O, let thy glories on me shine,
In earth beneath, from heaven above.

2 Thou art the weary wanderer's rest,
Give me the easy yoke to bear ;
With steadfast patience arm my breast,
With spotless love and lowly fear.

3 Be thou, O Rock of Ages, nigh !
So shall each murmuring thought be gone
And grief, and fear, and care shall fly,
As clouds before the mid-day sun.

4 Speak to my warring passions, "Peace" ;
Say to my trembling heart, "Be still" ;
Thy power my strength and fortress is,
For all things serve thy holy will.

318. 7s. M. FURNESS.

The Soul.

1 WHAT is this that stirs within,
Loving goodness, hating sin,
Always craving to be blest,
Finding here below no rest ?

2 Naught that charms the ear or eye
Can its hunger satisfy ;

Active, restless, it would pierce
Through the outward universe.

3 What is it ? and whither, whence ?
This unsleeping, secret sense,
Longing for its rest and food
In some hidden, untried good ?

4 'T is the Soul ! mysterious name !
Him it seeks from whom it came ;
It would, mighty God, like thee,
Holy, holy, holy be.

FAITH, HOPE, AND CHARITY.

319. C. M. WATTS

Faith the Evidence of Things not seen.

1 FAITH is the brightest evidence
Of things beyond our sight ;
It pierces through the veil of sense,
And dwells in heavenly light.

2 It sets time past in present view,
Brings distant prospects home,
Of things a thousand years ago,
Or thousand years to come.

3 By faith we know the world was made
By God's almighty word ;
We know the heavens and earth shall fade
And be again restored.

4 Abra'm obeyed the Lord's command,
From his own country driven ;
By faith he sought a promised land,
But found his rest in heaven.

5 Thus through life's pilgrimage we stray,
The promise in our eye ;
By faith we walk the narrow way
That leads to joy on high.

320. C. M. Bath Coll.

Prayer for strong Faith.

1 O, FOR a faith that will not shrink,
Though pressed by every foe,
That will not tremble on the brink
Of any earthly woe ! —

2 That will not murmur nor complain
Beneath the chastening rod,
But, in the hour of grief or pain,
Will lean upon its God ; —

3 A faith that shines more bright and clear
When tempests rage without ;
That when in danger knows no fear,
In darkness feels no doubt ; —

4 That bears, unmoved, the world's dread frown,
Nor heeds its scornful smile ;
That seas of trouble cannot drown,
Nor Satan's arts beguile ; —

5 A faith that keeps the narrow way
Till life's last hour is fled,
And with a pure and heavenly ray
Lights up a dying bed.

6 Lord, give us such a faith as this,
And then, whate'er may come,
We'll taste, e'en here, the hallowed bliss
Of an eternal home.

321. S. M. Noel's Coll.

Living by Faith.

1 IF on a quiet sea
Toward heaven we calmly sail,

With grateful hearts, O God, to thee,
We 'll own the favoring gale.

2 But should the surges rise,
And rest delay to come,
Blest be the sorrow, kind the storm,
Which drives us nearer home.

3 Soon shall our doubts and fears
All yield at thy control;
Thy tender mercies shall illume
The midnight of the soul.

4 Teach us, in every state,
To make thy will our own,
And, when the joys of sense depart,
To live by faith alone.

322. S. H. M. CHRISTIAN WATCHMAN.

Excellence of Faith.

1 FAITH is the Christian's prop,
Whereon his sorrows lean;
It is the substance of his hope,
His proof of things unseen;
It is the anchor of his soul
When tempests rage and billows roll.

2 Faith is the polar star
That guides the Christian's way,
Directs his wanderings from afar
To realms of endless day;
It points the course, where'er he roam,
And safely leads the pilgrim home.

3 Faith is the rainbow's form
Hung on the brow of heaven,
The glory of the passing storm,
The pledge of mercy given;
It is the bright, triumphal arch,
Through which the saints to glory march

4 The faith that works by love,
And purifies the heart,
A foretaste of the joys above
To mortals can impart;
It bears us through this earthly strife,
And triumphs in immortal life.

323. C. M. WATTS

A living Faith.

1 MISTAKEN souls, that dream of heaven,
And make their empty boast
Of inward joys, and sins forgiven,
While they are slaves to lust!

2 How vain are fancy's airy flights,
If faith be cold and dead;
None but a living power unites
To Christ, the living Head.

3 'T is faith that purifies the heart;
'T is faith that works by love;
That bids all sinful joys depart,
And lifts the thoughts above.

4 This faith shall every fear control
By its celestial power,
With holy triumph fill the soul
In death's approaching hour.

324. L. M. WATTS

Walking by Faith.

1 'T IS by the faith of joys to come
We walk through deserts dark as night;
Till we arrive at heaven, our home,
Faith is our guide, and faith our light.

2 The want of sight she well supplies;
She makes the pearly gates appear;
Far into distant worlds she pries,
And brings eternal glories near.

3 With joy we tread the desert through,
While faith inspires a heavenly ray,
Though lions roar, and tempests blow,
And rocks and dangers fill the way.

4 So Abra'm by divine command
Left his own house to walk with God;
His faith beheld the promised land,
And fired his zeal along the road.

325. L. M. DODDRIDGE

Faith in the invisible God.

1 ALMIGHTY and immortal King,
Thy peerless splendors none can bear;
But darkness veils seraphic eyes,
When God with all his glory 's there.

2 Yet faith can pierce the awful gloom,
The great Invisible can see,
And with its tremblings mingle joy,
In fixed regards, great God, to thee.

3 This one petition would it urge,
To bear thee ever in its sight;
In life, in death, in worlds unknown,
Its only portion and delight.

326. L. M. STEELE

Soaring by Faith.

1 THERE is a glorious world on high,
Resplendent with eternal day;
Faith views the blissful prospect nigh,
While God's own word reveals the way.

2 There shall the servants of the Lord
With never fading lustre shine;
Surprising honor! vast reward!
Conferred on man by love divine.

3 Rescued from that destructive way,
Where erring folly thoughtless roves,

The heavenly virtue they display,
Which Jesus taught, and God approves.

4 The shining firmament shall fade,
And sparkling stars resign their light;
But these shall know nor change nor shade,
For ever fair, for ever bright.

5 On wings of faith and strong desire,
O, may our spirits daily rise;
And reach at last the shining choir,
In the bright mansions of the skies.

327. C. M. TURNER

Power of Faith.

1 FAITH adds new charms to earthly bliss,
And saves us from its snares;
It yields support in all our toils
And softens all our cares.

2 The wounded conscience knows its power
The healing balm to give;
That balm the saddest heart can cheer,
And make the dying live.

3 Unveiling wide the heavenly world,
Where endless pleasures reign,
It bids us seek our portion there,
Nor bids us seek in vain.

4 There, still unshaken, would we rest,
Till this frail body dies,
And then, on faith's triumphant wing,
To endless glory rise.

328. C. M. WATTS.

Faith the Source of Triumph.

1 O, FOR an overcoming faith,
To cheer my dying hour,
To triumph o'er the monster, Death,
And all his frightful power.

2 Joyful, with all the strength I have,
My quivering lips would sing,
Where is thy boasted victory, Grave?
O Death! where is thy sting?

3 Pardon and life, — how dear each word!
God life and pardon sends,
And, by our dying, rising Lord,
Insures to all his friends.

4 All glory be to God on high,
And endless thanks be paid,
Who makes us conquerors though we die,
Through Christ, our living Head.

329. L. M. DRUMMOND

Faith without Works is dead.

1 AS body when the soul has fled,
As barren trees, decayed and dead,
Is faith; a hopeless, lifeless thing,
If not of righteous deeds the spring.

2 One cup of healing oil and wine,
One tear-drop shed on mercy's shrine,
Is thrice more grateful, Lord, to thee,
Than lifted eye or bended knee.

3 In true and heaven-born faith, we trace
The source of every Christian grace,
Within the pious heart it plays,
A living fount of joy and praise.

4 Kind deeds of peace and love betray
Where'er the stream has found its way;
But where these spring not rich and fair,
The stream has never wandered there.

330. C. M. STEELE.

Faith in Joys unseen.

1 O, COULD our thoughts and wishes fly,
Above these gloomy shades,

To those bright worlds beyond the sky,
Which sorrow ne'er invades ! —

2 There joys, unseen by mortal eyes,
Or reason's feeble ray,
In ever-blooming prospects rise,
Unconscious of decay.

3 Lord ! send a beam of light divine,
To guide our upward aim ;
With one reviving touch of thine,
Our languid hearts inflame.

4 O, then, on faith's sublimest wing,
Our ardent hope shall rise
To those bright scenes, where pleasures spring,
Immortal, in the skies.

331. L. M. ROSCOE

The Solace of Faith.

1 WHEN human hopes and joys depart,
I give thee, Lord, a contrite heart ;
And on my weary spirit steal
The thoughts that pass all earthly weal.

2 I cast above my tearful eyes,
And muse upon the starry skies ;
And think that He who governs there
Still keeps me in his guardian care.

3 I gaze upon the opening flower,
Just moistened with the evening shower ,
And bless the love which made it bloom,
To chase away my transient gloom.

4 I think, whene'er this mortal frame
Returns again to whence it came,
My soul shall wing its happy flight
To regions of eternal light.

332. C. M. BULFINCH

Help thou mine Unbelief.

1 FATHER, when o'er our trembling hearts
Doubt's shadows gathering brood,
When faith in thee almost departs,
And gloomiest fears intrude,
Forsake us not, O God of grace,
But send those fears relief;
Grant us again to see thy face;
Lord, help our unbelief.

2 When sorrow comes, and joys are flown,
And fondest hopes lie dead,
And blessings, long esteemed our own,
Are now for ever fled;
When the bright promise of our spring
Is but a withered leaf,
Lord, to thy truths still let us cling;
Help thou our unbelief.

3 And when the powers of nature fail
Upon the couch of pain,
Nor love nor friendship can avail
The spirit to detain;
Then, Father, be our closing eyes
Undimmed by tears of grief;
And, if a trembling doubt arise,
Help thou our unbelief.

333. C. M. STEELE.

God our Hope.

1 ETERNAL Source of joys divine,
To thee my soul aspires:
O, could I say, The Lord is mine!
'T is all my soul desires.

2 Thy smile can give me real joy,
Unmingled and refined,

Substantial bliss without alloy,
And lasting as the mind.

3 Thy smile can gild the shade of woe,
Bid stormy troubles cease,
And spread the dawn of heaven below,
And sweeten pain to peace.

4 My Hope, my Trust, my Life, my Lord,
Assure me of thy love ;
O, speak the kind, transporting word,
And bid my fears remove :

5 Then shall my thankful powers rejoice,
And triumph in my God,
Till heavenly rapture tune my voice
To sound thy praise abroad.

334. C. M. SIDNEY.

Hope.

1 BORNE o'er the ocean's stormy wave,
The beacon's light appears,
When yawns the seaman's watery grave,
And his lone bosom cheers.

2 Then, should the raging ocean foam,
His heart shall dauntless prove,
To reach, secure, his cherished home,
The haven of his love.

3 So, when the soul is wrapt in gloom,
To worldly grief a prey,
Thy beams, blest Hope, beyond the tomb,
Illume the pilgrim's way.

4 They point to that serene abode
Where holy faith shall rest,
Protected by the sufferer's God,
And be for ever blest.

5 O, still, though sorrow's rayless night
O'ershade our worldly way,

May pure religion's holy light
  Shine with o'erpowering ray.

335. C. M. WATTS.

The Hope of Heaven.

1 WHEN I can read my title clear
  To mansions in the skies,
I bid farewell to every fear,
  And wipe my weeping eyes.

2 Let cares like a wild deluge come,
  And storms of sorrow fall,
May I but safely reach my home,
  My God, my heaven, my all!

3 There shall I bathe my weary soul
  In seas of heavenly rest,
And not a wave of trouble roll
  Across my peaceful breast.

336. C. M. B W. NOEL.

Hope in Trouble.

1 WHEN musing sorrow weeps the past,
  And mourns the present pain,
'T is sweet to think of peace at last,
  And feel that death is gain.

2 'T is not that murmuring thoughts arise,
  And dread a Father's will;
'T is not that meek submission flies,
  And would not suffer still.

3 It is that heaven-born faith surveys
  The path that leads to light,
And longs her eagle plumes to raise,
  And lose herself in sight.

4 It is that troubled conscience feels
  The pangs of struggling sin,

And sees, though far, the hand that heals,
  And ends the strife within.

5 O, let me wing my hallowed flight
  From earthborn woe and care,
And soar above these clouds of night,
  My Saviour's bliss to share.

337. C. M. DRUMMOND.

God our only Hope.

1 WHEN reft of all, and hopeless care
  Would sink us to the tomb,
What power shall save us from despair,
  What dissipate the gloom?

2 No balm that earthly plants distil
  Can soothe the mourner's smart,
No mortal hand, with lenient skill,
  Bind up the broken heart.

3 But One alone, who reigns above,
  Our woe to joy can turn,
And light the lamp of life and love,
  That long has ceased to burn.

4 Then, O my soul! to that One flee,
  To God thy woes reveal;
His eye alone thy wounds can see,
  His power alone can heal.

338. 8 & 7s. M. MONTGOMERY.

Joyful Hope.

1 KNOW, my soul! thy full salvation;
  Rise o'er sin, and fear, and care,
Joy to find in every station,
  Something still to do or bear:
Think what spirit dwells within thee;
  Think what Father's smiles are thine;
Think what Jesus did to win thee; —
  Child of heaven! canst thou repine?

2 Haste thee on from grace to glory,
Armed with faith and winged with prayer,
Heaven's eternal day 's before thee,
God's own hand shall guide thee there:
Soon shall close thine earthly mission,
Soon shall pass thy pilgrim-days;
Hope shall change to glad fruition,
Faith to sight, and prayer to praise.

339. 7s. M. CENNICK

The Christian rejoicing in Hope.

1 CHILDREN of the Heavenly King,
As ye journey, sweetly sing;
Sing your Saviour's worthy praise,
Glorious in his works and ways.

2 Ye are travelling home to God,
In the way the fathers trod;
They are happy now, and ye
Soon their happiness shall see.

3 Shout, ye little flock and blest;
You on Jesus' throne shall rest;
There your seat is now prepared,
There your kingdom and reward.

4 Lord, submissive make us go,
Gladly leaving all below;
Only thou our Leader be,
And we still will follow thee.

340. C. M. DODDRIDGE

Gratitude and Hope.

1 MY soul, triumphant in the Lord,
Proclaim thy joys abroad,
And march with holy vigor on,
Supported by thy God.

2 Through every winding maze of life
His hand has been my guide;

And in his long-experienced care
My heart shall still confide.

3 Beyond the choicest joys of time,
Thy courts on earth I love;
But, O, I burn with strong desire
To dwell with thee above.

4 There, joined with all the shining band,
My soul would thee adore,
A pillar in thy temple fixed,
To be removed no more.

341. C. M. WATTS.

The Christian's Experience a Ground for Hope.

1 WHEN God revealed his gracious name,
And changed my mournful state,
My rapture seemed a pleasing dream,
The grace appeared so great.

2 The world beheld the glorious change,
And did thy hand confess;
My tongue broke out in unknown strains,
And sung surprising grace.

3 The Lord can clear the darkest skies,
Can give us day for night,
Make drops of sacred sorrow rise
To rivers of delight.

4 Let those that sow in sadness wait
Till the fair harvest come;
They shall confess their sheaves are great,
And shout the blessings home.

342. C. M. H. H. HAWLEY.

The Hope, the Star, the Voice.

1 THERE is a hope, a blessèd hope,
More precious and more bright
Than all the joyless mockery
The world esteems delight.

2 There is a star, a lovely star,
That lights the darkest gloom,
And sheds a peaceful radiance o'er
The prospects of the tomb.

3 There is a voice, a cheering voice,
That lifts the soul above,
Dispels the painful, anxious doubt,
And whispers, "God is love."

4 That voice, aloud from Calvary's height,
Proclaims the soul forgiven ;
That star is revelation's light ;
That hope, the hope of heaven.

343. C. M. ANONYMOUS.

Hope of Reunion above.

1 WHEN floating on life's troubled sea,
By storms and tempests driven,
Hope, with her radiant finger, points
To brighter scenes in heaven.

2 She bids the storms of life to cease,
The troubled breast be calm ;
And in the wounded heart she pours
Religion's healing balm.

3 Her hallowed influence cheers life's hours
Of sadness and of gloom ;
She guides us through this vale of tears,
To joys beyond the tomb.

4 And when our fleeting days are o'er,
And life's last hour draws near,
With still unwearied wing she hastes
To wipe the falling tear.

5 She bids the anguished heart rejoice :
Though earthly ties are riven,
We still may hope to meet again
In yonder peaceful heaven.

344. C. M. CHRISTIAN PSALMIST

Faith, Hope, and Charity.

1 FAITH, hope, and love now dwell on earth,
And earth by them is blest;
But faith and hope must yield to love,
Of all the graces best.

2 Hope shall to full fruition rise,
And faith be sight above;
These are the means, but this the end,
For saints for ever love.

345. L. M. WATTS

Religion vain without Love.

1 HAD I the tongues of Greeks and Jews,
And nobler speech than angels use,
If love be absent, I am found,
Like tinkling brass, an empty sound.

2 Were I inspired to preach and tell
All that is done in heaven and hell, —
Or could my faith the world remove, —
Still I am nothing without love.

3 Should I distribute all my store
To feed the hungry, clothe the poor, —
Or give my body to the flame,
To gain a martyr's glorious name, —

4 If love to God and love to men
Be absent, all my hopes are vain;
Nor tongues, nor gifts, nor fiery zeal,
The work of love can e'er fulfil.

346. L. M. WATTS.

Love to God and our Neighbour.

1 THUS saith the first, the great command:
"Let all thy inward powers unite
To love thy Maker and thy God
With utmost vigor and delight.

2 "Then shall thy neighbour next in place
Share thine affections and esteem;
And let thy kindness to thyself
Measure and rule thy love to him."

3 This is the sense that Moses spoke;
This did the prophets preach and prove;
For want of this the law is broke,
And the whole law 's fulfilled by love.

4 But, O, how base our passions are!
How cold our charity and zeal!
Lord, fill our souls with heavenly fire,
Or we shall ne'er perform thy will.

347. C. M. SWAIN

Brotherly Love.

1 HOW sweet, how heavenly, is the sight,
When those that love the Lord
In one another's peace delight,
And thus fulfil his word! —

2 When each can feel his brother's sigh,
And with him bear a part;
When sorrow flows from eye to eye,
And joy from heart to heart! —

3 When, free from envy, scorn, and pride,
Our wishes all above,
Each can his brother's failings hide,
And show a brother's love!

4 Love is the golden chain that binds
The happy souls above;
And he 's an heir of heaven that finds
His bosom glow with love.

348. S. M. WATTS.

Union and Peace.

1 BLEST are the sons of peace,
Whose hearts and hopes are one,

Whose kind designs to serve and please
Through all their actions run.

2 Blest is the pious house,
Where zeal and friendship meet;
Their songs of praise, their mingled vows,
Make their communion sweet.

3 From those celestial springs
Such streams of pleasure flow,
As no increase of riches brings,
Nor honors can bestow.

4 Thus, when on Aaron's head
They poured the rich perfume,
The oil through all his raiment spread,
And fragrance filled the room.

5 Thus, on the heavenly hills,
The saints are blest above,
Where joy, like morning dew, distils,
And all the air is love.

349. 7s. M. MONTGOMERY.

Joined to God's People.

1 PEOPLE of the living God,
I have sought the world around,
Paths of sin and sorrow trod,
Peace and comfort nowhere found.

2 Now to you my spirit turns, —
Turns, a fugitive unblest;
Brethren, where your altar burns,
O, receive me into rest.

3 Lonely I no longer roam,
Like the cloud, the wind, the wave;
Where you dwell shall be my home,
Where you die shall be my grave.

4 Mine the God whom you adore;
Your Redeemer shall be mine;

Earth can fill my soul no more ;
Every idol I resign.

350. L. M. MONTGOMERY.

The Christian Graces.

1 FAITH, hope, and charity, these three,
Yet is the greatest charity ;
Father of lights, these gifts impart
To mine and every human heart.

2 Faith, that in prayer can never fail,
Hope, that o'er doubting must prevail,
And charity, whose name above
Is God's own name, for God is love.

3 The morning star is lost in light,
Faith vanishes at perfect sight,
The rainbow passes with the storm
And hope with sorrow's fading form.

4 But charity, sêrene, sublime,
Beyond the reach of death and time,
Like the blue sky's all-bounding space,
Holds heaven and earth in its embrace.

351. H. M. MONTGOMERY

Christian Unity.

1 HOW beautiful the sight
Of brethren who agree
In friendship to unite,
And bonds of charity :
'T is like the precious ointment shed
O'er all his robes, from Aaron's head.

2 'T is like the dews that fill
The cups of Hermon's flowers,
Or Zion's fruitful hill,
Bright with the drops of showers,
When mingling odors breathe around,
And glory rests on all the ground.

3 For there the Lord commands
Blessings, a boundless store,
From his unsparing hands,
Yea, life for evermore .
Thrice happy they who meet above
To spend eternity in love.

352. S. M. BEDDOME

All one in Christ.

1 LET party names no more
The Christian world o'erspread ,
Gentile and Jew, and bond and free,
Are one in Christ their head.

2 Among the saints on earth
Let mutual love be found ;
Heirs of the same inheritance,
With mutual blessings crowned.

3 Envy and strife, be gone,
And only kindness known,
Where all one common father have,
One common master own.

4 Thus will the church below
Resemble that above ;
Where springs of purest pleasure rise,
And every heart is love.

353. L. M. BARBAULD

Christian Friendship.

1 HOW blest the sacred tie that binds
In union sweet according minds !
How swift the heavenly course they run,
Whose hearts, and faith, and hopes are one !

2 To each the soul of each how dear !
What jealous love, what holy fear !
How doth the generous flame within
Refine from earth and cleanse from sin !

3 Their streaming eyes together flow
For human guilt and mortal woe ;
Their ardent prayers together rise
Like mingling flames in sacrifice.

4 Together shall they seek the place
Where God reveals his awful face :
How high, how strong, their raptures swell,
There 's none but kindred souls can tell!

5 Nor shall the glowing flame expire
When nature droops her sickening fire ,
Then shall they meet in realms above,
A heaven of joy, — because of love.

354. C. M. DODDRIDGE

The Law of Love.

1 FAR from thy servants, God of grace,
Th' unfeeling heart remove,
And form in our obedient souls
The image of thy love.

2 O, may our sympathizing breasts
The generous pleasure know,
Kindly to share in others' joy,
And weep for others' woe !

3 Where'er the helpless sons of grief
In low distress are laid,
Soft be our hearts their pains to feel,
And swift our hands to aid.

4 O, be the law of love fulfilled
In every act and thought,
Each angry passion far removed,
Each selfish view forgot !

5 Be thou, my heart, dilated wide
With this kind, social grace,
And, in one grasp of fervent love,
All earth and heaven embrace.

355. C. M. DRENNAN.

The Law of Sympathy.

1 ALL nature feels attractive power,
A strong, embracing force ;
The drops that sparkle in the shower,
The planets in their course.

2 Thus in the universe of mind
Is felt the law of love ;
The charity, both strong and kind,
For all that live and move.

3 In this fine, sympathetic chain
All creatures bear a part ;
Their every pleasure, every pain,
Linked to the feeling heart.

4 More perfect bond, the Christian plan
Attaches soul to soul ;
Our neighbour is the suffering man,
Though at the farthest pole.

5 To earth below, from heaven above,
The faith in Christ professed
More clear reveals that God is love,
And whom he loves is blest

356. S. P. M. WATTS.

The Blessings of Friendship.

1 HOW pleasant 't is to see
Kindred and friends agree !
Each in his proper station move ;
And each fulfil his part,
With sympathizing heart,
In all the cares of life and love !

2 Like fruitful showers of rain,
That water all the plain,
Descending from the neighbouring hills ;

Such streams of pleasure roll
Through every friendly soul,
Where love, like heavenly dew, distils.

357. L. M. SCOTT

Charitable Judgment.

1 ALL-SEEING God ! 't is thine to know
The springs whence wrong opinions flow ;
To judge, from principles within,
When frailty errs, and when we sin.

2 Who among men, great Lord of all,
Thy servant to his bar shall call ?
Judge him, for modes of faith, thy foe,
And doom him to the realms of woe ?

3 Who with another's eye can read ?
Or worship by another's creed ?
Trusting thy grace, we form our own,
And bow to thy commands alone.

4 If wrong, correct ; accept, if right ;
While, faithful, we improve our light,
Condemning none, but zealous still
To learn and follow all thy will.

358. L. M. BROWNE

The Properties of Christian Charity.

1 LET men of high conceit and zeal
Their fervor and their faith proclaim :
If charity be wanting still,
The rest is but a sounding name.

2 Patient and meek, she suffers long,
And slowly her resentments rise :
Soon she forgets the greatest wrong,
And rage retires, and malice dies.

3 She envies none their better state,
But makes her neighbour's bliss her own :

Nor vaunts herself with mind elate,
But still a modest air puts on.

4 This is the grace that reigns on high,
And brightly will for ever burn,
When hope shall in fruition die,
And faith to sight triumphant turn.

359. L. M. BROWNE

Love to all Mankind.

1 O GOD, my Father and my King,
Of all I have, or hope, the spring!
Send down thy spirit from above,
And fill my heart with heavenly love.

2 May I from every act abstain,
That hurts or gives another pain:
And bear a sympathizing part,
Whene'er I meet a wounded heart.

3 And let my neighbour's prosperous state
A mutual joy in me create;
His virtuous triumph let me join;
His peace and happiness be mine.

4 And though my neighbour's hate I prove,
Still let me vanquish hate with love,
And every secret wish suppress,
That would abridge his happiness.

5 Let love through all my conduct shine,
An image fair, though faint, of thine;
Thus let me his disciple prove,
Who came to manifest thy love.

360. C. M. WATTS

Christ's Love to Enemies our Example.

1 GOD of our mercy and our praise,
Thy glory is our song;
We 'll speak the honors of thy grace
With a rejoicing tongue.

2 When Christ among the sons of men
In humble form was found,
With cruel slanders, false and vain,
They compassed him around.

3 Their miseries his compassion moved,
Their peace he still pursued ;
They rendered hatred for his love,
And evil for his good.

4 Their malice raged without a cause ;
Yet, with his dying breath,
He prayed for murderers on his cross
And blest his foes in death.

5 O, may his conduct, all divine,
To us a model prove :
Like his, O God, our hearts incline
Our enemies to love.

361. C. M. WATTS

Love to God.

1 HAPPY the heart where graces reign,
Where love inspires the breast :
Love is the brightest of the train,
And strengthens all the rest.

2 Knowledge, — alas ! 't is all in vain,
And all in vain our fear ;
Our stubborn sins will fight and reign,
If love be absent there.

3 This is the grace that lives and sings,
When faith and hope shall cease ;
'T is this shall strike our joyful strings
In realms of endless peace.

4 Before we quite forsake our clay,
Or leave this dark abode,
The wings of love bear us away
To see our gracious God.

362. L. M. WESLEYAN

For the Spirit of Love.

1 GIVER of peace and unity,
Send down thy mild, pacific Dove;
We all shall then in one agree,
And breathe the spirit of thy love.

2 We all shall think and speak the same
Delightful lesson of thy grace,
One undivided Christ proclaim,
And jointly glory in thy praise

3 O, let us take a softer mould,
Blended and gathered into thee;
Under one Shepherd make one fold,
Where all is love and harmony.

4 Subdue in us the carnal mind,
The enmity of sin destroy;
With cords of love our passions bind,
And gently melt us into joy.

5 Thus make us find the ancient way
The unbelieving world to move,
And force thy wondering foes to say,
"Behold these Christians, how they love!"

363. C. M. WATTS.

Kindness to the Poor.

1 HOW blest is he who fears the Lord,
And follows his commands,
Who lends the poor without reward,
Or gives with liberal hands.

2 As pity dwells within his breast
To all the sons of need,
So God shall answer his request
With blessings on his seed.

3 In times of danger and distress,
Some beams of light shall shine,

To show the world his righteousness,
And give him peace divine.

4 His works of piety and love
Remain before the Lord ;
Sweet peace on earth, and joys above,
Shall be his sure reward.

364. C. M. LUTHERAN COLL

Charity.

1 GO to the pillow of disease,
Where night gives no repose,
And on the cheek where sickness preys,
Bid health to plant the rose.

2 Go where the friendless stranger lies ;
To perish is his doom ;
Snatch from the grave his closing eyes,
And bring his blessing home.

3 Thus what our Heavenly Father gave
Shall we as freely give ;
Thus copy him who lived to save,
And died that we might live.

REPENTANCE AND REFORMATION

365. C. M. C. WESLEY

Prayer for Repentance.

1 O, FOR that tenderness of heart
Which bows before the Lord,
That owns how just and good thou art,
And trembles at thy word !

2 O, for those humble, contrite tears,
Which from repentance flow,

That sense of guilt, which, trembling, fears
The long-suspended blow!

3 O Lord, to me in pity give,
For sin the deep distress,
The pledge thou wilt at last receive,
And bid me die in peace.

4 O, fill my soul with faith and love,
And strength to do thy will;
Raise my desires and hopes above:
Thyself to me reveal.

366. L. M. STEELE

Sense of Sin.

1 JESUS demands this heart of mine,
Demands my love, my joy, my care;
But ah! how dead to things divine,
How cold, my best affections are!

2 'T is sin, alas! with dreadful power,
Divides my Saviour from my sight:
O, for one happy, shining hour
Of sacred freedom, sweet delight!

3 Come, gracious Lord; thy love can raise
My captive powers from sin and death,
And fill my heart and life with praise,
And tune my last, expiring breath.

367. C. M. ADDISON.

Solemn Apprehension.

1 WHEN, rising from the bed of death,
O'erwhelmed with guilt and fear,
I see my Maker face to face, —
O, how shall I appear!

2 If yet, while pardon may be found,
And mercy may be sought,
My heart with inward terror shrinks,
And trembles at the thought, —

3 When thou, O Lord, shall stand disclosed
In majesty severe,
And sit in judgment on my soul, —
O, how shall I appear !

4 But there 's forgiveness, Lord, with thee ;
Thy nature is benign ;
Thy pardoning mercy I implore,
For mercy, Lord, is thine.

5 O, let thy boundless mercy shine
On my benighted soul,
Correct my passions, mend my heart,
And all my fears control.

368. C. M. MIDDLETON

Painful Recollections.

1 AS o'er the past my memory strays,
Why heaves the secret sigh ?
'T is that I mourn departed days,
Still unprepared to die.

2 The world and worldly things beloved
My anxious thoughts employed ;
And time, unhallowed, unimproved,
Presents a fearful void.

3 Yet, Holy Father, wild despair
Chase from my laboring breast :
Thy grace it is which prompts the prayer ,
That grace can do the rest.

4 My life's brief remnant all be thine ;
And when thy sure decree
Bids me this fleeting breath resign,
O, speed my soul to thee.

369. 7s. M. J. TAYLOR.

Sins confessed and mourned.

1 GOD of mercy, God of love,
Hear our sad, repentant song ;

Sorrow dwells on every face,
Penitence on every tongue.

2 Deep regret for follies past,
Talents wasted, time misspent;
Hearts debased by worldly cares,
Thankless for the blessings lent;

3 Foolish fears, and fond desires,
Vain regrets for things as vain;
Lips too seldom taught to praise,
Oft to murmur and complain:

4 These, and every secret fault,
Filled with grief and shame we own,
Humbled at thy feet we lie,
Seeking pardon from thy throne.

5 God of mercy, God of grace,
Hear our sad, repentant songs;
O, restore thy suppliant race,
Thou to whom all praise belongs.

370. L. M. DODDRIDGE

Secret Self-examination.

1 RETURN, my roving heart, return,
And life's vain shadows chase no more;
Seek out some solitude to mourn,
And thy forsaken God implore.

2 O thou great God, whose piercing eye
Distinctly marks each deep retreat,
In these sequestered hours draw nigh,
And let me here thy presence meet.

3 Through all the windings of my heart,
My search let heavenly wisdom guide,
And still its radiant beams impart
Till all be known and purified.

4 Then let the visits of thy love
My inmost soul be made to share,

Till every grace combine to prove
That God has fixed his dwelling there.

371. C. M. Village Hymns

The Prodigal's Return.

1 THE long-lost son, with streaming eyes,
From folly just awake,
Reviews his wanderings with surprise;
His heart begins to break.

2 "I starve," he cries, "nor can I bear
The famine in this land,
While servants of my Father share
The bounty of his hand.

3 "With deep repentance I 'll return
And seek my Father's face;
Unworthy to be called a son,
I 'll ask a servant's place."

4 Far off the Father saw him move,
In pensive silence mourn,
And quickly ran, with arms of love,
To welcome his return.

5 Through all the courts the tidings flew,
And spread the joy around;
The angels tuned their harps anew;
The long-lost son is found!

372. S. M. Steele

Absence from God.

1 O THOU, whose mercy hears
Contrition's humble sigh;
Whose hand indulgent wipes the tears
From sorrow's weeping eye!

2 See, low before thy throne,
A wretched wanderer mourn;
Hast thou not bid me seek thy face?
Hast thou not said, "Return"?

3 Absent from thee, my light, —
Without one cheering ray, —
Through dangers, fears, and gloomy night,
How desolate my way !

4 On this benighted heart
With beams of mercy shine ;
And let thy healing voice impart
A taste of joys divine.

5 Thy presence can bestow
Delights which never cloy ;
Be this my solace here below,
And my eternal joy !

373. S. M. Belknap's Coll.

Obedience to God our Father.

1 MY Father ! I adore
That all commanding name ;
O, may it virtue's strength restore,
And raise devotion's flame !

2 I bow at thy commands,
And filial homage pay ;
With heart and life, with tongue and hands,
I 'll cheerfully obey.

3 No more will I transgress,
As I too oft have done ;
But every sinful thought suppress,
Each sinful action shun.

4 My Father thus I 'll claim,
And prove myself his son ;
And, while I bear the filial name,
The filial duties own.

5 Do thou the strength impart,
This purpose to fulfil :
Lord, write thy laws upon my heart,
That I may do thy will.

374. C. M. NEEDHAM

Sufficiency of Grace.

1 KIND are the words that Jesus speaks
To cheer the drooping saint:
"My grace sufficient is for you,
Though nature's powers may faint.

2 "My grace its glories shall display,
And make your griefs remove;
Your weakness shall the triumphs tell
Of boundless power and love."

3 What though my griefs are not removed?
Yet why should I despair?
For, if my Saviour's arm support,
I can the burden bear.

4 O thou, my Saviour and my Lord,
'T is good to trust thy name;
Thy power, thy faithfulness, and love,
Will ever be the same.

5 Weak as I am, yet through thy grace
I all things can perform,
And, smiling, triumph in thy name
Amid the raging storm.

375. S. M. BEDDOME

Mercy implored.

1 THOU Lord of all above
And all below the sky,
Before thy feet I prostrate fall,
And for thy mercy cry.

2 Guilt, like a heavy load,
Upon my conscience lies;
To thee I make my sorrows known,
And lift my weeping eyes.

3 The burden which I feel,
Thou only canst remove·

Display, O Lord, thy pardoning grace,
And thy unbounded love.

4 One gracious look of thine
Will ease my troubled breast;
O, let me know my sins forgiven,
And I shall then be blest.

376. C. M. WATTS

Deliverance from deep Distress.

1 I WAITED patient for the Lord;
He bowed to hear my cry;
He saw me resting on his word,
And brought salvation nigh.

2 He raised me from a gloomy pit,
Where, mourning, long I lay,
And from my bonds released my feet, —
Deep bonds of miry clay.

3 Firm on a rock he made me stand,
And taught my cheerful tongue
To praise the wonders of his hand,
In new and thankful song.

4 I 'll spread his works of grace abroad;
The saints with joy shall hear,
And sinners learn to make my God
Their only hope and fear.

5 How many are thy thoughts of love!
Thy mercies, Lord, how great!
We have not words nor hours enough
Their numbers to repeat.

377. C. M. DODDRIDGE.

"Cleanse thou me from secret Faults."

1 SEARCHER of hearts! before thy face
I all my soul display,

And, conscious of its innate arts,
  Entreat thy strict survey.
2 If, lurking in its inmost folds,
  I any sin conceal,
O, let a ray of light divine
  The secret guile reveal!
3 If, in these fatal fetters bound,
  A wretched slave I lie,
Smite off my chains, and wake my soul
  To light and liberty.
4 To humble penitence and prayer
  Be gentle pity given;
Speak ample pardon to my heart,
  And seal its claim to heaven.

378. L. M. 6 L. WESLEY'S COLL

Imploring Forgiveness and Renewal of Heart.

1 FORGIVE us, for thy mercy's sake,
  Our multitude of sins forgive;
And for thy own possession take,
  And bid us to thy glory live;
Live in thy sight, and gladly prove
Our faith by our obedient love.
2 The covenant of forgiveness seal,
  And all thy mighty wonders show;
Our hidden enemies expel,
  And conquering them to conquer go,
Till all of pride and wrath be slain,
And not one evil thought remain.
3 O, put it in our inward parts,
  The living law of perfect love;
Write the new precept on our hearts;
  We shall not then from thee remove,
Who in thy glorious image shine,
Thy people, and for ever thine.

379. L. M. BEDDOME

Inconstancy lamented.

1 THE wandering star and fleeting wind
Are emblems of the fickle mind ;
The morning cloud and early dew
Bring our inconstancy to view.

2 But cloud and wind, and dew and star,
Only a faint resemblance bear ;
Nor can there aught in nature be
So changeable and frail as we.

3 Our outward walk and inward frame
Are scarcely through an hour the same :
We vow, and straight our vows forget,
And then those very vows repeat.

4 With contrite hearts, Lord, we confess
Our folly and unsteadfastness :
When shall these hearts more stable be,
Fixed by thy grace alone on thee ?

380. S. M. JERVIS

God's Mercy to the Penitent.

1 SWEET is the friendly voice
Which speaks of life and peace ;
Which bids the penitent rejoice,
And sin and sorrow cease.

2 No balm on earth like this
Can cheer the contrite heart ;
No flattering dreams of earthly bliss
Such pure delight impart.

3 Still merciful and kind,
Thy mercy, Lord, reveal ;
The broken heart thy love can bind,
The wounded spirit heal.

4 Thy presence shall restore
Peace to my anxious breast :

Lord, let my steps be drawn no more
From paths which thou hast blessed.

381. C. M. MILMAN

Praying for Divine Help.

1 O, HELP us, Lord ! each hour of need
Thy heavenly succour give ;
Help us in thought, and word, and deed,
Each hour on earth we live.

2 O, help us, when our spirits bleed,
With contrite anguish sore ;
And when our hearts are cold and dead,
O, help us, Lord, the more.

3 O, help us, through the prayer of faith,
More firmly to believe ;
For still the more the servant hath,
The more shall he receive.

4 O, help us, Father, from on high ;
We know no help but thee ;
O, help us so to live and die,
As thine in heaven to be.

382. 6 & 4s. M. R. PALMER.

For Divine Guidance. *Altered, See Appendix.*

1 O GOD, thy grace impart ;
Revive my fainting heart ;
My zeal inspire ;
Reveal thyself to me,
And may my love to thee
Pure, warm, and changeless be, —
A living fire.

2 While life's dark maze I tread,
And griefs around me spread,
Be thou my guide ;

Bid darkness turn to day,
Wipe sorrow's tears away,
Nor let me ever stray
From thee aside.

3 When ends life's transient dream,
When death's cold, sullen stream
Shall o'er me roll,
O Father, then in love
Fear and distress remove,
And bear me safe above, —
A ransomed soul.

383. C. M. ANONYMOUS.

Aspiration after a holy Life.

1 ALMIGHTY Maker! Lord of all!
Of life the only spring!
Creator of unnumbered worlds!
Supreme, Eternal King!

2 Drive from the confines of my heart
Impenitence and pride;
Nor let me, in forbidden paths,
With thoughtless sinners glide.

3 Whate'er thine all-discerning eye
Sees for thy creature fit,
I 'll bless the good, and to the ill
Contentedly submit.

4 With generous pleasure let me view
The prosperous and the great;
Malignant envy let me fly,
And odious self-conceit.

5 Let not despair, nor fell revenge,
Be to my bosom known;
O, give me tears for others' woes,
And patience for my own.

6 May still my days serenely pass,
Without remorse or care;

And growing holiness my soul
For life's last hour prepare.

384. S. M. BULFINCH.

Regeneration.

1 THROUGH thee, O Lord, we own
A new and heavenly birth,
Kindred to spirits round thy throne,
Though sojourners of earth.

2 How glorious is the hour
When first our souls awake,
And, through thy Spirit's quickening power,
Of the new life partake.

3 With richer beauty glows
The world, before so fair;
Her holy light religion throws,
Reflected everywhere.

4 Amid repentant tears
We feel sweet peace within;
We know the God of mercy hears,
And pardons every sin.

5 Born of thy Spirit, Lord,
Thy spirit may we share;
Deep in our hearts inscribe thy word,
And place thine image there.

385. C. M. SPIRIT OF THE PSALMS

The Day-spring from on High.

1 GREAT God, wert thou extreme to mark
The deeds we do amiss,
Before thy presence who could stand?
Who claim thy promised bliss?
But, O, all merciful and just,
Thy love surpasseth thought;
A gracious Saviour has appeared,
And peace and pardon brought.

2 Thy servants in the temple watched
  The dawning of the day,
Impatient with its earliest beams
  Their holy vows to pay;
And chosen saints far off beheld
  That great and glorious morn,
When the glad day-spring from on high
  Auspiciously should dawn.

3 On us the Sun of Righteousness
  Its brightest beams hath poured;
With grateful hearts and holy zeal,
  Lord, be thy love adored;
And let us look with joyful hope
  To that more glorious day,
Before whose brightness sin and death
  And grief shall flee away.

386. 7s. M. MILMAN.

Prayer for Mercy in spiritual Need.

1 LORD, have mercy when we pray
Strength to seek a better way;
When our wakening thoughts begin
First to loathe their cherished sin;
When our weary spirits fail,
And our aching brows are pale;
When our tears bedew thy word;
Then, O, then, have mercy, Lord!

2 Lord, have mercy when we lie
On the restless bed and sigh, —
Sigh for death, yet fear it still,
From the thought of former ill;
When the dim, advancing gloom
Tells us that our hour has come;
When is loosed the silver cord;
Then, O, then, have mercy, Lord

3 Lord, have mercy when we know
First how vain this world below;
When its darker thoughts oppress,
Doubts perplex, and fears distress;
When the earliest gleam is given
Of the bright but distant heaven;
Then thy fostering grace afford;
Then, O, then, have mercy, Lord!

387. C. M. WATTS

Breathing after Holiness.

1 O, THAT the Lord would guide my ways
To keep his statutes still!
O, that my God would grant me grace
To know and do his will!

2 O, send thy Spirit down, to write
Thy law upon my heart!
Nor let my tongue indulge deceit,
Nor act the liar's part.

3 From vanity turn off mine eyes;
Let no corrupt design,
Nor covetous desires, arise
Within this soul of mine.

4 Order my footsteps by thy word,
And make my heart sincere;
Let sin have no dominion, Lord,
But keep my conscience clear.

5 Make me to walk in thy commands;
'T is a delightful road;
Nor let my head, nor heart, nor hands,
Offend against my God.

388. L. M. WATTS.

Pleasures of a good Conscience.

1 LORD, how secure and blest are they
Who feel the joys of pardoned sin!

Should storms of wrath shake earth and sea
  Their minds have heaven and peace within.

2 The day glides sweetly o'er their heads,
  Made up of innocence and love ;
And soft and silent as the shades,
  Their nightly minutes gently move.

3 Quick as their thoughts their joys come on,
  But fly not half so swift away !
Their souls are ever bright as noon,
  And calm as summer evenings be.

4 How oft they look to th' heavenly hills,
  Where groves of living pleasures grow !
And longing hopes and cheerful smiles
  Sit undisturbed upon their brow.

389. 7s. M. MERRICK

Freedom from Error, Guilt, and Folly.

1 BLEST Instructer ! from thy ways
Who can tell how oft he strays ?
Save from error's growth our mind,
Leave not, Lord, one root behind.

2 Purge us from the guilt that lies
Wrapt within our heart's disguise ;
Let us thence, by thee renewed,
Each presumptuous sin exclude.

3 Let our tongues, from error free,
Speak the words approved by thee :
To thine all-observing eyes
Let our thoughts accepted rise.

4 While we thus thy name adore,
And thy healing grace implore,
Blest Instructer ! bow thine ear :
God our strength ! propitious hear.

390. L. M. J. F. OBERLIN.

Christian Stability.

1 O LORD, thy heavenly grace impart,
And fix my frail, inconstant heart;
Henceforth my chief desire shall be
To dedicate myself to thee.

2 Whate'er pursuits my time employ,
One thought shall fill my soul with joy,
That silent, secret thought shall be,
That all my hopes are fixed on thee.

3 Thy glorious eye pervadeth space;
Thy presence, Lord, fills every place;
And, wheresoe'er my lot may be,
Still shall my spirit cleave to thee.

4 Renouncing every worldly thing,
And safe beneath thy spreading wing,
My sweetest thought henceforth shall be,
That all I want I find in thee.

391. C. P. M. HENRY MOORE

Pardon.

1 SOFT are the fruitful showers that bring
The welcome promise of the spring,
And soft the vernal gale:
Sweet the wild warblings of the grove,
The voice of nature and of love,
That gladden every vale.

2 But softer in the mourner's ear
Sounds the mild voice of mercy near,
That whispers sins forgiven;
And sweeter far the music swells,
When to the raptured soul she tells
Of peace and promised heaven.

3 Fair are the flowers that deck the ground;
And groves and gardens, blooming round,
Unnumbered charms unfold:

Bright is the sun's meridian ray,
And bright the beams of setting day,
That robe the clouds in gold.

4 But far more fair the pious breast,
In richer robes of goodness dressed,
Where heaven's own graces shine ;
And brighter far the prospects rise,
That burst on faith's delighted eyes,
From glories all divine.

392. 7s. M. BARBAULD

Devout Joy.

1 " JOY to those that love the Lord ! "
Saith the sure, eternal word ;
Not of earth the joy it brings,
Tempered in celestial springs.

2 'T is the joy of pardoned sin
When we feel 't is well within ;
'T is the joy that fills the breast
When the passions sink to rest.

3 'T is a joy that, seated deep,
Leaves not when we sigh and weep ;
Spreads itself in virtuous deeds,
Sighs for woe, in pity bleeds.

4 Stern and awful are its tones
When the patriot martyr groans,
And, the death-pulse beating high,
Rapture blends with agony.

5 Tend'rer is the form it wears,
Touched in love, dissolved in tears,
When, subdued, at Jesus' feet,
Sinners clasp the mercy-seat.

6 Joy e'en here ! a budding flower,
Struggling with the storm and shower,
Till its season to expand,
Planted in its native land.

CHRISTIAN AFFECTIONS AND LIFE.

393. C. M. MONTGOMERY

What is Prayer?

1 PRAYER is the soul's sincere desire,
Uttered or unexpressed,
The motion of a hidden fire,
That trembles in the breast.

2 Prayer is the burden of a sigh,
The falling of a tear,
The upward glancing of an eye,
When none but God is near.

3 Prayer is the simplest form of speech
That infant lips can try,
Prayer the sublimest strains that reach
The Majesty on high.

4 Prayer is the Christian's vital breath,
The Christian's native air,
The watchword at the gates of death ;
He enters heaven with prayer.

5 Prayer is the contrite sinner's voice,
Returning from his ways ;
While angels in their songs rejoice,
And cry, "Behold, he prays !"

6 In prayer, on earth, the saints are one
They 're one in word and mind ;
When with the Father and the Son
Sweet fellowship they find.

7 O Thou, by whom we come to God,
The Life, the Truth, the Way,
The path of prayer thyself hast trod ;
Lord, teach us how to pray !

394. C. M. BEDDOME.

Prayer.

1 PRAYER is the breath of God in man,
Returning whence it came;
Love is the sacred fire within,
And prayer the rising flame.

2 It gives the burdened spirit ease,
And soothes the troubled breast;
Yields comfort to the mourners here,
And to the weary rest.

3 When God inclines the heart to pray,
He hath an ear to hear;
To him there 's music in a sigh,
And beauty in a tear.

4 The humble suppliant cannot fail
To have his wants supplied,
Since he for sinners intercedes
Who once for sinners died.

395. L. M. STOWELL.

The Mercy-seat.

1 FROM every stormy wind that blows,
From every swelling tide of woes,
There is a calm, a sure retreat;
'T is found before the mercy-seat.

2 There is a place where Jesus sheds
The oil of gladness on our heads, —
A place of all on earth most sweet;
It is the heavenly mercy-seat.

3 There is a scene where spirits blend,
Where friend holds fellowship with friend;
Though sundered far, by faith they meet
Around one common mercy-seat.

4 There, there, on eagle wings we soar,
And sin and sense molest no more;

And heaven comes down our souls to greet,
And glory crowns the mercy-seat.

396. C. M. Mrs. Brown.

Secret Prayer.

1 I LOVE to steal awhile away
From every cumbering care,
And spend the hours of setting day
In humble, grateful prayer.

2 I love in solitude to shed
The penitential tear,
And all his promises to plead
Where none but God can hear.

3 I love to think on mercies past,
And future good implore,
And all my cares and sorrows cast
On him whom I adore.

4 I love by faith to take a view
Of brighter scenes in heaven;
The prospect doth my strength renew,
While here by tempests driven.

5 Thus, when life's toilsome day is o'er,
May its departing ray
Be calm as this impressive hour,
And lead to endless day.

397. 7 & 6s. M. Edin. Lit. Review

Pray without ceasing.

1 GO when the morning shineth,
Go when the noon is bright,
Go when the eve declineth,
Go in the hush of night;
Go with pure mind and feeling,
Fling earthly thought away,
And, in thy closet kneeling,
Do thou in secret pray.

2 Remember all who love thee,
All who are loved by thee ;
Pray, too, for those who hate thee,
If any such there be ;
Then for thyself, in meekness,
A blessing humbly claim,
And blend with each petition
Thy great Redeemer's name.

3 Or, if 't is e'er denied thee
In solitude to pray,
Should holy thoughts come o'er thee
When friends are round thy way,
E'en then the silent breathing,
Thy spirit raised above,
Will reach his throne of glory,
Where dwells eternal love.

4 O, not a joy or blessing
With this can we compare, —
The grace our Father gave us
To pour our souls in prayer :
Whene'er thou pin'st in sadness,
Before his footstool fall ;
Remember, in thy gladness,
His love, who gave thee all.

398. C. M. ANONYMOUS

Secret Prayer.

1 SWEET is the prayer whose holy stream
In earnest pleading flows ;
Devotion dwells upon the theme,
And warm and warmer glows.

2 Faith grasps the blessing she desires ;
Hope points the upward gaze ;
And love, celestial love, inspires
The eloquence of praise.

3 But sweeter far the still, small voice,
Unheard by human ear,
When God has made the heart rejoice,
And dried the bitter tear.

4 No accents flow, no words ascend ;
All utterance faileth there ;
But Christian spirits comprehend,
And God accepts the prayer.

399. C. M. DODDRIDGE

Secret Devotion.

1 FATHER divine, thy piercing eye
Sees through the darkest night ;
In deep retirement thou art nigh,
With heart-discerning sight.

2 May that observing eye survey
My faithful homage paid,
With every morning's dawning ray,
And every evening's shade

3 O, let thy own celestial fire
The incense still inflame,
While fervent vows to thee aspire,
Through my Redeemer's name.

4 So shall the visits of thy love
My soul in secret bless;
So wilt thou deign, in worlds above,
Thy suppliant to confess.

400. C. H. M. ANONYMOUS

Come, let us pray.

1 COME, let us pray : 't is sweet to feel
That God himself is near ;
That, while we at his footstool kneel,
His mercy deigns to hear :
Though sorrows cloud life's dreary way,
This is our solace, —let us pray.

2 Come, let us pray : the burning brow,
The heart oppressed with care,
And all the woes that throng us now,
Will be relieved by prayer :
Our God will chase our griefs away ;
O, glorious thought ! — come, let us pray.

3 Come, let us pray : the mercy-seat
Invites the fervent prayer ;
Our Heavenly Father waits to greet
The contrite spirit there :
O, loiter not, nor longer stay
From him who loves us ; — let us pray.

401. C. M. Urwick's Coll.

Prayer for Grace in Trial.

1 FATHER of all our mercies, thou
In whom we move and live,
Hear us in heaven, thy dwelling, now,
And answer, and forgive.

2 When, harassed by ten thousand foes,
Our helplessness we feel,
O, give the weary soul repose,
The wounded spirit heal.

3 When dire temptations gather round,
And threaten or allure,
By storm or calm, in thee be found
A refuge strong and sure.

4 When age advances, may we grow
In faith, in hope, and love,
And walk in holiness below
To holiness above.

5 Let earthly joys and cares depart ;
Let pain and sorrow cease ;
Be thou the portion of our heart ;
In thee may we have peace.

402. 8 & 7s. M. TOPLADY

Prayer for Light.

1 LIGHT of those whose dreary dwelling
Borders on the shades of death!
Rise on us, thyself revealing,
Rise, and chase the clouds beneath.

2 Thou, of life and light creator!
In our deepest darkness rise;
Scatter all the night of nature,
Pour the day upon our eyes.

3 Still we wait for thine appearing;
Life and joy thy beams impart;
Chasing all our fears, and cheering
Every meek and contrite heart.

4 Save us, in thy great compassion,
O thou God of peace and love!
Give the knowledge of salvation,
Fix our hearts on things above.

403. 6 & 4s. M. (Peculiar.) HEMANS

Prayer for Help in Necessity.

1 LOWLY and solemn be
Thy children's cry to thee,
Father divine, —
A hymn of suppliant breath,
Owning that life and death
Alike are thine.

2 O Father, in that hour
When earth all helping power
Shall disavow, —
When spear, and shield, and crown,
In faintness are cast down, —
Sustain us, thou!

3 By him who bowed to take
The death-cup for our sake,
The thorn, the rod, —
From whom the last dismay
Was not to pass away, —
Aid us, O God !

4 While trembling o'er the grave,
We call on thee to save,
Father divine !
Hear, hear our suppliant breath ;
Keep us, in life and death,
Thine, only thine

404. C. M. MONTGOMERY.

Prayer for Wisdom.

1 ALMIGHTY God, in humble prayer
To thee our souls we lift ;
Do thou our waiting minds prepare
For thy most needful gift.

2 We ask not golden streams of wealth
Along our path to flow ;
We ask not undecaying health,
Nor length of years below.

3 We ask not honors which an hour
May bring and take away ;
We ask not pleasure, pomp, and power,
Lest we should go astray.

4 We ask for wisdom : — Lord, impart
The knowledge how to live ;
A wise and understanding heart
To all before thee give.

5 The young remember thee in youth,
Before the evil days !
The old be guided by thy truth
In wisdom's pleasant ways !

405. C. M. Wesleyan

For Purity of Heart.

1 O, FOR a heart to praise my God,
A heart from sin set free ;
A heart that always feels how good,
Thou, Lord, hast been to me.

2 O, for a humble, contrite heart,
Believing, true, and clean,
Which neither life nor death can part
From him who dwells within ; —

3 A heart in every thought renewed,
And full of love divine,
Perfect, and right, and pure, and good,
Conformed, O Lord, to thine.

4 Thy temper, gracious Lord, impart ;
Come quickly from above ;
O, write thy name upon my heart ;
Thy name, O God, is love.

406. S. M. C. Wesley

Prayer for Self-consecration.

1 O GOD, my strength, my hope,
On thee I cast my care,
With humble confidence look up,
And know thou hearest prayer.

2 O, for a godly fear,
A quick-discerning eye,
That looks to thee when sin is near,
And sees the tempter fly ! —

3 A spirit still prepared,
And armed with jealous care,
For ever standing on its guard,
And watching unto prayer !

4 Lord, let me still abide,
Nor from my hope remove,

Till thou my patient spirit guide
To better worlds above.

407. C. M. C. Wesley

Prayer for Supplies of Grace.

1 THOU Fount of blessing, God of love,
To thee our hearts we raise ;
Thine all-sustaining power we prove,
And gladly sing thy praise.

2 Thine, wholly thine, we long to be ;
Our sacrifice receive ;
Made, and preserved, and saved, by thee,
To thee ourselves we give.

3 To thee our every wish aspires ;
For all thy mercy's store,
The sole return thy love requires
Is that we ask for more.

4 For more we ask ; we open, Lord,
Our hearts t' embrace thy will :
Renew us by thy quickening word,
And from thy fulness fill.

408. C. M. Exeter Coll

The Influence of habitual Piety.

1 BLEST is the man who fears the Lord !
His well established mind,
In every varying scene of life,
Shall true composure find.

2 Oft through the deep and stormy sea
The heavenly footsteps lie ;
But on a glorious world beyond
His faith can fix its eye.

3 Though dark his present prospects be,
And sorrows round him dwell,
Yet hope can whisper to his soul,
That all shall issue well.

4 Full in the presence of his God,
Through every scene he goes;
And, fearing him, no other fear
His steadfast bosom knows.

5 No dangers can his soul alarm,
No gloomy views affright;
For faith assures his humble heart,
Whatever is, is right.

409. C. M. ANONYMOUS

"Trust ye in the Lord."

1 WHEN grief and anguish press me down,
And hope and comfort flee,
I cling, O Father, to thy throne,
And stay my heart on thee.

2 When clouds of dark temptation rise,
And pour their wrath on me,
To thee for aid I turn my eyes,
And fix my trust on thee.

3 When death invades my peaceful home,
The sundered ties shall be
A closer bond, in time to come,
To bind my heart to thee.

4 Lord,—"Not my will but thine be done!"
My soul from fear set free,
Her faith shall anchor at thy throne,
And trust alone in thee.

410. C. M. WATTS

Confidence in God.

1 SOON as I heard my Father say,
"Ye children, seek my grace,"
My heart replied, without delay,
"I 'll seek my Father's face."

2 Let not thy face be hid from me,
Nor frown my soul away;

God of my life, I fly to thee
In each distressing day

3 Should friends and kindred, near and dear,
Leave me to want, or die,
My God will make my life his care,
And all my need supply.

4 Wait on the Lord, ye trembling saints,
And keep your courage up;
He 'll raise your spirit when it faints,
And far exceed your hope.

411. 8, 7, & 4s. M. OLIVER.

God the Pilgrim's Guide and Strength.

1 GUIDE me, O thou great Jehovah,
Pilgrim through this barren land:
I am weak, but thou art mighty;
Hold me with thy powerful hand:
Bread of heaven,
Feed me till I want no more.

2 Open now the crystal fountain,
Whence the healing streams do flow;
Let the fiery, cloudy pillar
Lead me all my journey through:
Strong Deliverer,
Be thou still my strength and shield.

3 When I tread the verge of Jordan,
Bid my anxious fears subside;
Bear me through the swelling current;
Land me safe on Canaan's side:
Songs of praises
I will ever give to thee.

412. C. M. RELIGIOUS SOUVENIR.

Trust in God.

1 O FATHER, good or evil send,
As seemeth best to thee,

And teach my stubborn soul to bend
In love to thy decree.

2 Whatever come, if thou wilt bless
The brightness and the gloom,
And temper joy, and soothe distress,
I fear no earthly doom.

3 Life cannot give a cureless sting;
Death can but crown my joy,
And waft me far, on angel's wing,
To heaven's divine employ.

413. S. M. WATTS.

Security and Comfort in God.

1 WHEN, overwhelmed with grief,
My heart within me dies,
Helpless, and far from all relief,
To heaven I lift mine eyes.

2 O, lead me to the Rock
That 's high above my head,
And make the covert of thy wings
My shelter and my shade.

3 Within thy presence, Lord,
For ever I 'll abide;
Thou art the tower of my defence,
The refuge where I hide.

4 Thou givest me the lot
Of those that fear thy name;
If endless life be their reward,
I shall possess the same.

414. 7s. M. SPIRIT OF THE PSALMS.

Safety in God.

1 THEY who on the Lord rely
Safely dwell, though danger 's nigh,
Lo! his sheltering wings are spread
O'er each faithful servant's head.

2 Vain temptation's wily snare;
Christians are Jehovah's care;
Harmless flies the shaft by day,
Or in darkness wings its way.

3 When they wake, or when they sleep,
Angel guards their vigils keep;
Death and danger may be near,
Faith and love have naught to fear.

415. C. M. STEELE

God the supreme Good.

1 IN vain we trace creation o'er
In search of sacred rest,
The whole creation is too poor
To make us fully blest.

2 In vain would this low world employ
Each flattering, specious wile;
For what can yield a real joy
But our Creator's smile?

3 Let earth with all her charms depart,
Unworthy of the mind;
In God alone this restless heart
An equal bliss can find.

4 Great Source of all felicity,
To whom our wishes tend!
Do not these wishes rise from thee,
And in thy favor end?

416. C. M. WATTS.

Secret Communion with God.

1 'T WAS in the watches of the night
I thought upon thy power;
I kept thy lovely face in sight,
Amid the darkest hour.

2 While I lay resting on my bed,
My soul arose on high;

My God, my life, my hope, I said,
Bring thy salvation nigh.

3 I strive to mount thy holy hill;
I walk the heavenly road;
Thy glories all my spirit fill,
While I commune with God.

4 Thy mercy stretches o'er my head
The shadow of thy wing;
My heart rejoices in thine aid,
And I thy praises sing.

417. L. M. 6 L. MORAVIAN

Seeking after God.

1 THOU hidden love of God, whose height,
Whose depth, unfathomed, no man knows,
I see from far thy beauteous light;
Inly I sigh for thy repose;
My heart is pained; nor can it be
At rest till it find rest in thee.

2 Thy secret voice invites me still
The sweetness of thy yoke to prove,
And fain I would; but though my will
Seem fixed, yet wide my passions rove,
Yet hindrances strow all the way;
I aim at thee, yet from thee stray.

3 'T is mercy all, that thou hast brought
My mind to seek her peace in thee;
Yet, while I seek, but find thee not,
No peace my wandering soul shall see.
O, when shall all my wanderings end,
And all my steps to thee-ward tend?

4 Is there a thing beneath the sun
That strives with thee my heart to share?
Ah, tear it thence, and reign alone,
The Lord of every motion there;
Then shall my heart from earth be free,
When it hath found repose in thee

418. C. M. DODDRIDGE

Walking with God.

1 THRICE happy souls, who, born from heaven,
While yet they sojourn here,
Do all their days with God begin,
And spend them in his fear.

2 'Midst hourly cares, may love present
Its incense to thy throne ;
And, while the world our hands employs,
Our hearts be thine alone.

3 As sanctified to noblest ends,
Be each refreshment sought ;
And by each various providence
Some wise instruction brought.

4 When to laborious duties called,
Or by temptations tried,
We 'll seek the shelter of thy wings,
And in thy strength confide.

5 As different scenes of life arise,
Our grateful hearts would be
With thee, amidst the social band,
In solitude with thee.

6 In solid, pure delights like these,
Let all our days be past ;
Nor shall we then impatient wish,
Nor shall we fear, the last.

419. C. M. COWPER

Walking with God.

1 O, FOR a closer walk with God,
A calm and heavenly frame,
A light to shine upon the road
That leads me to the Lamb !

2 What peaceful hours I once enjoyed !
How sweet their memory still !

But now I find an aching void
The world can never fill.

3 Return, O holy Dove, return,
Sweet messenger of rest;
I hate the sins that made thee mourn,
And drove thee from my breast.

4 The dearest idol I have known,
Whate'er that idol be,
Help me to tear it from thy throne,
And worship only thee.

5 So shall my walk be close with God,
Calm and serene my frame;
So purer light shall mark the road
That leads me to the Lamb.

420. L. M. 6 L. MORAVIAN.

Living to God.

1 O, DRAW me, Father, after thee,
So shall I run and never tire;
With gracious words still comfort me;
Be thou my hope, my sole desire:
Free me from every weight; nor fear
Nor sin can come, if thou art here.

2 From all eternity, with love
Unchangeable thou hast me viewed;
Ere knew this beating heart to move,
Thy tender mercies me pursued;
Ever with me may they abide,
And close me in on every side.

3 In suffering be thy love my peace,
In weakness be thy love my power;
And when the storms of life shall cease,
My God! in that important hour,
In death as life be thou my guide,
And bear me through death's whelming tide.

421. L. M. MONTGOMERY.

Following after God.

1 O GOD, thou art my God alone ;
Early to thee my soul shall cry,
A pilgrim in a land unknown,
A thirsty land, whose springs are dry.

2 Yet, through this rough and thorny maze,
I follow hard on thee, my God ;
Thine hand unseen upholds my ways ;
I lean upon thy staff and rod.

3 Thee, in the watches of the night,
When I remember, on my bed,
Thy presence makes the darkness light ;
Thy guardian wings are round my head.

4 Better than life itself thy love,
Dearer than all beside to me ;
For whom have I in heaven above,
Or what on earth, compared with thee ?

5 Praise with my heart, my mind, my voice,
For all thy mercy, I will give ;
My soul shall still in God rejoice ;
My tongue shall bless thee while I live.

422. 7s. M. 6 L. NEWTON.

The Child of God.

1 QUIET, Lord, my froward heart ;
Make me teachable and mild,
Upright, simple, free from art ;
Make me as a little child ;
From distrust and envy free,
Pleased with all that pleases thee.

2 What thou shalt to-day provide,
Let me as a child receive ;
What to-morrow may betide,
Calmly to thy wisdom leave ;

'T is enough that thou wilt care ;
Why should I the burden bear ?

3 As a little child relies
On a care beyond his own,
Knows he 's neither strong nor wise,
Fears to stir a step alone, —
Let me thus with thee abide,
As my Father, Guard, and Guide.

423. C. M. DODDRIDGE

Joy in the Presence of God.

1 SHINE on our souls, Eternal God !
With rays of beauty shine ;
O, let thy favor crown our days,
And all their round be thine.

2 Did we not raise our hands to thee,
Our hands might toil in vain ;
Small joy success itself could give,
If thou thy love restrain.

3 With thee let every week begin,
With thee each day be spent,
For thee each fleeting hour improved,
Since each by thee is lent.

4 Thus cheer us through this desert road,
Till all our labors cease,
And heaven refresh our weary souls
With everlasting peace.

424. L. M. BOWRING.

God's sustaining Presence.

1 FATHER and Friend, thy light, thy love,
Beaming through all thy works, we see ,
Thy glory gilds the heavens above,
And all the earth is full of thee.

2 Thy voice we hear, thy presence feel,
Whilst thou, too pure for mortal sight,

Involved in clouds, invisible,
  Reignest the Lord of life and light.

3 We know not in what hallowed part
  Of the wide heavens thy throne may be,
But *this* we know, — that where thou art,
  Strength, wisdom, goodness, dwell with thee.

4 And through the various maze of time,
  And through th' infinity of space,
We follow thy career sublime,
  And all thy wondrous footsteps trace.

5 Thy children shall not faint nor fear,
  Sustained by this delightful thought, —
Since thou, their God, art everywhere,
  They cannot be where thou art not.

425. S. M. COWPER.

Dependence on God.

1 TO keep the lamp alive,
  With oil we fill the bowl;
'T is water makes the willow thrive,
  And grace that feeds the soul.

2 The Lord's unsparing hand
  Supplies the living stream;
It is not at our own command,
  But still derived from him.

3 Man's wisdom is to seek
  His strength in God alone;
And e'en an angel would be weak,
  Who trusted in his own.

4 Retreat beneath his wings,
  And in his grace confide;
This more exalts the King of kings
  Than all your works beside.

5 In God is all our store,
  Grace issues from his throne;

Whoever says, "I want no more,"
  Confesses he has none.

426. L. M. 6 L. J. QUARLES

Self-abandonment to God.

1 FOUNTAIN of light and living breath,
  Whose mercies never fail nor fade,
Fill us with life that hath no death,
  Fill us with light that hath no shade ;
Appoint the remnant of our days
To see thy power and sing thy praise.

2 Lord God of gods ! before whose throne
  Stand storms and fire, O, what shall we
Return to heaven that is our own,
  When all the world belongs to thee ?
We have no offering to impart
But praises and a wounded heart.

3 Great God, whose kingdom hath no end,
  Into whose secrets none can dive,
Whose mercy none can apprehend,
  Whose justice none can feel and live ;
What our weak minds cannot aspire
To know, Lord, teach us to admire.

427. L. M. SIR WALTER SCOTT

Imploring the constant Presence of God.

1 WHEN Israel, of the Lord beloved,
  Out from the land of bondage came,
Her father's God before her moved,
  An awful guide in smoke and flame.

2 By day, along th' astonished lands,
  The cloudy pillar glided slow ;
By night, Arabia's crimsoned sands
  Returned the fiery column's glow.

3 Thus present still, though now unseen,
  When brightly shines the prosperous day,

Be thoughts of thee a cloudy screen,
To temper the deceitful ray !

4 And, O, when gathers on our path,
In shade and storm, the frequent night,
Be thou, long suffering, slow to wrath,
A burning and a shining light !

428. C. M. DODDRIDGE.

God speaking Peace to his People.

1 UNITE, my roving thoughts, unite
In silence soft and sweet ;
And thou, my soul, sit gently down
At thy great Sovereign's feet.

2 Jehovah's awful voice is heard ;
Yet gladly I attend ;
For, lo ! the everlasting God
Proclaims himself my friend.

3 Harmonious accents to my soul
The sound of peace convey ;
The tempest at his word subsides,
And winds and seas obey.

4 By all its joys, I charge my heart
To grieve his love no more,
But, charmed by melody divine,
To give its follies o'er.

5 Let this my every hour employ,
Till I thy glory see,
Enter into my Master's joy,
And find my heaven in thee !

429. 7 & 6s. M. (Peculiar.) WESLEYAN.

Confidence in God's Protection.

1 O MY soul, unceasing pray ;
In God alone confide ;
He thy feeble steps shall stay,
Nor suffer thee to slide ;

Lean on thy Redeemer's breast
He thy spirit safely keeps ;
Rest in him, securely rest ;
Thy Watchman never sleeps.

2 Neither sin, nor earth, nor hell,
Thy Keeper can surprise ;
Careless slumbers cannot steal
On his all-seeing eyes ;
He is Israel's sure Defence ;
Israel all his care shall prove,
Kept by watchful Providence,
And ever-waking Love.

3 See the Lord, thy Keeper, stand
Omnipotently near ;
Lo, he holds thee by thy hand,
And banishes thy fear ;
He shall bless thy going out,
He shall bless thy coming in,
Kindly compass thee about,
And guard from every sin.

430. C. M. HEGINBOTHAM.

Rejoicing in God, our Father.

1 COME, shout aloud the Father's grace,
And sing the Saviour's love ;
Soon shall ye join the glorious theme,
In loftier strains, above.

2 God, the eternal, mighty God,
To dearer names descends ;
Calls you his treasure and his joy,
His children and his friends.

3 My Father, God ! and may these lips
Pronounce a name so dear ?
Not thus could heaven's sweet harmony
Delight my listening ear.

4 Thanks to my God for every gift
His bounteous hands bestow ;
And thanks eternal for that love
Whence all these comforts flow.

431. 7s. M. 6 L. MONTGOMERY.

The Soul panting for God.

1 AS the hart, with eager looks,
Panteth for the water-brooks.
So my soul, athirst for thee,
Pants the living God to see ;
When, O, when, with filial fear,
Lord, shall I to thee draw near ?

2 Why art thou cast down, my soul ?
God, thy God, shall make thee whole :
Why art thou disquieted ?
God shall lift thy fallen head,
And his countenance benign
Be the saving health of thine.

432. C. M. STEELE.

Refuge in God.

1 O FATHER, to thy mercy-seat
My soul for shelter flies :
'T is here I find a safe retreat
When storms and tempests rise.

2 My cheerful hope can never die,
If thou, my God, art near ;
Thy grace can raise my comforts high,
And banish every fear.

3 My great Protector and my Lord,
Thy constant aid impart,
O, let thy kind, thy gracious word
Sustain my trembling heart.

4 O, never let my soul remove
From this divine retreat ;

Still let me trust thy power and love,
And dwell beneath thy feet.

433. L. M. 6 L. C. Wesley

Rejoicing in God.

1 THOU hidden Source of calm repose,
Thou all-sufficient Love divine,
My Help and Refuge from my foes,
Secure I am if thou art mine.
And, lo! from sin, and grief, and shame,
I hide me, Father, in thy name.

2 Thy mighty name salvation is;
And keeps my happy soul above;
Comfort it brings, and power, and peace,
And joy, and everlasting love:
To me, through thy dear Son, are given
Pardon and holiness and heaven.

3 Father my all in all thou art,
My rest in toil, my ease in pain;
The balm to heal each broken heart;
In storms my peace, in loss my gain,
My joy beneath the worldling's frown;
In shame my glory and my crown;—

4 In want my plentiful supply;
In weakness my almighty power;
In bonds my perfect liberty;
My refuge in temptation's hour;
My comfort 'midst all grief and pain,
My life in death, my endless gain.

434. S. M. J. W

Trust in God under Affliction.

1 COMMIT thou all thy griefs
And ways into his hands,
To his sure trust and tender care,
Who earth and heaven commands:

2 Who points the clouds their course,
Whom winds and seas obey,
He shall direct thy wandering feet,
He shall prepare thy way.

3 No profit canst thou gain
By self-consuming care;
To him commend thy cause, — his ear
Attends the softest prayer.

4 Thou on the Lord rely,
So safe shalt thou go on;
Fix on his work thy steadfast eye,
So shall thy work be done.

435. L: M. HENRY MOORE

Wisdom and Virtue sought from God.

1 SUPREME and universal Light!
Fountain of reason! Judge of right!
Parent of good! whose blessings flow
On all above, and all below:

2 Assist us, Lord, to act, to be,
What nature and thy laws decree;
Worthy that intellectual flame,
Which from thy breathing spirit came!

3 Our moral freedom to maintain,
Bid passion serve, and reason reign,
Self-poised and independent still
On this world's varying good or ill.

4 No slave to profit, shame, or fear,
O, may our steadfast bosoms bear,
The stamp of heaven, — an upright heart,
Above the mean disguise of art!

5 May our expanded souls disclaim
The narrow view, the selfish aim;
But with a Christian zeal embrace
Whate'er is friendly to our race.

6 O Father, grace and virtue grant!
No more we wish, no more we want:
To know, to serve thee, and to love,
Is peace below, — is bliss above.

436. S. M. C. Wesley

Watching, Prayer, and Perseverance.

1 A CHARGE to keep I have,
A God to glorify,
A never dying soul to save,
And fit it for the sky;
To serve the present age,
My calling to fulfil:
O, may it all my powers engage
To do my Master's will!

2 Arm me with jealous care,
As in thy sight to live;
And, O, thy servant, Lord, prepare
The strict account to give:
Help me to watch and pray,
And on thyself rely,
Assured, if I my trust betray,
I shall forsaken die.

437. C. M. C. Wesley.

Watchfulness.

1 I WANT a principle within
Of jealous, godly fear;
A sensibility of sin,
A pain to find it near.

2 I want the first approach to feel
Of pride, or fond desire;
To catch the wandering of my will,
And quench the kindling fire.

3 From thee that I no more may part,
No more thy goodness grieve,

The filial awe, the fleshly heart,
The tender conscience give.

4 Quick as the apple of an eye,
O God ! my conscience make ;
Awake my soul when sin is nigh,
And keep it still awake.

438. C. M. LOGAN

The Ways of Wisdom.

1 O, HAPPY is the man who hears
Instruction's faithful voice ;
And who celestial wisdom makes
His early, only choice !

2 Wisdom has treasures greater far
Than east or west unfold ;
And her rewards more precious are
Than is the gain of gold.

3 In her right hand she holds to view
A length of happy years ;
And in her left, the prize of fame
And honor bright appears.

4 She guides the young, with innocence,
In pleasure's path to tread ;
A crown of glory she bestows
Upon the hoary head.

5 According as her labors rise,
So her rewards increase ;
Her ways are ways of pleasantness,
And all her paths are peace.

439. C. M CAMPBELL'S COLL

They shall walk and not faint.

1 SUPREME in wisdom, as in power,
The Rock of Ages stands,
Though him thou canst not see, nor trace
The workings of his hands.

2 He gives the conquest to the weak,
Supports the sinking heart,
And courage, in the evil hour,
His heavenly aids impart.

3 Mere human power shall fast decay,
And youthful vigor cease ;
But they who wait upon the Lord
In strength shall still increase.

4 They with unwearied feet shall tread
The path of life divine,
With growing ardor onward move,
With growing brightness shine.

5 On eagles' wings they mount, they soar ;
Their wings are faith and love ;
Till, past the cloudy regions here,
They rise to heaven above.

440. S. M. EPISCOPAL COLL.

Ark of Safety.

1 O, CEASE, my wandering soul,
On restless wing to roam ;
All this wide world, to either pole,
Has not for thee a home.

2 Behold the ark of God ;
Behold the open door ;
O, haste to gain that dear abode,
And rove, my soul, no more.

3 There, safe thou shalt abide,
There, sweet shall be thy rest,
And every longing satisfied,
With full salvation blest.

441. C. M. BEDDOME.

Fear not.

1 YE trembling souls, dismiss your fears ;
Be mercy all your theme ;

For mercy like a river flows,
In one perpetual stream.

2 Fear not the powers of earth and hell;
God will those powers restrain;
His arm will all their rage repel,
And make their efforts vain.

3 Fear not the want of outward good;
For his he will provide,
Grant them supplies of daily food,
And give them heaven beside.

4 Fear not that he will e'er forsake,
Or leave his work undone;
He 's faithful to his promises,
And faithful to his Son.

5 Fear not the terrors of the grave,
Nor death's relentless sting;
He will from endless wrath preserve,
To endless glory bring.

442. 8, 6, & 4s. M. HEMANS

Imploring Succour.

1 FATHER, who in the olive shade,
When the dark hour came on,
Didst, with a breath of heavenly aid,
Strengthen thy Son, —

2 O, by the anguish of that night,
Send us down blest relief;
Or, to the chastened, let thy might
Hallow this grief.

3 And thou, that, when the starry sky
Saw the dread strife begun,
Didst teach adoring faith to cry,
"Thy will be done!" —

4 By thy meek spirit, thou, of all
That e'er have mourned the chief,

Blest Saviour, if the stroke must fall,
Hallow this grief.

443. L. M. E. Taylor.

Love to Christ.

1 THERE 'S not a hope with comfort fraught,
Triumphant over death and time,
But Jesus mingles in the thought,
Forerunner of our course sublime.

2 His image meets me in the hour
Of joy, and brightens every smile ,
I see him, when the tempests lower,
Each terror soothe, each grief beguile.

3 I see him in the daily round
Of social duty, mild and meek ;
With him I tread the hallowed ground
Communion with my God to seek.

4 I see his pitying, gentle eye,
When lonely want appeals for aid ;
I hear him in the frequent sigh,
That mourns the waste which sin has made.

5 I meet him at the lowly tomb ;
I weep where Jesus wept before ;
And there, above the grave's dark gloom,
I see him rise, and weep no more.

444. L. M. Anonymous.

Christ the Way, the Truth, and the Life

1 THOU art the Way ; and he who sighs,
Amid this starless waste of woe,
To find a pathway to the skies,
A light from heaven's eternal glow,
By thee must come, thou Gate of love,
Through which the saints undoubting trod,
Till faith discovers, like the dove,
An ark, a resting-place in God.

2 Thou art the Truth, whose steady day
Shines on through earthly blight and bloom ,
The pure, the everlasting Ray,
The Lamp that shines e'en in the tomb ;
The Light that out of darkness springs,
And guideth those that blindly go ;
The Word whose precious radiance flings
Its lustre upon all below.

3 Thou art the Life, the blessèd Well
With living waters gushing o'er,
Which those that drink shall ever dwell
Where sin and thirst are known no more.
Thou art the mystic Pillar given,
Our Lamp by night, our Light by day ;
Thou art the sacred Bread from heaven ;
Thou art the Life, the Truth, the Way.

445. L. M. C. Wesley

Enjoyment of Christ's Love.

1 JESUS, thy boundless love to me
No thought can reach, no tongue declare ,
Unite my thankful heart to thee,
And reign without a rival there.

2 Thy love, how cheering is its ray !
All pain before its presence flies ;
Care, anguish, sorrow, melt away,
Where'er its healing beams arise.

3 O, let thy love my soul inflame,
And to thy service sweetly bind ;
Transfuse it through my inmost frame,
And mould me wholly to thy mind.

4 Thy love, in sufferings, be my peace ;
Thy love, in weakness, make me strong ;
And, when the storms of life shall cease,
Thy love shall be in heaven my song.

446. 6 & 10s. M. MARTINEAU'S COLL

Looking unto Jesus.

1 THOU, who didst stoop below,
To drain the cup of woe,
And wear the form of frail mortality, —
Thy blessèd labors done,
Thy crown of victory won, —
Hast passed from earth, — passed to thy home on high.

2 It was no path of flowers,
Through this dark world of ours,
Belovèd of the Father, thou didst tread;
And shall we in dismay
Shrink from the narrow way,
When clouds and darkness are around it spread?

3 O Thou, who art our life,
Be with us through the strife;
Thy own meek head by rudest storms was bowed;
Raise thou our eyes above,
To see a Father's love
Beam, like a bow of promise, through the cloud.

4 E'en through the awful gloom,
Which hovers o'er the tomb,
That light of love our guiding star shall be;
Our spirits shall not dread
The shad'wy way to tread,
Friend, Guardian, Saviour, which doth lead to thee.

447. L. M. SIR J. E. SMITH.

"It is I; be not afraid."

1 WHEN power divine, in mortal form,
Hushed with a word the raging storm,
In soothing accents, Jesus said,
"Lo, it is I; be not afraid."

2 So, when in silence nature sleeps,
And his lone watch the mourner keeps,

One thought shall every pang remove, —
Trust, feeble man, thy Maker's love.

3 God calms the tumult and the storm ;
He rules the seraph and the worm ;
No creature is by him forgot,
Of those who know, or know him not.

4 And when the last dread hour shall come,
While trembling nature waits her doom,
This voice shall wake the pious dead, —
" Lo, it is I ; be not afraid."

448. C. M. AVELING

Fear not.

1 WHENE'ER the clouds of sorrow roll,
And trials whelm the mind, —
When, faint with grief, thy wearied soul
No joys on earth can find, —
Then lift thy voice to God on high,
Dry up the trembling tear,
And hush the low, complaining sigh :
" Fear not" ; thy God is near.

2 When dark temptations spread their snares,
And earth with charms allures,
And when thy soul, oppressed with fears,
The world's assault endures,
Then let thy Father's friendly voice
Thy fainting spirit cheer,
And bid thy trembling heart rejoice :
" Fear not" ; thy God is near.

3 And when the final hour shall come,
That calls thee to thy rest,
To dwell within thy heavenly home,
A welcome, joyful guest,
Be calm ; though Jordan's waves may roll,
No ills shall meet thee there ;

Angels shall whisper to thy soul,
  "Fear not"; thy God is near.

449. C. M. COWPER

Submission to the Divine Disposal.

1 O LORD! my best desires fulfil,
  And help me to resign
Life, health, and comfort to thy will,
  And make thy pleasure mine.

2 Why should I shrink at thy command,
  Whose love forbids my fears;
Or tremble at thy gracious hand,
  That wipes away my tears?

3 No! let me rather freely yield
  What most I prize to thee;
Who never hast a good withheld,
  Nor wilt withhold from me.

4 Wisdom and mercy guide my way;
  Shall I resist them both;
Short-sighted creature of a day,
  And crushed before the moth?

5 But, ah! my heart within me cries,
  Still bind me to thy sway;
Else the next cloud that veils the skies,
  Drives all these thoughts away.

450. C. M. MERRICK

Holy Resignation.

1 AUTHOR of good, to thee we turn:
  Thine ever wakeful eye
Alone can all our wants discern,
  Thy hand alone supply.

2 O, let thy love within us dwell,
  Thy fear our footsteps guide;
That love shall vainer loves expel,
  That fear all fears beside.

3 And, O, by error's force subdued,
Since oft, with stubborn will,
We blindly shun the latent good,
And grasp the specious ill, —

4 Not what we wish, but what we want,
Let mercy still supply :
The good we ask not, Father, grant ;
The ill we ask, deny.

451. L. M. ROSCOE

The Peace of God in Affliction.

1 WHEN anguish bows me down, I turn,
O God, with trusting heart, to thee ;
And holy thoughts still shine and burn,
And cheer my cold, sad destiny.

2 The stars of heaven are shining on,
Though these frail eyes are dim with tears ;
The hopes of earth, indeed, are gone ;
But are not ours th' immortal years ?

3 Father, forgive the heart that clings,
Thus trembling, to the joys of time :
And bid my soul on angel wings
Ascend into a purer clime.

4 There shall no doubts disturb its trust,
No sorrow dim celestial love ;
But these afflictions of the dust
Like shadows of the night remove.

5 E'en now, above, there 's radiant day,
While clouds and darkness brood below ;
Then, Father, joyful on my way
To drink the bitter cup I go.

452. C. M. MRS. FOLLEN.

Resignation.

1 HOW sweet to be allowed to pray,
To God the Holy One,

With filial love and trust to say,
O God, thy will be done !

2 We in these sacred words can find
A cure for every ill ;
They calm and soothe the troubled mind,
And bid all care be still.

3 O, let that will, which gave me breath
And an immortal soul,
In joy or grief, in life or death,
My every wish control.

4 O, teach my heart the blessèd way
To imitate thy Son !
Teach me, O God, in truth to pray,
" Thy will, not mine, be done."

453. C. H. M. CONDER

Blessedness of Submission in Trials.

1 WHEN I can trust my all with God,
In trial's fearful hour,
Bow, all resigned, beneath his rod,
And bless his sparing power,
A joy springs up amid distress,
A fountain in the wilderness.

2 O, blessèd be the hand that gave, —
Still blessèd when it takes ;
Blessèd be he who smites to save, —
Who heals the heart he breaks :
Perfect and true are all his ways,
Whom heaven adores and death obeys.

454. C. P. M. COTTON

Contentment and Resignation.

1 IF solid happiness we prize,
Within our breasts the jewel lies ;
Nor need we roam abroad :

The world has little to bestow;
From well formed hearts our joys must flow,
Hearts that delight in God.

2 Then let us, with a grateful mind,
Take what our Father, ever kind,
Doth graciously bestow;
The blessings which he sends, enjoy,
And in his praise find sweet employ,
From whom our comforts flow.

3 To be resigned, when ills betide,
Patient, when favors are denied,
And pleased with favors given;
This is the wise, the virtuous part:
This is that incense of the heart,
Whose fragrance reaches heaven.

4 Thus through life's changing scenes we 'll go,
Its checkered paths of joy and woe
With holy care we 'll tread;
Quit its vain scenes without a tear,
Without a trouble or a fear,
And mingle with the dead.

5 For conscience, like a faithful friend,
Shall through the gloomy vale attend,
And cheer our dying breath;
Shall, when all other comforts cease,
Like a kind angel, whisper peace,
And smooth the bed of death.

455. S. M. Sacred Songs.

Affliction Blessed.

1 HOW tender is thy hand,
O thou most gracious Lord!
Afflictions come at thy command,
And leave us at thy word.

2 How gentle was the rod,
That chastened us for sin!

How soon we found a gracious God,
Where deep distress had been!

3 A Father's hand we felt,
A Father's heart we knew;
'Mid tears of penitence we knelt,
And found his word was true.

4 Now we will bless the Lord,
And in his strength confide
For ever be his name adored
For there is none beside.

456. C. M. ANONYMOUS

The Benefit of Affliction.

1 O GOD, to thee my sinking soul
In deep distress doth fly;
Thy love can all my griefs control
And all my wants supply.

2 How oft, when dark misfortune's band
Around their victim stood,
The seeming ill, at thy command,
Hath changed to real good!

3 The tempest that obscured the sky
Hath set my bosom free
From earthly care and sensual joy,
And turned my thoughts to thee.

4 Affliction's blast hath made me learn
To feel for others' woe,
And humbly seek, with deep concern
My own defects to know.

5 Then rage, ye storms; ye billows, roar
My heart defies your shock;
Ye make me cling to God the more,—
To God, my sheltering Rock.

457. 8s. M. BATH COLL

Our Salvation in Trouble.

1 O THOU whose compassionate care
Forbids my sad heart to complain,
Now graciously teach me to bear
The weight of affliction and pain.

2 Though cheerless my days seem to flow,
Though weary and wakeful my nights,
What comfort it gives me to know
'T is the hand of a Father that smites !

3 A tender physician thou art,
Who woundest in order to heal,
And comfort divine dost impart
To soften the anguish we feel.

4 O, let this correction be blest,
And answer thy gracious design ;
Then grant that my soul may find rest
In comforts so healing as thine.

458. C. M. EDMESTON

Asking Mercy in Affliction.

1 O THOU whose mercy guides my way,
Though now it seem severe,
Forbid my unbelief to say
There is no mercy here.

2 O, grant me to desire the pain
That comes in kindness down,
More than the world's alluring gain
Succeeded by a frown.

3 Then, though thou bow my spirit low,
Love only shall I see ;
A Father's hand directs the blow,
In mercy chastens me.

459. L. M. 6 L. HEBER

" Though he slay me, yet will I trust in him."

1 THOUGH sorrows rise and dangers roll
In waves of darkness o'er my soul ;
Though friends are false, and love decays
And few and evil are my days ;
Yet e'en in nature's utmost ill,
I 'll love thee, Lord, I 'll love thee still

2 Though conscience, fiercest of my foes,
Swells with remembered guilt my woes ,
And memory points, with busy pain,
To grace and mercy given in vain ;
Though every thought has power to kill,
I 'll love thee, Lord, I 'll love thee still.

3 O, by the woes Messiah bore,
And in his griefs was loved the more ;
By these my pangs, whose healing smart
Thy grace hath planted in my heart ;
I know, I feel, thy gracious will,
Thou lov'st me, Lord, thou lov'st me still.

460. C. M. PERCY CHAPEL COLL

" Thy Will be done."

1 FATHER, I know thy ways are just,
Although to me unknown ;
O, grant me grace thy love to trust,
And cry, " Thy will be done."

2 If thou shouldst hedge with thorns my path,
Should wealth and friends be gone,
Still, with a firm and lively faith,
I 'll cry, " Thy will be done."

3 Although thy steps I cannot trace,
Thy sovereign right I 'll own ;
And, as instructed by thy grace,
I 'll cry, " Thy will be done."

4 'T is sweet thus passively to lie
Before thy gracious throne,
Concerning every thing to cry,
"My Father's will be done."

461. 8 & 6s. M. (Peculiar.) ANONYMOUS

"Thy Will be done."

1 MY God, my Father, while I stray
Far from my home on life's rough way,
O, teach me from my heart to say,
"Thy will, my God, be done."

2 Though dark my path, and sad my lot,
Let me be still, and murmur not,
And breathe the prayer divinely taught,
"Thy will, my God, be done."

3 What though in lonely grief I sigh
For friends beloved no longer nigh;
Submissive still would I reply,
"Thy will, my God, be done."

4 If thou shouldst call me to resign
What most I prize, — it ne'er was mine, —
I only yield thee what is thine;
"Thy will, my God, be done."

5 Should pining sickness waste away
My life in premature decay,
In life or death teach me to say,
"Thy will, my God, be done."

6 Renew my will from day to day,
Blend it with thine, and take away
Whate'er now makes it hard to say,
"Thy will, my God, be done."

462. C. M. STEELE.

Filial Submission.

1 AND can my heart aspire so high,
To say, "My Father, God"?

Lord, at thy feet I fain would lie,
And learn to kiss the rod.

2 I would submit to all thy will,
For thou art good and wise;
Let each rebellious thought be still,
Nor one faint murmur rise.

3 Thy love can cheer the darkest gloom,
And bid me wait serene,
Till hopes and joys immortal bloom,
And brighten all the scene.

4 "My Father, God," permit my heart
To plead her humble claim,
And ask the bliss those words impart,
In my Redeemer's name.

463. C. M. Sabbath Recreations

Resignation.

1 IN trouble and in grief, O God,
Thy smile hath cheered my way;
And joy hath budded from each thorn,
That round my footsteps lay.

2 The hours of pain have yielded good,
Which prosperous days refused;
As herbs, though scentless when entire,
Spread fragrance when they 're bruised.

3 The oak strikes deeper, as its boughs
By furious blasts are driven;
So life's tempestuous storms the more
Have fixed my heart in heaven.

4 All-gracious Lord, whate'er my lot
In other times may be,
I 'll welcome still the heaviest grief,
That brings me near to thee.

464. S. M. TOPLADY

Encouragement.

1 YOUR harps, ye trembling saints,
Down from the willows take;
Loud to the praise of love divine,
Bid every string awake.

2 Though in a foreign land,
We are not far from home;
And nearer to our house above,
We every moment come.

3 His grace will to the end
Stronger and brighter shine;
Nor present things, nor things to come,
Shall quench the spark divine.

465. L. M. COWPER.

"God is Love."

1 WHEN darkness long has veiled my mind,
And smiling day once more appears;
Then, my Creator! then I find
The folly of my doubts and fears.

2 Straight I upbraid my wandering heart,
And blush that I should ever be
Thus prone to act so base a part,
Or harbour one hard thought of thee.

3 O, let me then at length be taught
What I am still so slow to learn, —
That God is love, and changes not,
Nor knows the shadow of a turn.

4 Sweet truth, and easy to repeat!
But, when my faith is sharply tried,
I find myself a learner yet,
Unskilful, weak, and apt to slide.

5 But, O my God! one look from thee
Subdues the disobedient will,

Drives doubt and discontent away,
And thy rebellious child is still.

466. L. M. WATTS

The Gospel exemplified in the Conduct.

1 SO let our lips and lives express
The holy gospel we profess;
So let our works and virtues shine,
To prove the doctrine all divine.

2 Thus shall we best proclaim abroad
The honors of our Maker, God,
When his salvation reigns within,
And grace subdues the power of sin.

3 Our flesh and sense must be denied,
Ambition, envy, lust, and pride;
While justice, temperance, truth, and love
Our inward piety approve.

4 Religion bears our spirits up,
While we expect that blesséd hope,
The bright appearance of the Lord,
And faith stands leaning on his word.

467. L. M. RIPPON'S COLL.

Patience.

1 PATIENCE, O, 't is a grace divine,
Sent from the God of peace and love,
That leans upon its father's arm,
As through the wilds of life we rove.

2 By patience, we serenely bear
The troubles of our mortal state,
And wait, contented, our discharge,
Nor think our glory comes too late.

3 O, for this grace to aid us on,
And arm with fortitude the breast,
Till, life's tumultuous voyage o'er,
We reach the shores of endless rest.

4 Faith into vision shall resign,
Hope shall in full fruition die,
And patience in possession end,
In the bright worlds of bliss on high.

468. S. M. HEATH.

Watchfulness and Prayer inculcated.

1 MY soul, be on thy guard ;
Ten thousand foes arise ;
The hosts of sin are pressing hard
To draw thee from the skies.

2 O, watch, and fight, and pray ;
The battle ne'er give o'er ;
Renew it boldly every day,
And help divine implore.

3 Ne'er think the victory won,
Nor lay thine armor down :
Thy arduous work will not be done
Till thou obtain thy crown.

4 Fight on, my soul, till death
Shall bring thee to thy God ;
He 'll take thee, at thy parting breath,
To his divine abode.

469. C. M. WATTS.

Humility and Submission.

1 IS there ambition in my heart ?
Search, gracious God, and see ;
Or do I act a haughty part ?
Lord, I appeal to thee.

2 I charge my thoughts, be humble still,
And all my carriage mild ;
Content, my Father, with thy will,
And quiet as a child.

3 The patient soul, the lowly mind,
Shall have a large reward :

Let saints in sorrow lie resigned,
And trust a faithful Lord.

470. L. M. ENFIELD.

Humility.

1 WHEREFORE should man, frail child of clay,
Who, from the cradle to the shroud,
Lives but the insect of a day, —
O, why should mortal man be proud?

2 His brightest visions just appear,
Then vanish, and no more are found;
The stateliest pile his pride can rear,
A breath may level with the ground.

3 By doubt perplexed, in error lost,
With trembling step he seeks his way:
How vain of wisdom's gift the boast!
Of reason's lamp, how faint the ray!

4 Follies and sins, a countless sum,
Are crowded in life's little span:
How ill, alas! does pride become
That erring, guilty creature, man!

5 God of my life! Father divine!
Give me a meek and lowly mind:
In modest worth, O, let me shine,
And peace in humble virtue find.

471. C. M. WATTS

Prudence.

1 O, 'T IS a lovely thing to see
A man of prudent heart,
Whose thoughts, and lips, and life agree
To act a useful part.

2 When envy, strife, and wars begin,
In fierce, contentious souls,
Mark how the sons of peace come in,
And quench the kindling coals.

3 Their minds are humble, mild, and meek,
Nor let their anger rise ;
Nor passion moves their lips to speak,
Nor pride exalts their eyes.

4 Their lives are prudence mixed with love ,
Good works employ their day ;
They join the serpent with the dove,
But cast the sting away.

472. L. M. SCOTT.

The Blessing of Meekness.

1 HAPPY the meek, whose gentle breast,
Clear as the summer's evening ray,
Calm as the regions of the blest,
Enjoys on earth celestial day.

2 His heart no broken friendships sting,
No storms his peaceful tent invade ;
He rests beneath th' Almighty wing,
Hostile to none, of none afraid.

3 Spirit of grace, all meek and mild,
Inspire our breasts, our souls possess ;
Repel each passion rude and wild,
And bless us as we aim to bless.

473. C. M. ADDISON

Gratitude.

1 WHEN all thy mercies, O my God,
My rising soul surveys,
Transported with the view, I 'm lost
In wonder, love, and praise.

2 Unnumbered comforts on my soul
Thy tender care bestowed,
Before my infant heart conceived
From whom those comforts flowed.

3 When in the slippery paths of youth
With heedless steps I ran,

Thine arm, unseen, conveyed me safe,
And led me up to man.

4 When worn with sickness, oft hast thou
With health renewed my face ;
And, when in sin and sorrow sunk,
Revived my soul with grace.

5 Ten thousand thousand precious gifts
My daily thanks employ ;
Nor is the least a cheerful heart,
That tastes those gifts with joy.

6 Through every period of my life,
Thy goodness I 'll pursue ;
And after death, in distant worlds,
The glorious theme renew.

474. C. M. WATTS.

Hidden Life of the Christian.

1 O HAPPY soul that lives on high,
While men lie grovelling here !
His hopes are fixed above the sky,
And faith forbids his fear.

2 His conscience knows no secret stings,
While grace and joy combine
To form a life whose holy springs
Are hidden and divine.

3 He waits in secret on his God,
His God in secret sees ;
Let earth be all in arms abroad,
He dwells in heavenly peace.

4 His pleasures rise from things unseen,
Beyond this world and time,
Where neither eyes nor ears have oeen,
Nor thoughts of mortals climb.

5 He wants no pomp nor royal throne
To raise his honors here :

Content and pleased to live unknown,
Till Christ his life appear.

475. C. M. WATTS

Christian Courage and Self-denial.

1 AM I a soldier of the cross,
A follower of the Lamb ?
And shall I fear to own his cause,
Or blush to speak his name ?

2 Must I be carried to the skies
On flowery beds of ease,
While others fought to win the prize,
And sailed through bloody seas ?

3 Are there no foes for me to face ?
Must I not stem the flood ?
Is this vile world a friend to grace,
To help me on to God ?

4 Sure I must fight, if I would reign ;
Increase my courage, Lord !
I 'll bear the toil, endure the pain,
Supported by thy word.

5 Thy saints, in all this glorious war,
Shall conquer, though they 're slain :
They see the triumph from afar,
And soon with Christ shall reign.

6 When that illustrious day shall rise,
And all thy armies shine
In robes of victory through the skies,
The glory shall be thine.

476. S. M. MORAVIAN.

The Christian encouraged.

1 GIVE to the winds thy fears ;
Hope and be undismayed ;
God hears thy sighs, and counts thy tears ;
God shall lift up thy head.

2 Through waves, through clouds, and storms,
He gently clears thy way;
Wait thou his time; so shall the night
Soon end in joyous day.

3 Thou seest our weakness, Lord,
Our hearts are known to thee;
O, lift thou up the sinking hand,
Confirm the feeble knee!

4 Let us, in life or death,
Boldly thy truth declare!
And publish, with our latest breath,
Thy love and guardian care.

477. C. M. ANONYMOUS.

The whole Armor.

1 O, SPEED thee, Christian, on thy way,
And to thy armor cling;
With girded loins the call obey
That grace and mercy bring.

2 There is a battle to be fought,
An upward race to run,
A crown of glory to be sought,
A victory to be won.

3 O, faint not, Christian, for thy sighs
Are heard before His throne;
The race must come before the prize,
The cross before the crown.

478. C. M. GISBORNE.

The Christian's Life.

1 A SOLDIER'S course, from battles won
To new commencing strife;
A pilgrim's, restless as the sun;—
Behold the Christian's life.

2 O, let us seek our heavenly home,
Revealed in sacred lore;

The land whence pilgrims never roam,
  Where soldiers war no more ;—

3 Where grief shall never wound, nor death,
  Beneath the Saviour's reign ;
Nor sin, with pestilential breath,
  His holy realm profane ;—

4 The land where, suns and moons unknown,
  And night's alternate sway,
Jehovah's ever-burning throne
  Upholds unbroken day ;—

5 Where they who meet shall never part ,
  Where grace achieves its plan ;
And God, uniting every heart,
  Dwells face to face with man.

479. L. M. BARBAULD

The Christian Warfare.

1 AWAKE, my soul ! lift up thine eyes ;
See where thy foes against thee rise,
In long array, a numerous host ;
Awake, my soul ! or thou art lost.

2 Here giant danger threatening stands,
Mustering his pale, terrific bands ;
There pleasure's silken banners spread,
And willing souls are captive led.

3 See where rebellious passions rage,
And fierce desires and lusts engage ;
The meanest foe of all the train
Has thousands and ten thousands slain.

4 Thou tread'st upon enchanted ground ;
Perils and snares beset thee round ;
Beware of all ; guard every part ;
But most, the traitor in thy heart.

5 Come, then, my soul ! now learn to wield
The weight of thine immortal shield ;

Put on the armor from above,
Of heavenly truth, and heavenly love.

6 The terror and the charm repel,
And powers of earth, and powers of hell;
The Man of Calvary triumphed here;—
Why should his faithful followers fear?

480. C. M. DODDRIDGE

The Way to the Heavenly City.

1 SING, ye redeeméd of the Lord,
Your great Deliverer sing;
Pilgrims, for Zion's city bound,
Be joyful in your King.

2 A hand divine shall lead you on
Through all the blissful road,
Till to the sacred mount you rise,
And see your Father, God.

3 There, garlands of immortal joy
Shall bloom on every head;
While sorrow, sighing, and distress
Like shadows all are fled.

4 March on in your Redeemer's strength,
Pursue his footsteps still,
And let the prospect cheer your eye,
While laboring up the hill.

481. L. M. WATTS

The heavenly Race.

1 AWAKE, our souls; away, our fears;
Let every trembling thought be gone;
Awake, and run the heavenly race,
And put a cheerful courage on.

2 True, 't is a strait and thorny road,
And mortal spirits tire and faint;
But they forget the mighty God,
Who feeds the strength of every saint;—

3 The mighty God, whose matchless powei
Is ever new and ever young,
And firm endures, while endless years
Their everlasting circles run.

4 From thee, the overflowing spring,
Our souls shall drink a full supply;
While those who trust their native strength
Shall melt away, and droop, and die.

5 Swift as an eagle cuts the air,
We 'll mount aloft to thine abode;
On wings of love our souls shall fly,
Nor tire amid the heavenly road.

482. C. M. DODDRIDGE

The Christian Race.

1 AWAKE, my soul! stretch every nerve,
And press with vigor on;
A heavenly race demands thy zeal,
And an immortal crown.

2 A cloud of witnesses around
Hold thee in full survey;
Forget the steps already trod,
And onward urge thy way.

3 'T is God's all-animating voice
That calls thee from on high;
'T is his own hand presents the prize
To thine uplifted eye; —

4 That prize, with peerless glories bright,
Which shall new lustre boast,
When victors' wreaths and monarchs' gems
Shall blend in common dust.

483. S. M. L. H. SIGOURNEY.

Active Piety.

1 LABORERS of Christ, arise,
And gird you for the toil;

The dew of promise from the skies
Already cheers the soil.

2 Go where the sick recline,
Where mourning hearts deplore;
And, where the sons of sorrow pine,
Dispense your hallowed lore.

3 Urge, with a tender zeal,
The erring child along,
Where peaceful congregations kneel,
And pious teachers throng.

4 Be faith, which looks above,
With prayer, your constant guest,
And wrap the Saviour's changeless love
A mantle round your breast.

5 So shall you share the wealth,
That earth may ne'er despoil,
And the blest gospel's saving health
Repay your arduous toil.

484. S. M. BULFINCH

The Use of present Opportunities.

1 CHILDREN of light, awake!
At Jesus' call arise,
Forth with your leader to partake
His toils, his victories.

2 Ye must not idly stand,
His sacred voice who hear,
Arm for the strife the feeble hand,
The holy standard rear.

3 Naught doth the world afford,
But toil must be the price;
Wilt thou not, servant of the Lord,
Then toil for paradise?

4 Awake, ye sons of light!
Strive till the prize be won;

Far spent already is the night ;
  The day comes brightening on.

485. S. M. STEELE

Religion a Support in Life.

1 WHEN gloomy thoughts and fears
  The trembling heart invade,
And all the face of nature wears
  A universal shade, —

2 Religion can assuage
  The tempest of the soul ;
And every fear shall lose its rage
  At her divine control.

3 Through life's bewildered way,
  Her hand unerring leads ;
And o'er the path her heavenly ray
  A cheering lustre sheds.

4 When reason, tired and blind,
  Sinks helpless and afraid,
Thou blest supporter of the mind,
  How powerful is thine aid !

5 O, let us feel thy power,
  And find thy sweet relief,
To brighten every gloomy hour
  And soften every grief.

486. C. M. DODDRIDGE.

Sickness and Recovery.

1 MY God, thy service well demands
  The remnant of my days ;
Why was this fleeting breath renewed,
  But to renew thy praise ?

2 Thine arms of everlasting love
  Did this weak frame sustain,
When life was hovering o'er the grave,
  And nature sunk with pain.

3 I calmly bowed my fainting head
On thy dear, faithful breast,
And waited for my Father's call
To his eternal rest.

4 Back from the borders of the grave,
At thy command, I come;
Nor will I ask a speedier flight
To my celestial home.

5 Where thou appointest mine abode
There would I choose to be;
For in thy presence death is life,
And earth is heaven with thee.

487. C. M. HEGINBOTHAM

Comfort in Sickness and Death.

1 WHEN sickness shakes the languid frame,
Each dazzling pleasure flies;
Phantoms of bliss no more obscure
Our long-deluded eyes.

2 The tottering frame of mortal life
Shall crumble into dust;
Nature shall faint — but learn, my soul,
On nature's God to trust.

3 The man whose pious heart is fixed
On his all-gracious God,
In every frown may comfort find,
And kiss the chastening rod.

4 Nor him shall death itself alarm;
On heaven his soul relies;
With joy he views his Maker's love,
And with composure dies.

488. C. M. WATTS.

Trusting God in old Age.

1 MY God, my everlasting hope,
I live upon thy truth;

Thy hands have held my childhood up,
And strengthened all my youth.

2 Still has my life new wonders seen
Repeated every year;
Behold my days that yet remain,
I trust them to thy care.

3 Cast me not off when strength declines,
When hoary hairs arise;
And round me let thy glory shine,
Whene'er thy servant dies.

4 Then, in the history of my age,
When men review my days,
They 'll read thy love in every page,
In every line thy praise.

489. C. M. ANONYMOUS.

Old Age anticipated.

1 WHEN in the vale of lengthened years
My feeble feet shall tread,
And I survey the various scenes
Through which I have been led, —

2 How many mercies will my life
Before my view unfold!
What countless dangers will be passed,
What tales of sorrow told!

3 But yet, my soul, if thou canst say,
I 've seen my God in all,
In every blessing owned his hand,
In every loss his call; —

4 If piety has marked my steps,
And love my actions formed,
And purity possessed my heart,
And truth my lips adorned; —

5 If I an aged servant am
Of Jesus and of God,

I need not fear the closing scene,
Nor dread th' appointed road.

6 This scene will all my labors end,
This road conduct on high;
With comfort I 'll review the past,
And triumph though I die.

490. C. M. WATTS

Sustaining Grace in old Age implored.

1 GOD of my childhood and my youth,
The Guide of all my days,
I have declared thy heavenly truth,
And told thy wondrous ways.

2 Wilt thou forsake my hoary hairs,
And leave my fainting heart?
Who shall sustain my sinking years,
If God, my strength, depart?

3 Let me thy power and truth proclaim
Before the rising age,
And leave a savor of thy name
When I shall quit the stage.

4 The land of silence and of death
Attends my next remove;
O, may these poor remains of breath
Teach all the world thy love.

491. L. M. WATTS

Blessedness of the Righteous.

1 BLEST are the humble souls that see
Their emptiness and poverty:
Treasures of grace to them are given,
And crowns of joy laid up in heaven.

2 Blest are the meek, who stand afar
From rage and passion, noise and war;
God will secure their happy state,
And plead their cause against the great.

3 Blest are the souls that thirst for grace,
Hunger and long for righteousness ;
They shall be well supplied, and fed
With living streams and living bread.

4 Blest are the pure, whose hearts are clean,
Who never tread the ways of sin ;
With endless pleasure they shall see
A God of spotless purity.

5 Blest are the men of peaceful life,
Who quench the coals of growing strife ;
They shall be called the heirs of bliss,
The sons of God, — the God of peace

6 Blest are the faithful, who partake
Of pain and shame for Jesus' sake ;
Their souls shall triumph in the Lord ;
Eternal life is their reward.

MOURNING AND CONSOLATION.

492. L. M. STEELE

Death of an Infant.

1 SO fades the lovely, blooming flower,
Frail, smiling solace of an hour ;
So soon our transient comforts fly,
And pleasure only blooms to die.

2 Is there no kind, no healing art,
To soothe the anguish of the heart ?
Spirit of grace, be ever nigh :
Thy comforts are not made to die.

3 Let gentle patience smile on pain,
Till dying hope revives again ;
Hope wipes the tear from sorrow's eye,
And faith points upward to the sky.

493. C. M. STEELE

Death of a Child.

1 LIFE is a span, — a fleeting hour :
How soon the vapor flies !
Man is a tender, transient flower,
That e'en in blooming dies.

2 The once-loved form, now cold and dead,
Each mournful thought employs ;
And nature weeps, her comforts fled,
And withered all her joys.

3 Hope looks beyond the bounds of time,
When what we now deplore
Shall rise in full, immortal prime,
And bloom to fade no more.

4 Cease, then, fond nature, cease thy tears ,
Thy Saviour dwells on high ;
There everlasting spring appears ;
There joys shall never die.

494. L. M. J. Q. ADAMS

Death of Children.

1 SURE, to the mansions of the blest
When infant innocence ascends,
Some angel brighter than the rest
The spotless spirit's flight attends.

2 On wings of ecstasy they rise,
Beyond where worlds material roll,
Till some fair sister of the skies
Receives the unpolluted soul.

3 There, at th' Almighty Father's hand,
Nearest the throne of living light,
The choirs of infant seraphs stand,
And dazzling shine, where all are bright.

4 For when the Lord of mortal breath
Decrees his bounty to resume,

And points the silent shaft of death,
Which speeds an infant to the tomb, —
5 No passion fierce, no low desire,
Has quenched the radiance of the flame;
Back to its God the living fire
Returns, unsullied, as it came.

495. L. M. ANONYMOUS.

Death of an Infant.

1 AS the sweet flower that scents the morn,
But withers in the rising day,
Thus lovely was this infant's dawn,
Thus swiftly fled its life away.

2 It died ere its expanding soul
Had ever burnt with wrong desires,
Had ever spurned at Heaven's control,
Or ever quenched its sacred fires.

3 It died to sin, it died to cares,
But for a moment felt the rod:
O mourner! such, the Lord declares,
Such are the children of our God!

496. C. M. STEELE

Death of a young Person.

1 WHEN blooming youth is snatched away
By death's resistless hand,
Our hearts the mournful tribute pay,
Which pity must demand.

2 While pity prompts the rising sigh,
O, may this truth, impressed
With awful power, "I, too, must die,"
Sink deep in every breast.

3 Let this vain world delude no more;
Behold the opening tomb!
It bids us seize the present hour, —
To-morrow death may come.

4 Great God, thy sovereign grace impart,
Wiht cleansing, healing power ;
This only can prepare the heart
For death's surprising hour.

497. L. M. S. Wesley.

The Young cut off in their Prime.

1 THE morning flowers display their sweets,
And gay their silken leaves unfold,
As careless of the noontide heats,
As fearless of the evening cold.

2 Nipped by the wind's untimely blast,
Parched by the sun's directer ray,
The momentary glories waste,
The short-lived beauties die away.

3 So blooms the human face divine,
When youth its pride of beauty shows ,
Fairer than spring the colors shine,
And sweeter than the virgin rose.

4 Or worn by slowly rolling years,
Or broke by sickness in a day,
The fading glory disappears,
The short-lived beauties die away.

5 Yet these, new rising from the tomb,
With lustre brighter far shall shine ;
Revive with ever-during bloom,
Safe from diseases and decline.

6 Let sickness blast, let death devour,
If heaven must recompense our pains .
Perish the grass, and fade the flower,
If firm the word of God remains.

498. 8 & 7s. M. S. F. Smith

Interment of a pious young Female.

1 SISTER, thou wast mild and lovely,
Gentle as the summer breeze,

Pleasant as the air of evening,
When it floats among the trees.

2 Peaceful be thy silent slumber, —
Peaceful in the grave so low;
Thou no more wilt join our number;
Thou no more our songs shalt know.

3 Dearest sister, thou hast left us;
Here thy loss we deeply feel;
But 't is God that hath bereft us:
He can all our sorrows heal.

4 Yet again we hope to meet thee,
When the day of life is fled,
Then in heaven with joy to greet thee,
Where no farewell tear is shed.

499. C. M. L. H. Sigourney

Burial of a Friend.

1 AS, bowed by sudden storms, the rose
Sinks on the garden's breast,
Down to the grave our brother goes,
In silence there to rest.

2 No more with us his tuneful voice
The hymn of praise shall swell;
No more his cheerful heart rejoice
When peals the Sabbath bell.

3 Yet, if, in yonder cloudless sphere,
Amid a sinless throng,
He utters in his Saviour's ear
The everlasting song, —

4 No more we 'll mourn the absent friend,
But lift our earnest prayer,
And daily every effort bend
To rise and join him there.

500. C. M. DALE

Death of a Christian.

1 DEAR as thou wert, and justly dear,
We will not weep for thee :
One thought shall check the starting tear ,
It is, that thou art free.

2 And thus shall faith's consoling power
The tears of love restrain :
O, who that saw thy parting hour
Could wish thee here again !

3 Triumphant in thy closing eye
The hope of glory shone ;
Joy breathed in thy expiring sigh,
To think the race was run.

4 The passing spirit gently fled,
Sustained by grace divine ;
O, may such grace on us be shed,
And make our end like thine.

501. 7s. M. J. H. BANCROFT

The Christian's Burial.

1 BROTHER, though from yonder sky
Cometh neither voice nor cry,
Yet we know for thee to-day
Every pain hath passed away.

2 Not for thee shall tears be given,
Child of God and heir of heaven ;
For he gave thee sweet release ;
Thine the Christian's death of peace.

3 Well we know thy living faith
Had the power to conquer death ;
As a living rose may bloom
By the border of the tomb.

4 Brother, in that solemn trust
We commend thee, dust to dust ;

In that faith we wait, till, risen,
Thou shalt meet us all in heaven.

5 While we weep as Jesus wept,
Thou shalt sleep as Jesus slept;
With thy Saviour thou shalt rest,
Crowned, and glorified, and blest.

502. 7s. M. ANONYMOUS

Funeral Hymn.

1 CLAY to clay, and dust to dust!
Let them mingle, — for they must!
Give to earth the earthly clod,
For the spirit 's fled to God.

2 Never more shall midnight's damp
Darken round this mortal lamp;
Never more shall noonday's glance
Search this mortal countenance.

3 Deep the pit and cold the bed,
Where the spoils of death are laid:
Stiff the curtains, chill the gloom,
Of man's melancholy tomb.

4 Look aloft! The spirit 's risen; —
Death cannot the soul imprison:
'T is in heaven that spirits dwell,
Glorious, though invisible.

5 Thither let us turn our view:
Peace is there, and comfort too:
There shall those we love be found,
Tracing joy's eternal round.

503. C. P. M. W. BOSTON COLL.

The dying Christian.

1 WHEN life's tempestuous storms are o'er,
How calm he meets the friendly shore,
Who lived averse from sin!

Such peace on virtue's paths attends,
That, where the sinner's pleasure ends,
The Christian's joys begin.

2 See smiling patience smooth his brow!
See bending angels downward bow,
To cheer his way on high!
While, eager for the blest abode,
He joins with them to praise the God
Who taught him how to die.

3 No sorrow drowns his lifted eyes;
No horror wrests the struggling sighs,
As from the sinner's breast;
His God, the God of peace and love,
Pours kindly solace from above,
And soothes his soul to rest.

4 O, grant, my Father and my Friend,
Such joys may gild my peaceful end,—
So calm my evening close;
While, loosed from every earthly tie,
With steady confidence I fly
To thee from whom I rose.

504. L. M. WATTS

At a Funeral.

1 UNVEIL thy bosom, faithful tomb;
Take this new treasure to thy trust,
And give these sacred relics room,
To slumber in the silent dust.

2 Nor pain, nor grief, nor anxious fear,
Invade thy bounds; no mortal woes
Can reach the peaceful sleeper here,
While angels watch the soft repose.

3 So Jesus slept; God's dying Son
Passed through the grave, and blest the oed;
Rest, then, dear saint, till from his throne
The morning break, and pierce the shade.

4 Break from his throne, illustrious morn!
Attend, O earth, his sovereign word;
Restore thy trust; a glorious form
Shall then arise to meet the Lord.

505. 8 & 7s. M. Bap. Memorial.

Burial of a Christian.

1 BROTHER, rest from sin and sorrow;
Death is o'er and life is won;
On thy slumber dawns no morrow;
Rest; thine earthly race is run.

2 Brother, wake; the night is waning;
Endless day is round thee poured;
Enter thou the rest remaining
For the people of the Lord.

3 Brother, wake; for he who loved thee,—
He who died that thou mightst live,—
He who graciously approved thee,—
Waits thy crown of joy to give.

4 Fare thee well; though woe is blending
With the tones of earthly love,
Triumph high and joy unending
Wait thee in the realms above.

506. C. M. Watts

At a Funeral.

1 WHY do we mourn departing friends,
Or shake at death's alarms?
'T is but the voice that Jesus sends
To call them to his arms.

2 Why should we tremble to convey
Their bodies to the tomb?
'T was there the Saviour's body lay,
And left a long perfume.

3 The graves of all his saints he blest,
And softened every bed:

Where should the dying members rest,
But with their dying Head?

507. L. M. WATTS

Death disarmed.

1 WHY should we start, and fear to die?
What timorous worms we mortals are!
Death is the gate of endless joy,
And yet we dread to enter there.

2 The pains, the groans, and dying strife,
Fright our approaching souls away;
Still we shrink back again to life,
Fond of our prison and our clay.

3 O, if my Lord would come and meet,
My soul would stretch her wings in haste,
Fly, fearless, through death's iron gate,
Nor feel the terrors as she passed.

4 Jesus can make a dying bed
Feel soft as downy pillows are,
While on his breast I lean my head,
And breathe my life out sweetly there.

508. L. M. W. BOSTON COLL

Weep not.

1 WHY weep for those, frail child of woe,
Who 've fled and left thee mourning here!
Triumphant o'er their latest foe,
They glory in a brighter sphere.

2 Weep not for them; — beside thee now
Perhaps they watch with guardian care,
And witness tears that idly flow
O'er those who bliss of angels share.

3 Or round their Father's throne above,
With raptured voice, his praise they sing,
Or on his messages of love
They journey with unwearied wing.

4 Space cannot check, thought cannot bound,
The high exulting souls, whom He,
Who formed these million worlds around,
Takes to his own eternity.

5 Weep, weep no more ; their voices raise
The song of triumph high to God,
And, wouldst thou join their song of praise,
Walk humbly in the path they trod.

509. L. M. BARBAULD.

Blessedness of the Righteous in Death.

1 HOW blest the righteous when he dies !
When sinks a weary soul to rest !
How mildly beam the closing eyes !
How gently heaves th' expiring breast !

2 So fades a summer cloud away ;
So sinks the gale when storms are o'er ;
So gently shuts the eye of day ;
So dies a wave along the shore.

3 A holy quiet reigns around,
A calm which life nor death destroys ;
And naught disturbs that peace profound,
Which his unfettered soul enjoys.

4 Farewell, conflicting hopes and fears,
Where lights and shades alternate dwell ;
How bright th' unchanging morn appears !
Farewell, inconstant world, farewell !

5 Life's duty done, as sinks the clay,
Light from its load the spirit flies,
While heaven and earth combine to say,
" How blest the righteous when he dies ! "

510. L. M. BRYANT

Blessed are they that mourn.

1 DEEM not that they are blest alone,
Whose days a peaceful tenor keep ;

The God, who loves our race, has shown
  A blessing for the eyes that weep.

2 The light of smiles shall fill again
  The lids that overflow with tears,
And weary hours of woe and pain
  Are earnests of serener years.

3 O, there are days of hope and rest
  For every dark and troubled night!
And grief may bide, an evening guest,
  But joy shall come with early light.

4 And thou, who o'er thy friend's low bier,
  Dost shed the bitter drops like rain,
Hope that a brighter, happier sphere,
  Will give him to thy arms again.

5 Nor let the good man's trust depart,
  Though life its common gifts deny;
Though with a pierced and broken heart,
  And spurned of men, he goes to die.

6 For God hath marked each anguished day,
  And numbered every secret tear;
And heaven's long age of bliss shall pay
  For all his children suffer here.

511. C. M. COTTON

God the Refuge of the Afflicted.

1 AFFLICTION is a stormy deep,
  Where wave resounds to wave;
Though o'er our heads the billows roll,
  We know the Lord can save.

2 When darkness and when sorrows rose,
  And pressed on every side,
The Lord hath still sustained our steps,
  And still hath been our Guide.

3 Perhaps, before the morning dawn,
  He will restore our peace;

For he who bade the tempest roar
Can bid the tempest cease.

4 Here will we rest, here build our hopes,
Nor murmur at his rod;
He 's more to us than all the world,
Our Health, our Life, our God.

512. C. M. BARBAULD

The Mourner's Thoughts of Heaven.

1 NOT for the pious dead we weep;
Their sorrows now are o'er;
The sea is calm, the tempest past,
On that eternal shore.

2 Their peace is sealed, their rest is sure,
Within that better home;
Awhile we weep and linger here,
Then follow to the tomb.

3 O, might some dream of visioned bliss,
Some trance of rapture, show
Where, on the bosom of their God,
They rest from human woe!

4 Thence may their pure devotion's flame
On us, on us descend;
To us their strong aspiring hopes,
Their faith, their fervors lend.

5 Let these our shadowy path illume,
And teach the chastened mind
To welcome all that 's left of good,
To all that 's lost resigned.

513. C. M. WATTS.

Human Frailty and Divine Support.

1 LET others boast how strong they be,
Nor death nor danger fear;
But we 'll confess, O Lord, to thee,
What feeble things we are.

2 Fresh as the grass our bodies stand,
And flourish bright and gay ;
A blasting wind sweeps o'er the land,
And fades the grass away.

3 Our life contains a thousand springs,
And dies if one be gone ;
Strange ! that a harp of thousand strings
Should keep in tune so long.

4 But 't is our God supports our frame,
The God who built us first ;
Salvation to th' almighty name,
That reared us from the dust.

5 While we have breath, or use our tongues,
Our Maker we 'll adore ;
His spirit moves our heaving lungs,
Or they would breathe no more.

514. 7, 6, & 8s. M. Noel's Coll.

The Land of Rest.

1 BROTHER, thou art gone to rest ;
We will not weep for thee ;
For thou art now where oft on earth
Thy spirit longed to be.

2 Brother, thou art gone to rest ;
Thine is an early tomb ;
But God hath summoned thee away ;
Thy Father called thee home.

3 Brother thou art gone to rest ;
Thy toils and cares are o'er ;
And sorrow, pain, and suffering, now
Shall ne'er distress thee more.

4 Brother, thou art gone to rest ;
Thy sins are all forgiven ;
And saints in light have welcomed thee
To share the joys of heaven.

5 Brother, thou art gone to rest;
And this shall be our prayer, —
That, when we reach our journey's end,
Thy glory we may share.

515. 11 & 10s. M. SPIRITUAL SONGS.

Invitation to the Mercy-seat.

1 COME, ye disconsolate, where'er ye languish;
Come, at the mercy-seat fervently kneel;
Here bring your wounded hearts, here tell your anguish;
Earth has no sorrow that heaven cannot heal.

2 Joy of the desolate, light of the straying,
Hope of the penitent, fadeless and pure,
Here speaks the Comforter, tenderly saying,
Earth has no sorrow that heaven cannot cure.

3 Here see the bread of life; see waters flowing
Forth from the throne of God, pure from above;
Come to the feast of love; come, ever knowing
Earth has no sorrow but heaven can remove.

516. L. M. J. N. BROWN.

Address to the dying Christian.

1 GO, spirit of the sainted dead,
Go to thy longed-for, happy home:
The tears of man are o'er thee shed;
The voice of angels bids thee come.

2 If life be not in length of days,
In silvered locks and furrowed brow,
But living to the Saviour's praise,
How few have lived so long as thou!

3 Though earth may boast one gem the less,
May not e'en heaven the richer be?
And myriads on thy footsteps press,
To share thy blest eternity.

517. S. H. M. Montgomery

The Christian's tranquil Death.

1 THIS place is holy ground ;
World, with its cares, away ;
A holy, solemn stillness round
This lifeless, mouldering clay ;
Nor pain, nor grief, nor anxious fear,
Can reach the peaceful sleeper here.

2 Behold the bed of death, —
The pale and mortal clay ;
Heard ye the sob of parting breath ?
Marked ye the eye's last ray ?
No ; life so sweetly ceased to be,
It lapsed in immortality.

3 Why mourn the pious dead ?
Why sorrows swell our eyes ?
Can sighs recall the spirit fled ?
Shall vain regrets arise ?
Though death has caused this altered mien,
In heaven the ransomed soul is seen.

4 Bury the dead, and weep
In stillness o'er the loss :
Bury the dead ; in Christ they sleep
Who bore on earth his cross ;
And from the grave their dust shall rise,
In his own image, to the skies.

518. C. M. Watts.

God the Author of Mercies and Afflictions.

1 NAKED, as from the earth we came,
And rose to life at first,
We to the earth return again,
And mingle with the dust.

2 The dear delights we here enjoy,
And fondly call our own,

Are only favors borrowed now,
To be repaid anon.

3 'T is God who lifts our comforts high,
Or sinks them in the grave;
He gives, and, blessèd be his name,
He takes but what he gave.

4 Peace, all our angry passions, then;
Let each rebellious sigh
Be silent at his sovereign will,
And every murmur die.

5 If smiling mercy crown our lives,
Its praises shall be spread;
And we 'll adore the justice, too,
That strikes our comforts dead.

519. 7s. M. Toplady.

The dying Christian to his Soul.

1 DEATHLESS spirit, now arise;
Soar, thou native of the skies, —
Go to shine before the throne;
Deck the Mediator's crown.

2 Go, his triumphs to adorn,
Made for God, to God return;
Lo! he beckons from on high;
Fearless to his presence fly.

3 Burst thy shackles; drop thy clay;
Sweetly breathe thyself away;
Singing, to thy crown remove,
Swift of wing and fired with love.

4 See the haven full in view;
Love divine shall bear thee through;
Trust to that propitious gale;
Weigh thy anchor, spread thy sail.

5 Saints in glory, perfect made,
Wait thy passage through the shade;

Swiftly to their wish be given;
Kindle higher joy in heaven.

520. 12 & 11s. M. HEBER.

Farewell to a Friend departed.

1 THOU art gone to the grave; but we will not deplore thee;
Though sorrows and darkness encompass the tomb;
The Saviour has passed through its portals before thee,
And the lamp of his love is thy guide through the gloom.

2 Thou art gone to the grave; we no longer behold thee,
Nor tread the rough paths of the world by thy side;
But the wide arms of mercy are spread to enfold thee,
And sinners may hope, since the Saviour hath died.

3 Thou art gone to the grave; and, its mansion forsaking,
Perchance thy weak spirit in doubt lingered long;
But the sunshine of heaven beamed bright on thy waking,
And the sound thou didst hear was the seraphim's song.

4 Thou art gone to the grave; but we will not deplore thee;
Since God was thy Refuge, thy Guardian, thy Guide;
He gave thee, he took thee, and he will restore thee;
And death has no sting, since the Saviour hath died.

521. C. M. WATTS.

Those blessed who die in the Lord.

1 HEAR what the voice from heaven proclaims
For all the pious dead;

"Sweet is the savor of their names,
And soft their sleeping bed.

2 "They die in Jesus and are blest;
How kind their slumbers are!
From suffering and from sin released,
They 're freed from every snare.

3 "Far from this world of toil and strife,
They 're present with the Lord;
The labors of their mortal life
End in a large reward."

522. 7 & 8s. M. (Peculiar.) DOANE.

Weep not.

1 LIFT not thou the wailing voice;
Weep not; 't is a Christian dieth:
Up, where blessèd saints rejoice,
Ransomed now, the spirit flieth:
High in Heaven's own light she dwelleth,
Full the song of triumph swelleth:
Freed from earth, and earthly failing,
Lift for her no voice of wailing.

2 They who die in Christ are blest:
Ours be, then, no thought of grieving
Sweetly with their God they rest,
All their toils and troubles leaving:
So be ours the faith that saveth,
Hope that every trial braveth,
Love that to the end endureth,
And, through Christ, the crown secureth.

523. C. M. PEABODY.

Peaceful Death of the Pious.

1 BEHOLD the western evening light!
It melts in deepening gloom;
So calmly Christians sink away,
Descending to the tomb.

2 The winds breathe low ; the yellow leaf
Scarce whispers from the tree ;
So gently flows the parting breath,
When good men cease to be.

3 How beautiful, on all the hills,
The crimson light is shed !
'T is like the peace the Christian gives
To mourners round his bed.

4 How mildly on the wandering cloud
The sunset beam is cast !
So sweet the memory left behind,
When loved ones breathe their last.

5 And, lo ! above the dews of night
The vesper star appears :
So faith lights up the mourner's heart,
Whose eyes are dim with tears.

6 Night falls, but soon the morning light
Its glories shall restore ;
And thus the eyes that sleep in death
Shall wake to close no more.

524. L. M. NORTON

Trust and Submission.

1 MY God, I thank thee ; may no thought
E'er deem thy chastisements severe ;
But may this heart, by sorrow taught,
Calm each wild wish, each idle fear.

2 Thy mercy bids all nature bloom ;
The sun shines bright, and man is gay ;
Thine equal mercy spreads the gloom,
That darkens o'er his little day.

3 Full many a throb of grief and pain
Thy frail and erring child must know :
But not one prayer is breathed in vain,
Nor does one tear unheeded flow.

4 Thy various messengers employ,
Thy purposes of love fulfil;
And, 'mid the wreck of human joy,
Let kneeling faith adore thy will.

525. S. H. M. Montgomery

Friends separated by Death.

1 FRIEND after friend departs:
Who hath not lost a friend?
There is no union here of hearts
That finds not here an end:
Were this frail world our final rest,
Living or dying, none were blest.

2 Beyond the flight of time,
Beyond the reign of death,
There surely is some blessèd clime
Where life is not a breath,
Nor life's affections transient fire,
Whose sparks fly upward and expire.

3 There is a world above,
Where parting is unknown;
A long eternity of love,
Formed for the good alone;
And faith beholds the dying here
Translated to that glorious sphere.

4 Thus star by star declines,
Till all are passed away;
As morning high and higher shines,
To pure and perfect day;
Nor sink those stars in empty night,
But hide themselves in heaven's own light.

526. L. M. 6 l. Winchell's Sel

The Hope of Christian Friendship.

1 SWEET is the thought, the promise sweet,
That friends, long-severed friends, shall meet,—

That kindred souls, on earth disjoined,
Shall meet, from earthly dross refined,
Their mortal cares and sorrows o'er,
And mingle hearts to part no more.

2 But for this hope, this blessèd stay,
When earthly comforts all decay,
O, who could view th' expiring eye,
Nor wish, with those they love, to die?
Who could receive their parting breath,
Nor long to follow them in death?

3 But we have brighter hopes; we know
Short is this pilgrimage of woe;
We know that our Redeemer lives;
We trust the promises he gives;
And part in hope to meet above,
Where all is joy, and all is love.

527. L. M. NORTON.

Blessedness of the pious Dead.

1 O, STAY thy tears; for they are blest,
Whose days are past, whose toil is done:
Here midnight care disturbs our rest;
Here sorrow dims the noonday sun.

2 How blest are they whose transient years
Pass like an evening meteor's flight!
Not dark with guilt, nor dim with tears;
Whose course is short, unclouded, bright.

3 O, cheerless were our lengthened way;
But Heaven's own light dispels the gloom,
Streams downward from eternal day,
And casts a glory round the tomb.

4 O, stay thy tears; the blest above
Have hailed a spirit's heavenly birth,
And sung a song of joy and love;
Then why should anguish reign on earth?

528. C. M. ANONYMOUS

Peaceful Death of the Righteous.

1 I LOOKED upon the righteous man
And saw his parting breath,
Without a struggle or a sigh,
Serenely yield to death :
There was no anguish on his brow,
Nor terror in his eye :
The spoiler aimed a fatal dart,
But lost the victory.

2 I looked upon the righteous man,
And heard the holy prayer
Which rose above that breathless form,
To soothe the mourners' care,
And felt how precious was the gift
He to his loved ones gave, —
The stainless memory of the just,
The wealth beyond the grave.

3 I looked upon the righteous man ;
And all our earthly trust
Of pleasure, vanity, or pride
Seemed lighter than the dust,
Compared with his celestial gain, —
A home above the sky :
O, grant us, Lord, his life to live,
That we like him may die !

529. L. M. BATHURST

The Christian's parting Hour.

1 HOW sweet the hour of closing day,
When all is peaceful and serene,
And when the sun, with cloudless ray,
Sheds mellow lustre o'er the scene !

2 Such is the Christian's parting hour ;
So peacefully he sinks to rest ;

When faith, indued from heaven with power,
Sustains and cheers his languid breast.

3 Mark but that radiance of his eye,
That smile upon his wasted cheek:
They tell us of his glory nigh,
In language that no tongue can speak.

4 A beam from heaven is sent to cheer
The pilgrim on his gloomy road;
And angels are attending near,
To bear him to their bright abode.

5 Who would not wish to die like those
Whom God's own Spirit deigns to bless?
To sink into that soft repose,
Then wake to perfect happiness?

530. 8 & 7s. M. COLLYER

Comfort in the Death of the Christian.

1 CEASE, ye mourners, cease to languish
O'er the grave of those you love;
Pain, and death, and night, and anguish
Enter not the world above.

2 While our silent steps are straying,
Lonely, through night's deepening shade,
Glory's brightest beams are playing
Round the happy Christian's head.

3 Light and peace at once deriving
From the hand of God most high,
In his glorious presence living,
They shall never, never die.

4 Endless pleasure, pain excluding,
Sickness, there, no more can come;
There, no fear of woe, intruding,
Sheds o'er heaven a moment's gloom.

531. C. M. DODDRIDGE.

The Christian's Farewell.

1 YE golden lamps of heaven, farewell,
With all your feeble light!
Farewell, thou ever-changing moon,
Pale empress of the night!

2 And thou, refulgent orb of day,
In brighter flames arrayed!
My soul, that springs beyond thy sphere,
No more demands thy aid.

3 Ye stars are but the shining dust
Of my divine abode,
The pavement of those heavenly courts
Where I shall see my God.

4 The Father of eternal light
Will there his beams display;
Nor shall one moment's darkness blend
With that unvaried day.

532. S. M. CH. PSALMODY

The peaceful Death of the Righteous.

1 O, FOR the death of those
Who slumber in the Lord!
O, be like theirs my last repose,
Like theirs my last reward!

2 Their ransomed spirits soar,
On wings of faith and love,
To meet the Saviour they adore,
And reign with him above.

3 With us their names shall live
Through long-succeeding years,
Embalmed with all our hearts can give,—
Our praises and our tears.

4 O, for the death of those
Who slumber in the Lord!

O, be like theirs my last repose,
Like theirs my last reward!

533. C. P. M. C. WESLEY

Reunion of Friends in Heaven.

1 IF death my friend and me divide,
Thou dost not, Lord, my sorrow chide,
Or frown my tears to see;
Restrained from passionate excess,
Thou bidd'st me mourn in calm distress
For them that rest in thee.

2 I feel a strong, immortal hope,
Which bears my mournful spirit up
Beneath its mountain load;
Redeemed from death, and grief, and pain,
I soon shall find my friend again,
Within the arms of God.

3 Pass a few fleeting moments more,
And death the blessing shall restore,
Which death hath snatched away;
For me thou wilt the summons send,
And give me back my parted friend,
In that eternal day.

534. C. M. R. TURNBULL

My Father's House.

1 THERE is a place of sacred rest,
Far, far beyond the skies,
Where beauty smiles eternally,
And pleasure never dies;—
My Father's house, my heavenly nome,
Where "many mansions" stand,
Prepared, by hands divine, for all
Who seek the better land.

2 When tossed upon the waves of life,
With fear on every side,—

When fiercely howls the gathering storm
And foams the angry tide, —
Beyond the storm, beyond the gloom,
Breaks forth the light of morn,
Bright beaming from my Father's house,
To cheer the soul forlorn.

3 Yes, even at that fearful hour,
When death shall seize its prey
And from the place that knows us now,
Shall hurry us away, —
The vision of that heavenly home
Shall cheer the parting soul,
And o'er it, mounting to the skies,
A tide of rapture roll.

4 In that pure home of tearless joy
Earth's parted friends shall meet,
With smiles of love that never fade,
And blessedness complete :
There, there adieus are sounds unknown ;
Death frowns not on that scene,
But life and glorious beauty shine,
Untroubled and serene.

535. C. M. LOGAN

The Creation, an Emblem of the Resurrection.

1 ALL nature dies, and lives again :
The flowers that paint the field,
The trees that crown the mountain's brow,
And boughs and blossoms yield, —

2 Resign the honors of their form
At winter's stormy blast ;
And leave the naked, leafless plain,
A desolated waste.

3 Yet soon reviving plants and flowers
Anew shall deck the plain ;

The woods shall hear the voice of spring,
And flourish green again.

4 So, to the dreary grave consigned,
Man sleeps in death's dark gloom,
Until th' eternal morning wake
The slumbers of the tomb.

5 O, may the grave become to us
The bed of peaceful rest ;
Whence we shall gladly rise at length,
And mingle with the blest.

6 Cheered by this hope, with patient mind
We 'll wait Heaven's high decree ;
Till the appointed period come
When death shall set us free.

536. L. M. TUCK.

The Dwelling-place of God.

1 THERE is a region lovelier far
Than sages tell or poets sing,
Brighter than noonday glories are,
And softer than the tints of spring.

2 It is not fanned by summer's gale ;
'T is not refreshed by vernal showers ,
It never needs the moonbeam pale, —
For there are known no evening hours.

3 No ; for that world is ever bright
With purest radiance all its own :
The streams of uncreated light
Flow round it from th' eternal throne.

4 It is all holy and serene,
The land of glory and repose ;
No cloud obscures the radiant scene
There not a tear of sorrow flows.

5 In vain the curious, searching eye
May seek tc view the fair abode,

Or find it in the starry sky :
  It is the dwelling-place of God.

537. C. M. W. B. Tappan

The Peace and Repose of Heaven.

1 THERE is an hour of hallowed peace
  For those with cares oppressed,
When sighs and sorrowing tears shall cease,
  And all be hushed to rest.

2 'T is then the soul is freed from fears
  And doubts which here annoy ;
Then they that oft had sown in tears
  Shall reap again in joy.

3 There is a home of sweet repose,
  Where storms assail no more ;
The stream of endless pleasure flows
  On that celestial shore.

4 There purity with love appears,
  And bliss without alloy ;
There they that oft had sown in tears
  Shall reap again in joy.

538. L. P. M. Watts

Source of Consolation.

1 I 'LL praise my Maker with my breath ;
And, when my voice is lost in death,
  Praise shall employ my nobler powers ;
My days of praise shall ne'er be past,
While life, and thought, and being last,
  Or immortality endures.

2 How blest the man whose hopes rely
On Israel's God ! He made the sky,
  And earth, and seas, with all their train ;
His truth for ever stands secure ;
He saves th' oppressed, he feeds the poor,
  And none shall find his promise vain.

3 I 'll praise him while he lends me breath ,
And, when my voice is lost in death,
Praise shall employ my nobler powers ,
My days of praise shall ne'er be past,
While life, and thought, and being last,
Or immortality endures.

539. L. M. ANONYMOUS

The better Land.

1 THERE is a land mine eye hath seen,
In visions of enraptured thought,
So bright that all which spreads between
Is with its radiant glory fraught ; —

2 A land upon whose blissful shore
There rests no shadow, falls no stain ;
There those who meet shall part no more,
And those long parted meet again.

3 Its skies are not like earthly skies,
With varying hues of shade and light ;
It hath no need of suns to rise,
To dissipate the gloom of night.

4 There sweeps no desolating wind
Across that calm, serene abode ;
The wanderer there a home may find,
Within the paradise of God.

540. 8 & 6s. M. W. B. TAPPAN.

Heaven anticipated.

1 THERE is an hour of peaceful rest
To mourning wanderers given ;
There is a joy for souls distressed,
A balm for every wounded breast ;
'T is found alone in heaven.

2 There is a home for weary souls,
By sins and sorrows driven,

When tossed on life's tempestuous shoals,
Where storms arise, and ocean rolls,
And all is drear ; — 't is heaven.

3 There faith lifts up the tearless eye, —
The heart no longer riven, —
And views the tempest passing by,
Sees evening shadows quickly fly,
And all serene in heaven.

4 There fragrant flowers immortal bloom,
And joys supreme are given ;
There rays divine disperse the gloom ;
Beyond the dark and narrow tomb
Appears the dawn of heaven.

541. C. M. NEWTON.

The Death of a Believer.

1 IN vain our fancy strives to paint
The moment after death, —
The glories that surround the saints,
When yielding up their breath.

2 One gentle sigh their fetters breaks !
We scarce can say, " They 're gone ! "
Before the willing spirit takes
Her mansion near the throne.

3 Faith strives, but all its efforts fail
To trace her in its flight ;
No eye can pierce within the veil
Which hides that world of light.

4 Thus much, and this is all we know,
They are completely blest ;
Have done with sin, and care, and woe,
And with their Saviour rest.

542. L. P. M. Watts

Life, Death, and Resurrection.

1 ETERNAL God! how frail is man!
Few are the hours, and short the span,
Between the cradle and the grave:
Who can prolong his vital breath?
Who from the bold demands of death
Hath skill to fly, or power to save?

2 But let no murmuring heart complain,
That, therefore, man is made in vain,
Nor the Creator's grace distrust;
For though his servants, day by day,
Go to their graves, and turn to clay,
A bright reward awaits the just.

3 Jesus hath made thy purpose known,
A new and better life hath shown,
And we the glorious tidings hear:
For ever blessèd be the Lord,
That we can read his holy word,
And find a resurrection there.

543. L. M. Fawcett

Death of Parents.

1 THE God of mercy will indulge
The flowing tear, the heaving sigh,
When honored parents fall around,
When friends beloved and kindred die.

2 Yet not one anxious, murmuring thought
Should with our mourning passions blend;
Nor should our bleeding hearts forget
Their mighty, ever-living Friend.

3 Parent, Protector, Guardian, Guide,
Thou art each tender name in one;
On thee we cast our every care,
And comfort seek from thee alone.

4 To thee, our Father, would we look,
Our Rock, our Portion, and our Friend,
And on thy gracious love and truth
With humble, steadfast hope depend.

544. C. M. DODDRIDGE.

Death of a Minister.

1 WHAT though the arm of conquering death
Does God's own house invade ;
What though our teacher and our friend
Is numbered with the dead ; —

2 Though earthly shepherds dwell in dust,
The agéd and the young ;
The watchful eye in darkness closed,
And dumb th' instructive tongue ; —

3 Th' eternal Shepherd still survives,
His teaching to impart :
Lord, be our Leader and our Guide,
And rule and keep our heart.

4 Yes, while the dear Redeemer lives,
We have a boundless store,
And shall be fed with what he gives,
Who lives for evermore.

545. 10s. M. MONTGOMERY

Death of a Minister in his Prime.

1 GO to the grave in all thy glorious prime,
In full activity of zeal and power ;
A Christian cannot die before his time ;
The Lord's appointment is the servant's hour.

2 Go to the grave ; at noon from labor cease ;
Rest on thy sheaves ; thy harvest-task is done ;
Come from the heat of battle, and in peace,
Soldier, go home ; with thee the fight is won.

3 Go to the grave ; for there thy Saviour lay
In death's embrace, ere he arose on high :

And all the ransomed, by that narrow way,
Pass to eternal life beyond the sky.

4 Go to the grave ; — no ; take thy seat above ;
Be thy pure spirit present with the Lord,
Where thou for faith and hope hast perfect love,
And open vision for the written word.

546. 8 & 7s. M. L. H. SIGOURNEY.

Death of a Pastor.

1 PASTOR, thou art from us taken
In the glory of thy years,
As the oak, by tempests shaken,
Falls ere time its verdure sears.

2 Pale and cold we see thee lying
In God's temple, once so dear,
And the mourners' bitter sighing
Falls unheeded on thine ear.

3 All thy love and zeal, to lead us
Where immortal fountains flow,
And on living bread to feed us,
In our fond remembrance glow.

4 May the conquering faith, that cheered thee
When thy foot on Jordan pressed,
Guide our spirits while we leave thee
In the tomb that Jesus blessed.

547. S. M. MONTGOMERY

The Death of an aged Minister.

1 " SERVANT of God, well done !
Rest from thy loved employ ;
The battle fought, the victory won,
Enter thy Master's joy."

2 The voice at midnight came ;
He started up to hear ;
A mortal arrow pierced his frame ,
He fell, but felt no fear.

3 Tranquil amid alarms,
It found him on the field,
A veteran slumbering on his arms,
Beneath his red-cross shield.

4 The pains of death are past;
Labor and sorrow cease;
And, life's long warfare closed at last,
His soul is found in peace.

5 Soldier of Christ, well done!
Praise be thy new employ;
And, while eternal ages run,
Rest in thy Saviour's joy.

548. L. M. LUTHERAN COLL.

Death of a Parent.

1 WHILE you with mournful thoughts deplore
The parent gone, removed the friend,
With hearts resigned his grace adore
On whom your noblest hopes depend.

2 Does he not bid his children come
Through death's dark shades to realms of light
Yet, when he calls them to their home,
Shall fond survivors mourn their flight?

3 His word — here let your souls rely —
Immortal consolation gives:
Your Heavenly Father cannot die,
Th' Eternal Friend for ever lives.

549. L. M. ANONYMOUS.

"Thy Will be done."

1 WHEN called, O Lord, to mourn the doom
Of one affection held most dear, —
While o'er the closing, silent tomb,
The bleeding heart distils the tear, —
Though love its tribute sure will pay,
And early streams of solace shun,

Still, still the humble soul would say,
  In lowly dust, " Thy will be done."

2 Whate'er, O Lord, thou hast designed
  To bring my soul to thee in trust,
If mercies or afflictions kind, —
  For all thy dealings Lord are just, —
Take all, but grant, in goodness free,
  That love which ne'er thy stroke would shun
Support this heart and strengthen me
  To say in faith, " Thy will be done."

550. C. M. WATTS

The Christian's Triumph over Death.

1 O, FOR a firm and lively faith,
  Which may the grave defy,
And, trusting what the gospel saith,
  May triumph when we die !

2 Joyful, with all the strength we have,
  Our feeble lips would sing,
" Where is thy boasted victory, Grave ?
  O Death, where is thy sting ? "

3 Pardon and life, how dear each word !
  God life and pardon sends,
And, by our dying, rising Lord,
  Insures to all his friends.

4 All glory be to God on high,
  And endless thanks be paid,
Who makes us conquerors, though we die,
  Through Christ our living Head.

551. L. M. GASKELL

The Light of the Gospel on the Tomb.

1 DARK, dark indeed, the grave would be,
Had we no light, O God, from thee ;
If all we saw were all we knew,
Or hope from reason only grew.

2 But fearless now we rest in faith,
A holy life makes happy death ;
'T is but a change ordained by thee,
To set th' imprisoned spirit free.

3 Sad, sad indeed, 't would be to part
From those who long had shared our heart,
If thou hadst left us still to fear
Love's only heritage was here.

4 But calmly now we see them go
From out this world of pain and woe ;
We follow to a home on high,
Where pure affections never die.

552. 7 & 6s. M. ANONYMOUS.

Children in Heaven.

1 IN the broad fields of heaven, —
In the immortal bowers
By life's clear river dwelling,
Amid undying flowers, —
There hosts of beauteous spirits,
Fair children of the earth,
Linked in bright bands celestial,
Sing of their human birth.

2 They sing of earth and heaven, —
Divinest voices rise
To God, their gracious Father,
Who called them to the skies :
They all are there, — in heaven, —
Safe, safe, and sweetly blest ;
No cloud of sin can shadow
Their bright and holy rest.

553. 7s. M. H. S. WASHBURN.

The Pastor's Funeral.

1 FATHER, gathered round the bier,
Aid thy weeping children here ;

All our stricken hearts deplore
Loss of him we meet no more.

2 Tender are the rites we pay,
Pastor, o'er thy sleeping clay;
We, who late the welcome gave,
Must we bear thee to thy grave?

3 Earth, unto thy faithful trust
We commit this precious dust,
There, by pain no more oppressed,
Brother, thou wilt sweetly rest.

4 Glorious will that morning break,
When the dead in Christ shall wake;
Joy and grief our bosoms swell,
Brother, pastor, guide, farewell.

554. P. M. MILMAN.

Funeral Hymn.

1 BROTHER, thou art gone before us,
And thy saintly soul is flown,
Where tears are wiped from every eye,
And sorrow is unknown:
From the burden of the flesh,
And from care and fear released,
Where the wicked cease from troubling
And the weary are at rest.

2 Brother, yes, thy course is finished;
Thou hast borne earth's heavy load,
But Christ has taught thy languid feet
To reach his blest abode:
Sweetly art thou sleeping now,
On thy Father's faithful breast,
Where the wicked cease from troubling
And the weary are at rest.

3 Sin no more can taint thy spirit,
Nor can doubt thy faith assail;

Thy soul its welcome has received,
Thy strength shall never fail :
And thou 'rt sure to meet the good,
Whom on earth thou lovedst best,
Where the wicked cease from troubling
And the weary are at rest.

4 To thy grave we sadly bear thee,
There in dust we place thy head,
We lay the turf above thee now,
And seal thy narrow bed ;
But thy spirit soars away,
Free, among the faithful blest,
Where the wicked cease from troubling
And the weary are at rest.

5 When the Lord shall send his summons
Unto us who 're left behind,
May we, untainted by the world,
As sure a welcome find ;
Each like thee depart in peace
To the kingdom of the blest,
Where the wicked cease from troubling
And the weary are at rest.

LIFE, DEATH, AND FUTURITY.

555. C. M. WATTS

Brevity and Frailty of Life.

1 HOW short and hasty is our life !
How vast our soul's affairs !
Yet foolish mortals vainly strive
To lavish out their years.

2 Our days run thoughtlessly along,
Without a moment's stay ;
Just like a story or a song,
We pass our lives away.

3 God from on high invites us home ;
But we march heedless on,
And, ever hastening to the tomb,
Stoop downward as we run.

4 Draw us, O God, with sovereign grace,
And lift our thoughts on high,
That we may end this mortal race,
And see salvation nigh.

556. S. M. WATTS

Man hastening to the Grave.

1 LORD, what a feeble piece
Is this our mortal frame !
Our life, how poor a trifle 't is,
That scarce deserves the name !

2 Alas ! 't was brittle clay
That formed our body first ;
And every month, and every day,
'T is mouldering back to dust,

3 Our moments fly apace ;
Nor will our minutes stay ;
Just like a flood our hasty days
Are sweeping us away.

4 Then, if our days must fly,
We 'll keep their end in sight ;
We 'll spend them all in wisdom's way,
And let them speed their flight.

5 They 'll waft us sooner o'er
This life's tempestuous sea :
We soon shall reach the peaceful shore
Of blest eternity.

557. C. M. WATTS.

Life short, and Man frail.

1 TEACH me the measure of my days,
Thou Maker of my frame ;

I would survey life's narrow space,
And learn how frail I am.

2 A span is all that we can boast;
How short the fleeting time!
Man is but vanity and dust,
In all his flower and prime.

3 Some walk in honor's gaudy show,
Some dig for golden ore;
They toil for heirs, they know not who,
And straight are seen no more.

4 What should I wish, or wait for, then,
From creatures, — earth and dust?
They make our expectations vain,
And disappoint our trust.

5 Now I resign my earthly hope,
My fond desire recall;
I give my mortal interest up,
And make my God my all.

558. 7 & 6s. M. S. F. SMITH

Life rapidly passing away.

1 AS flows the rapid river,
With channel broad and free,
Its waters rippling ever,
And hasting to the sea,
So life is onward flowing,
And days of offered peace,
And man is swiftly going
Where calls of mercy cease.

2 As moons are ever waning,
As hastes the sun away,
As stormy winds, complaining,
Bring on the wintry day,
So fast the night comes o'er us, —
The darkness of the grave;

And death is just before us :
  God takes the life he gave.

3 Say, hath thy heart its treasure
  Laid up in worlds above ?
And is it all thy pleasure
  Thy God to praise and love ?
Beware, lest death's dark river
  Its billows o'er thee roll,
And thou lament for ever
  The ruin of thy soul.

559. 7 & 6s. (Peculiar.) J. BARTON

Life a Winter's Day.

1 TIME is winging us away
  To our eternal home ;
Life is but a winter's day, —
  A journey to the tomb :
Youth and vigor soon will flee,
  Blooming beauty lose its charms ;
All that 's mortal soon shall be
  Inclosed in death's cold arms.

2 Time is winging us away
  To our eternal home ;
Life is but a winter's day, —
  A journey to the tomb ;
But the Christian shall enjoy
  Health and beauty soon above,
Where no worldly griefs annoy,
  Secure in Jesus' love.

560. S. M. WATTS.

Reflections on past Generations.

1 HOW swift the torrent rolls,
  That bears us to the sea !
The tide which hurries thoughtless souls
  To vast eternity !

2 Our fathers ! — where are they,
With all they called their own ? —
Their joys and griefs, and hopes and cares,
And wealth and honor ? — gone !

3 God of our fathers ! hear, —
Thou everlasting Friend ! —
While we, as on life's utmost verge,
Our souls to thee commend.

4 Of all the pious dead
May we the footsteps trace,
Till with them, in the land of light,
We dwell before thy face.

561. C. M. J. Q. Adams.

Swiftness of Time.

1 HOW swift, alas ! the moments fly !
How rush the years along !
Scarce here, yet gone already by, —
The burden of a song.

2 See childhood, youth, and manhood pass,
And age, with furrowed brow ;
Time was, — time shall be, — but, a.as !
Where, where, in time, is now ?

3 Time is the measure but of change ;
No present hour is found ;
The past, the future, fill the range
Of time's unceasing round.

4 Then, pilgrim, let thy joys and fears
On time no longer lean ;
But henceforth all thy hopes and fears
From earth's affections wean.

5 To God let grateful accents rise :
With truth, with virtue, live ;
So all the bliss that time denies,
Eternity shall give.

562. L. M. LOGAN

The Christian summoned to depart.

1 THE hour of my departure 's come ;
I hear the voice that calls me home :
At last, O Lord, let trouble cease,
And let thy servant die in peace.

2 The race appointed I have run ;
The combat 's o'er, the prize is won ;
And now my witness is on high,
And now my record 's in the sky.

3 I leave the world without a tear,
Save for the friends I held so dear :
To heal their sorrows, Lord, descend,
And to the friendless prove a friend.

4 I come, I come ; at thy command,
I give my spirit to thy hand ;
Stretch forth thine everlasting arms,
And shield me in the last alarms.

5 The hour of my departure 's come ;
I hear the voice that calls me home :
Now, O my God, let trouble cease ;
Now let thy servant die in peace.

563. C. M. H K. WHITE.

Journeying through Death to Life.

1 THROUGH sorrow's night and danger's path,
Amid the deepening gloom,
We, soldiers of a Heavenly King,
Are marching to the tomb.

2 There, when the turmoil is no more,
And all our powers decay,
Our cold remains, in solitude,
Shall sleep the years away.

3 Our labors done, securely laid
In this our last retreat,

Unheeded, o'er our silent dust
The storms of life shall beat.

4 Yet not thus lifeless, thus inane,
The vital spark shall lie :
For o'er life's wreck that spark shall rise,
To seek its kindred sky.

564. L. M. J. Taylor

True Length of Life.

1 LIKE shadows gliding o'er the plain,
Or clouds that roll successive on,
Man's busy generations pass ;
And while we gaze, their forms are gone.

2 " He lived, — he died " ; behold the sum,
The abstract, of th' historian's page .
Alike, in God's all-seeing eye,
The infant's day, the patriarch's age.

3 O Father, in whose mighty hand
The boundless years and ages lie,
Teach us thy boon of life to prize,
And use the moments as they fly ; —

4 To crowd the narrow span of life
With wise designs and virtuous deeds :
So shall we wake from death's dark night,
To share the glory that succeeds.

565. C. H. M. J. Taylor

What is your Life?

1 O, WHAT is life ? — 't is like a flower
That blossoms and is gone ;
It flourishes its little hour,
With all its beauty on :
Death comes, and, like a wintry day,
It cuts the lovely flower away.

2 O, what is life ? — 't is like the bow
That glistens in the sky :

We love to see its colors glow ;
  But, while we look, they die :
Life fails as soon : — to-day 't is here ;
To-morrow it may disappear.

3 Lord, what is life ? — if spent with thee,
  In humble praise and prayer,
How long or short our life may be,
  We feel no anxious care :
Though life depart, our joys shall last
When life and all its joys are past.

566. C. M. HEBER

Man's Mortality.

1 BENEATH our feet and o'er our head
  Is equal warning given ;
Beneath us lie the countless dead,
  Above us is the heaven.

2 Their names are graven on the stone,
  Their bones are in the clay ;
And ere another day is done,
  Ourselves may be as they.

3 Death rides on every passing breeze ;
  He lurks in every flower ;
Each season has its own disease,
  Its peril every hour.

4 Our eyes have seen the rosy light
  Of youth's soft cheek decay,
And fate descend in sudden night
  On manhood's middle day ; —

5 Our eyes have seen the steps of age
  Halt feebly towards the tomb ; —
And yet shall earth our hearts engage,
  And dreams of days to come ?

6 Turn, mortal, turn ; thy danger know ;
  Where'er thy foot can tread,

The earth rings hollow from below,
And warns thee of her dead!

567. L. M. WATTS

Life.

1 LIFE is the time to serve the Lord, —
The time t' insure the great reward;
And while the lamp holds out to burn,
To thee the sinner may return.

2 Life is the hour that thou hast given
To fit us for the joys of heaven;
The day of grace, and mortals may
Secure the blessings of the day.

3 Then the great work we have to do,
Let us, with all our might, pursue;
And wisely every hour employ,
Till faith and hope are lost in joy.

568. 8 & 4s. M. ANONYMOUS.

Vanity of the World.

1 ALAS! how poor and little worth
Are all those glittering toys of earth
That lure us here! —
Dreams of a sleep that death must break:
Alas! before it bids us wake,
They disappear.

2 Where is the strength that spurned decay,
The step that rolled so light and gay,
The heart's blithe tone?
The strength is gone, the step is slow,
And joy grows weariness and woe
When age comes on.

Our birth is but a starting-place;
Life is the running of the race,
And death the goal:

There all those glittering toys are brought;
That path alone, of all unsought,
Is found of all.

4 O, let the soul its slumbers break,
Arouse its senses, and awake
To see how soon
Life, like its glories, glides away,
And the stern footsteps of decay
Come stealing on.

569. C. M. COWPER

Human Frailty.

1 WEAK and irresolute is man:
The purpose of to-day,
Woven with pains into his plan,
To-morrow rends away.

2 Some foe to his upright intent
Finds out his weaker part;
Virtue engages his assent,
But pleasure wins his heart.

3 Bound on a voyage of awful length,
Through dangers little known,
A stranger to superior strength,
Man vainly trusts his own.

4 But oars alone can ne'er prevail
To reach the distant coast;
The breath of heaven must swell the sail,
Or all the toil is lost.

570. C. M. WATTS

Frail Life and succeeding Eternity.

1 THEE we adore, Eternal Name,
And humbly own to thee
How feeble is our mortal frame,
What dying worms are we.

2 Our wasting lives grow shorter still,
As months and days increase;

And every beating pulse we tell
  Leaves but the number less.

3 The year rolls round, and steals away
  The breath that first it gave ;
Whate'er we do, where'er we be,
  We 're travelling to the grave.

4 Dangers stand thick through all the grouna,
  To push us to the tomb ;
And fierce diseases wait around,
  To hurry mortals home.

5 Waken, O Lord, our drowsy sense,
  To walk this dangerous road ;
And, if our souls are hurried hence,
  May they be found with God !

571. 11s. M. MUHLENBURG.

I would not live alway.

1 I WOULD not live alway ; I ask not to stay
Where storm after storm rises dark o'er the way
I would not live alway ; no, welcome the tomb ;
Since Jesus hath lain there, I dread not its gloom

2 Who, who would live alway, away from his God,
Away from yon heaven, that blissful abode,
Where the rivers of pleasure flow o'er the brigl
  plains,
And the noontide of glory eternally reigns ?—

3 Where the saints of all ages in harmony meet,
Their Saviour and brethren transported to greet,
While the anthems of rapture unceasingly roll,
And the smile of the Lord is the life of the soul !

572. P. M. POPE.

The dying Christian to his Soul.

1 VITAL spark of heavenly flame,
Quit, O, quit this mortal frame !

Trembling, hoping, lingering, flying,
O, the pain, the bliss of dying !
Cease, fond nature, cease thy strife,
And let me languish into life.

2 Hark ! they whisper ! angels say,
" Sister spirit, come away."
What is this absorbs me quite,
Steals my senses, shuts my sight,
Drowns my spirit, draws my breath ?
Tell me, my soul, can this be death ?

3 The world recedes ; it disappears ;
Heaven opens on my eyes ; my ears
With sounds seraphic ring.
Lend, lend your wings ! I mount, I fly !
O Grave, where is thy victory ?
O Death, where is thy sting ?

573. 7s. M. MONTGOMERY

The Summons.

1 " SPIRIT, leave thy house of clay ;
Lingering dust, resign thy breath ;
Spirit, cast thy chains away ;
Dust, be thou dissolved in death ":
Thus the blessèd Saviour speaks,
While the faithful Christian dies ;
Thus the bonds of life he breaks,
And the ransomed captive flies.

2 " Prisoner, long detained below,
Prisoner now with freedom blest,
Welcome from a world of woe ;
Welcome to a land of rest " :
Thus the choir of angels sing,
As they bear the soul on high,
While with hallelujahs ring
All the regions of the sky.

574. C. M. WATTS.

Meditation on the Tomb.

1 HARK ! from the tombs a warning sound ;
My ears, attend the cry : —
" Ye living men, come view the ground
Where you must shortly lie.

2 " Princes, this clay must be your bed,
In spite of all your towers ;
The tall, the wise, the reverend head
Must lie as low as ours."

3 Great God, is this our certain doom ?
And are we still secure ? —
Still walking downward to the tomb,
And yet prepare no more ?

4 Grant us the power of quickening grace,
To fit our souls to fly ;
Then, when we drop this dying flesh,
We 'll rise above the sky.

575. L. M. BROWNE

Fear of Death overcome.

1 I CANNOT shun the stroke of death ;
Lord, help me to surmount the fear ;
That, when I must resign my breath,
Serene my summons I may hear.

2 'T is sin gives venom to the dart ;
In me let every sin be slain ;
From secret faults, Lord, cleanse my heart,
From wilful sins my hands restrain.

3 May I, my God, with holy zeal,
Closely the ends of life pursue,
Seek thy whole pleasure to fulfil,
And honor thee in all I do.

4 Let all my bliss and treasure lie
Where, in thy light, I light may see ;

The soul may freely dare to die,
That longs to be possessed of thee.

576. 8 & 4s. M. MONTGOMERY

The Grave.

1 THERE is a calm for those who weep,
A rest for weary pilgrims found :
They softly lie and sweetly sleep,
Low in the ground.

2 The storm that sweeps the wintry sky
No more disturbs their deep repose,
Than summer evening's latest sigh,
That shuts the rose.

3 Then, traveller in the vale of tears
To realms of everlasting light,
Through time's dark wilderness of years
Pursue thy flight.

4 Thy soul, renewed by grace divine,
In God's own image, freed from clay,
In heaven's eternal sphere shall shine,
A star of day.

577. 7 & 4s. M. MRS. GILBERT.

Prayer for Support in Death.

1 WHEN the vale of death appears,
Faint and cold this mortal clay,
O my Father, soothe my fears,
Light me through the gloomy way ;
Break the shadows,
Usher in eternal day ; —

2 Upward from this dying state
Bid my waiting soul aspire ;
Open thou the crystal gate ;
To thy praise attune my lyre :
Then, triumphant,
I will join th' immortal choir.

578. 6 & 5s. M. ANONYMOUS

The Knell of Death.

1 THROUGH the night-air stealing,
Hark ! the bell is pealing
Mournfully and slow ;
Rest to the soul departed,
Peace to the broken-hearted,
In this vale of woe.

2 Say, for whom thou ringest,
Say, if to him thou bringest
Hopes beyond the tomb ;
Or if the sound appalls him,
When death's summons calls him
To uncertain doom.

579. C. M. COLLYER

Prayer for Support in Death.

1 WHEN, bending o'er the brink of life,
My trembling soul shall stand,
And wait to pass death's awful flood,
Great God, at thy command, —

2 Thou Source of life and joy supreme,
Whose arm alone can save,
Dispel the darkness that surrounds
The entrance to the grave.

3 Lay thy supporting, gentle hand
Beneath my sinking head,
And let a beam of light divine
Illume my dying bed.

580. L. M. R. HILL.

Prayer for the Dying Christian.

1 GENTLY, my Father, let me down,
To slumber in the arms of death :
I rest my soul on thee alone,
E'en till my last expiring breath.

2 Soon will the storms of life be o'er,
   And I shall enter endless rest :
There I shall live to sin no more,
   And bless thy name, for ever blest.

3 Bid me possess sweet peace within ;
   Let childlike patience keep my heart ;
Then shall I feel my heaven begin,
   Before my spirit hence depart.

4 Hasten thy chariot, God of love !
   And take me from this world of woe.
I long to reach those joys above,
   And bid farewell to all below.

5 There shall my raptured spirit raise
   Still louder notes than angels sing, —
Extol the riches of thy grace,
   My God, my Father, and my King.

581. C. M. WATTS

Rest in Heaven from Sin and Trouble.

1 OUR sins, alas ! how strong they be !
   And, like a raging flood,
They break our duty, Lord, to thee,
   And force us from our God.

2 The waves of trouble, how they rise !
   How loud the tempests roar !
But death shall land our weary souls
   Safe on the heavenly shore.

3 Fulfilling there his high commands,
   Our cheerful feet shall move ;
No sins shall clog our active zeal,
   Or cool our burning love.

4 We there shall ever sing and tell
   The wonders of his grace,
While heavenly raptures fire our hearts,
   And smile in every face.

582. S. M. MONTGOMERY.

Home in Heaven.

1 MY Father's house on high!
Home of my soul! how near,
At times, to faith's foreseeing eye
Thy golden gates appear!

2 I hear at morn and even,
At noon and midnight hour,
The choral harmonies of heaven
Seraphic music pour.

3 O, then my spirit faints
To reach the land I love, —
The bright inheritance of saints,
My glorious home above.

583. C. M. BARBAULD.

The Pilgrimage of Life.

1 OUR country is Immanuel's ground;
We seek that promised soil;
The songs of Zion cheer our hearts,
While strangers here we toil.

2 Oft do our eyes with joy o'erflow,
And oft are bathed in tears;
Yet naught but heaven our hopes can raise,
And naught but sin our fears.

3 We tread the path our Master trod;
We bear the cross he bore;
And every thorn that wounds our feet,
His temples pierced before.

4 Our powers are oft dissolved away
In ecstasies of love;
And while our bodies wander here,
Our souls are fixed above.

5 We purge our mortal dross away,
Refining as we run ;
But while we die to earth and sense,
Our heaven is here begun.

584. L. M. 6 L. CHRISTIAN PSALMIST

Foretaste of Heaven.

1 WHAT must it be to dwell above,
At God's right hand, where Jesus reigns,
Since the sweet earnest of his love
O'erwhelms us on these earthly plains !
No heart can think, no tongue explain,
What bliss it is with Christ to reign.

2 When sin no more obstructs our sight,
When sorrow pains our hearts no more,
How shall we view the Prince of Light
And all his works of grace explore !
What heights and depths of love divine
Will there through endless ages shine !

3 This is the heaven I long to know ;
For this, with patience, I would wait,
Till, weaned from earth, and all below,
I mount to my celestial seat,
And wave my palm, and wear my crown,
And, with the elders, cast them down.

585. C. M. T. MOORE.

Heaven desired.

1 THE dove let loose in eastern skies,
Returning fondly home,
Ne'er stoops to earth her wing, nor flies,
Where idle warblers roam ;—

2 But high she shoots through air and light,
Above all low delay,
Where nothing earthly bounds her flight,
Nor shadow dims her way.

3 So grant me, Lord, from every snare
Of sinful passion free,
Aloft, through faith's serener air,
To urge my course to thee ; —

4 No sin to cloud, no lure to stay
My soul, as home she springs,
Thy sunshine on her joyful way,
Thy freedom on her wings.

586. 8 & 7s. M. 6 L. KELLY

Close of the Christian Warfare.

1 WHEN we pass through yonder river,
When we reach the farther shore,
There 's an end of war for ever ;
We shall see our foes no more :
All our conflicts then shall cease,
Followed by eternal peace.

2 After warfare, rest is pleasant :
O, how sweet the prospect is !
Though we toil and strive at present,
Let us not repine at this :
Toil, and pain, and conflict past,
All endear repose at last.

3 When we gain the heavenly regions,
When we touch the heavenly shore, —
Blessèd thought ! — no hostile legions
Can alarm or trouble more :
Far beyond the reach of foes,
We shall dwell in sweet repose.

4 O, that hope ! how bright, how glorious !
'T is his people's blest reward ;
In the Saviour's strength victorious,
They at length behold their Lord :
In his kingdom they shall rest,
In his love be fully blest.

587. L. M. WATTS

The Christian's Prospect.

1 WHAT sinners value I resign;
Lord, 't is enough that thou art mine;
I shall behold thy blissful face,
And stand complete in righteousness.

2 This life 's a dream, — an empty show;
But that bright world to which I go
Hath joys substantial and sincere:
When shall I wake, and find me there?

3 O, glorious hour! O, blest abode!
I shall be near and like my God,
And flesh and sin no more control
The sacred pleasures of my soul.

4 My flesh shall slumber in the ground
Till the last trumpet's joyful sound,
Then burst the chains, with glad surprise,
And in my Saviour's image rise.

588. C. M. CHRISTIAN PSALMIST.

The Society of Heaven.

1 JERUSALEM! my glorious home!
  Name ever dear to me!
When shall my labors have an end
  In joy, and peace, and thee?

2 When shall these eyes thy heaven-built walls
  And pearly gates behold?
Thy bulwarks, with salvation strong,
  And streets of shining gold?

3 There happier bowers than Eden's bloom,
  Nor sin nor sorrow know:
Blest seats! through rude and stormy scenes
  I onward press to you.

4 Why should I shrink at pain and woe?
  Or feel at death dismay?

I 've Canaan's goodly land in view,
And realms of endless day.

5 Apostles, martyrs, prophets, there,
Around my Saviour stand ;
And soon my friends in Christ below
Will join the glorious band.

6 Jerusalem ! my glorious home !
My soul still pants for thee ;
Then shall my labors have an end,
When I thy joys shall see.

589. L. M. PEABODY.

Heaven.

1 O, WHEN the hours of life are past,
And death's dark shade arrives at last, —
It is not sleep, — it is not rest, —
'T is glory opening to the blest.

2 Their way to heaven was pure from sin,
And Christ shall there receive them in ;
There each shall wear a robe of light
Like his, divinely fair and bright.

3 There parted hearts again shall meet
In union holy, calm, and sweet ;
There grief find rest, and never more
Shall sorrow call them to deplore.

4 There angels will unite their prayers
With spirits bright and blest as theirs,
And light shall glance on every crown,
From suns that never more go down.

5 For there the God of mercy sheds
His purest influence on their heads,
And gilds the spirits round the throne
With glory radiant as his own.

590. C. M. WATTS

A Prospect of Heaven.

1 THERE is a land of pure delight,
Where saints immortal reign ;
Infinite day excludes the night,
And pleasures banish pain.

2 There everlasting spring abides,
And never-withering flowers :
Death, like a narrow sea, divides
This heavenly land from ours.

3 Sweet fields beyond the swelling flood
Stand dressed in living green :
So to the Jews old Canaan stood,
And Jordan rolled between.

4 But timorous mortals start and shrink,
To cross this narrow sea ;
And linger shivering on the brink,
And fear to launch away.

5 O, could we make our doubts remove, —
Those gloomy doubts that rise, —
And see the Canaan that we love
With unbeclouded eyes, —

6 Could we but climb where Moses stood,
And view the landscape o'er, —
Not Jordan's stream, nor death's cold flood,
Should fright us from the shore.

591. 7s. M. RAFFLES

The Saints in Glory.

1 HIGH, in yonder realms of light,
Dwell the raptured saints above,
Far beyond our feeble sight,
Happy in Immanuel's love.

2 Pilgrims in this vale of tears,
Once they knew, like us below,

Gloomy doubts, distressing fears,
Torturing pain, and heavy woe.

3 Happy spirits, ye are fled
Where no grief can entrance find,
Lulled to rest the aching head,
Soothed the anguish of the mind.

4 'Mid the chorus of the skies,
'Mid th' angelic lyres above,
Hark ! their songs melodious rise, —
Songs of praise to Jesus' love.

592. C. M. STENNETT

Heaven in Prospect.

1 ON Jordan's stormy banks I stand,
And cast a wishful eye
To Canaan's fair and happy land,
Where my possessions lie.

2 O, the transporting, rapturous scene
That rises to my sight ! —
Sweet fields, arrayed in living green
And rivers of delight.

3 No chilling winds, nor poisonous breath,
Can reach that healthful shore ;
Sickness and sorrow, pain and death,
Are felt and feared no more.

4 When shall I reach that happy place,
And be for ever blest ?
When shall I see my Father's face,
And in his bosom rest ?

5 Filled with delight, my raptured soul
Would here no longer stay ;
Though Jordan's waves should round me roll,
I 'd fearless launch away.

593. C. M. Sir J. E. Smith.

The Changes of Nature Types of Immortality.

1 AS twilight's gradual veil is spread
Across the evening sky;
So man's bright hours decline in shade,
And mortal comforts die.

2 The bloom of spring, the summer rose,
In vain pale winter brave;
Nor youth, nor age, nor wisdom knows
A ransom from the grave.

3 But morning dawns, and spring revives,
And genial hours return;
So man's immortal soul survives,
And scorns the mouldering urn.

4 When this vain scene no longer charms,
Or swiftly fades away,
He sinks into a Father's arms,
Nor dreads the coming day.

594. C. M. Steele

Glories of Heaven.

1 FAR from these narrow scenes of night,
Unbounded glories rise,
And realms of joy and pure delight,
Unknown to mortal eyes.

2 Fair, distant land! — could mortal eyes
But half its charms explore,
How would our spirits long to rise,
And dwell on earth no more!

3 No cloud those blissful regions know, —
Realms ever bright and fair;
For sin, the source of mortal woe,
Can never enter there.

4 O, may the heavenly prospect fire
Our hearts with ardent love,

Till wings of faith, and strong desire,
Bear every thought above.

5 Prepare us, Lord, by grace divine,
For thy bright courts on high;
Then bid our spirits rise and join
The chorus of the sky.

595. L. M. STEELE.

The Worship of Heaven.

1 O, FOR a sweet, inspiring ray,
To animate our feeble strains,
From the bright realms of endless day,
The blissful realms where Jesus reigns.

2 There, low before his glorious throne,
Adoring saints and angels fall;
And, with delightful worship, own
His smile their bliss, their heaven, their all.

3 Immortal glories crown his head,
While tuneful hallelujahs rise,
And love, and joy, and triumph spread
Through all th' assemblies of the skies.

4 He smiles, — and seraphs tune their songs
To boundless rapture, while they gaze;
Ten thousand thousand joyful tongues
Resound his everlasting praise.

5 There all the followers of the Lamb
Shall join at last the heavenly choir;
O, may the joy-inspiring theme
Awake our faith and warm desire.

596. S. M. MONTGOMERY.

The Issues of Life and Death.

1 O, WHERE shall rest be found, —
Rest for the weary soul?
'T were vain the ocean depths to sound,
Or pierce to either pole.

2 The world can never give
The bliss for which we sigh;
'T is not the whole of life to live,
Nor all of death to die.

3 Beyond this vale of tears,
There is a life above,
Unmeasured by the flight of years;
And all that life is love: —

4 There is a death, whose pang
Outlasts the fleeting breath;
O, what appalling horrors hang
Around the "second death"!

5 Lord God of truth and grace!
Teach us that death to shun,
Lest we be banished from thy face,
And utterly undone.

6 Here would we end our quest;
Alone are found in thee
The life of perfect love, — the rest
Of immortality.

597. 7s. M. MONTGOMERY

The Redeemed in Heaven.

1 WHO are these in bright array,
This exulting, happy throng,
Round the altar, night and day,
Hymning one triumphant song? —
"Worthy is the Lamb, once slain,
Blessing, honor, glory, power,
Wisdom, riches, to obtain,
New dominion every hour."

2 These through fiery trials trod;
These from great affliction came;
Now, before the throne of God,
Sealed with his almighty name,

Clad in raiment pure and white,
  Victor-palms in every hand,
Through their great Redeemer's might,
  More than conquerors they stand.

3 Hunger, thirst, disease, unknown,
  On immortal fruits they feed;
Them the Lamb, amidst the throne,
  Shall to living fountains lead;
Joy and gladness banish sighs;
  Perfect love dispels all fears;
And for ever from their eyes
  God shall wipe away their tears.

598. L. M. 6 L. HEBER.

The visible World a Shadow of the invisible.

I PRAISED the earth in beauty seen,
With garlands gay, of various green;
I praised the sea, whose ample field
Shone glorious as a silver shield;
And earth and ocean seemed to say,
"Our beauties are but for a day."

2 I praised the sun, whose chariot rolled
On wheels of amber and of gold;
I praised the moon, whose softer eye
Gleamed sweetly through the summer sky;
And moon and sun in answer said,
"Our years are told, when we must fade."

3 O God! O good beyond compare!
If thus thy meaner works are fair, —
If thus thy bounties gild the span
Of sinful earth and mortal man, —
How glorious must thy mansion be
Where thy redeemed shall dwell with thee!

599. C. M. WATTS

Death and immediate Glory.

1 THERE is a house not made with hands,
Eternal and on high ;
And here my spirit waiting stands,
Till God shall bid it fly.

2 We walk by faith of joys to come ;
Faith lives upon his word ;
But while the body is our home,
We 're absent from the Lord.

3 Shortly this prison of my clay
Must be dissolved and fall ;
Then, O my soul, with joy obey
Thy Heavenly Father's call.

600. C. M. COWPER

The Christian in the Prospect of Death.

1 O, MOST delightful hour by man
Experienced here below,
The hour that terminates his span,
His folly, and his woe.

2 Worlds should not bribe me back to tread
Again life's dreary waste,
To see again my day o'erspread
With all the gloomy past.

3 My home henceforth is in the skies ;
Earth, seas, and sun, adieu !
All heaven unfolded to my eyes,
I have no sight for you.

4 So speaks the Christian, firm possessed
Of faith's supporting rod,
Then breathes his soul into its rest,
The bosom of his God.

601. S. M. MONTGOMERY

Heaven and Earth.

1 BEHOLD yon bright array
Before the heavenly throne!
There young nor old, there rich nor poor,
There bond nor free, are known

2 At once they strike their lyres;
At once break off, — and all,
With trembling joy and silent love,
In adoration fall.

3 Whate'er their lot below,
As fellow-heirs of bliss,
In heaven their services are one:
Let earth be heaven in this.

4 As brethren so may we
Worship with one accord;
In stillness wait, in prayer bow down,
And bless and praise the Lord.

5 As pilgrims on the way,
God's earthly courts we fill;
And travel on from strength to strength,
Abreast, to Zion's hill.

6 There may our spirits meet,
When faith is changed to sight,
Where God the Lord himself shall be
The temple, life, and light.

602. S. M. R. PALMER

Heavenly Rest. *Altered, See Appendix.*

1 AND is there, Lord, a rest
For weary souls designed,
Where not a care shall stir the breast,
Or sorrow entrance find?

2 Is there a blissful home,
Where kindred minds shall meet,

And live and love, nor ever roam
From that serene retreat?

3 For ever blessèd they,
Whose joyful feet shall stand,
While endless ages waste away,
Amid that glorious land.

4 My soul would thither tend,
While toilsome years are given;
Then let me, gracious God, ascend
To sweet repose in heaven.

THE CHURCH, BAPTISM, AND CHRISTIAN FELLOWSHIP.

603. S. M. WATTS.

Gospel Order.

1 FAR as thy name is known
The world declares thy praise;
Thy saints, O Lord, before thy throne,
Their songs of honor raise.

2 With joy thy people stand
On Zion's chosen hill,
Proclaim the wonders of thy hand,
And counsels of thy will.

3 Let strangers walk around
The city where we dwell,
Survey with care thine holy ground,
And mark the building well, —

4 The order of thy house,
The worship of thy court,
The cheerful songs, the solemn vows,
And make a fair report.

5 How decent, and how wise!
How glorious to behold!
Beyond the pomp that charms the eyes,
And rites adorned with gold.

6 The God we worship now
Will guide us till we die, —
Will be our God while here below,
And ours above the sky.

604. C. M. MONTGOMERY

Saints on Earth and in Heaven.

1 IN one fraternal bond of love,
One fellowship of mind,
The saints below and saints above
Their bliss and glory find.

2 Here, in their house of pilgrimage,
Thy statutes are their song;
There, through one bright eternal age,
Thy praises they prolong.

3 Lord, may our union form a part
Of that thrice happy whole,
Derive its pulse from thee, the heart,
Its life from thee, the soul.

605. C. M. C. WESLEY

Union of Saints in Heaven and on Earth.

1 COME, let us join our friends above,
Who have obtained the prize,
And on the eagle wings of love
To joy celestial rise.

2 Let saints below in concert sing
With those to glory gone;
For all the servants of our King
In heaven and earth are one.

3 E'en now to their eternal home
Some happy spirits fly;

And we are to the margin come,
And soon expect to die.

4 O God, be thou our constant guide!
Then, when the word is given,
Bid death's cold flood its waves divide,
And land us safe in heaven.

606. 8 & 7s. M. NEWTON.

The Church God's chosen Residence.

1 GLORIOUS things of thee are spoken,
Zion, city of our God;
He whose word can ne'er be broken
Chose thee for his own abode.

2 Lord, thy church is still thy dwelling,
Still is precious in thy sight,
Judah's temple far excelling,
Beaming with the gospel's light.

3 On the Rock of Ages founded,
What can shake her sure repose?
With salvation's wall surrounded,
She can smile at all her foes.

4 See, the streams of living waters,
Springing from eternal love,
Well supply her sons and daughters,
And all fear of want remove.

5 Round her habitation hovering,
See the cloud and fire appear,
For a glory and a covering,
Showing that the Lord is near.

607. 11s. M. ANONYMOUS.

The Church victorious.

1 DAUGHTER of Zion, awake from thy sadness;
Awake, for thy foes shall oppress thee no more:
Bright o'er thy hills dawns the daystar of gladness;
Arise, for the night of thy sorrow is o'er.

2 Strong were thy foes ; but the arm that subdued them,
And scattered their legions, was mightier far ;
They fled like the chaff from the scourge that pursued them ;
Vain were their steeds and their chariots of war.

3 Daughter of Zion, the power that hath saved thee
Extolled with the harp and the timbrel should be ;
Shout, for the foe is destroyed that enslaved thee ;
Th' oppressor is vanquished, and Zion is free.

608. C. M. FROTHINGHAM.

The Church.

1 O LORD of life, and truth, and grace,
Ere nature was begun !
Make welcome to our erring race
Thy Spirit and thy Son.

2 We hail the church built high o'er all
The heathen's rage and scoff ;
Thy providence its fencéd wall, —
" The Lamb the light thereof."

3 Thy Christ hath reached his heavenly seat
Through sorrows and through scars ;
The golden lamps are at his feet,
And in his hand the stars.

4 O, may he walk among us here,
With his rebuke and love ;
A brightness o'er this lower sphere,
A ray from worlds above.

609. C. M. BEDDOME.

The Church Triumphant.

1 A HOST of spirits round the throne
In humble posture stand,
On every head a starry crown,
A palm in every hand.

2 From different regions of the globe
These happy spirits came ;
In Jesus they their trust reposed,
And triumphed in his name.

3 One glorious body now they make, —
More glorious far their Head ;
Their souls to rapturous joys awake ;
Their sorrows all are fled.

4 Without a jarring note, they join
In ceaseless songs of praise,
And to Jehovah, holy One,
Loud hallelujahs raise.

610. C. M. DODDRIDGE

Dedication of Children to God and Christ.

1 SEE Israel's gentle Shepherd stand,
With all-engaging charms ,
Hark ! how he calls the tender lambs,
And folds them in his arms !

2 " Permit them to approach," he cries,
" Nor scorn their humble name ;
For 't was to bless such souls as these
The Lord of angels came."

3 We bring them, Lord, in thankful hands,
And yield them up to thee ;
Joyful that we ourselves are thine,
Thine let our offspring be.

4 Ye little flock, with pleasure hear ;
Ye children, seek his face,
And fly with transport to receive
The blessings of his grace.

5 If orphans they are left behind,
God's guardian care we trust ;
That care shall heal our bleeding hearts,
If weeping o'er their dust.

611. 8 & 7s. M. ANONYMOUS.

Children commended to Christ.

1 SAVIOUR, who thy flock art feeding
With the shepherd's kindest care,
All the feeble gently leading,
While the lambs thy bosom share,—

2 Now, these little ones receiving,
Fold them in thy gracious arm;
There, we know,—thy word believing,
Only there secure from harm.

3 Never, from thy pasture roving,
Let them be the lion's prey;
Let thy tenderness, so loving,
Keep them all life's dangerous way.

4 Then within thy fold eternal
Let them find a resting-place,
Feed in pastures ever vernal,
Drink the rivers of thy grace.

612. C. M. WATTS

Children included in God's Covenant.

1 HOW large the promise, how divine,
To Abraham and his seed!—
"I 'll be a God to thee and thine,
Supplying all their need."

2 The words of his extensive love
From age to age endure;
The angel of the covenant proves
And seals the blessing sure.

3 Jesus the ancient faith confirms,
To our great fathers given;
He takes young children to his arms,
And calls them heirs of heaven.

4 Our God, how faithful are his ways!
His love endures the same,

Nor from the promise of his grace
Blots out his children's name.

613. C. M. STENNETT

Infants, living or dying, in the Arms of Christ.

1 THY life I read, my dearest Lord,
With transport all-divine ;
Thine image trace in every word,
Thy love, in every line.

2 With joy, I see a thousand charms
Spread o'er thy lovely face ;
While infants in thy tender arms
Receive the smiling grace.

3 "I take these little lambs," said he,
"And lay them on my breast ;
Protection they shall find in me, —
In me be ever blest.

4 "Death may the bands of life unloose,
But can't dissolve my love ;
Millions of infant souls compose
The family above."

5 His words, ye happy parents, hear,
And shout, with joys divine,
"Dear Saviour ! all we have and are
Shall be for ever thine."

614. C. M. ANONYMOUS

Christ blessing Children.

1 ON, through Judea's palmy plain,
By Jordan's silvery shore,
The Saviour leads the thronging train,
Who follow to implore.

2 'Midst youth, and sire, and blooming maid,
He marked the listening child ;
His hand upon its head he laid,
And blest in accents mild.

3 Lord, though no more thy hallowed form
Can greet our children's sight,
O, grant, whilst life their breasts shall warm,
Thy words may guide them right.

4 They may not feel thine earthly touch ;
But be thy Spirit given,
To make them holy ; "for of such
The kingdom is of heaven."

615. L. M. STEELE

Infant Baptism.

1 O LORD ! encouraged by thy grace,
We bring our infant to thy throne ;
Give it within thy heart a place,
Let it be thine, and thine alone.

2 We ask not for it earthly bliss,
Or earthly honors, wealth, or fame :
The sum of our request is this, —
That it may love and fear thy name.

3 This infant we by faith commit
To thy kind love and guardian care ;
We lay it at the Saviour's feet,
He will not let it perish there.

616. C. M. S. F. SMITH

Baptism.

1 COME, blessèd Spirit, come to-day
To our baptismal scene :
Let thoughts of earth be far away,
And every mind serene.

2 This day we give to holy joy ;
This day to heaven belongs :
Raised to new life, we will employ
In melody our tongues.

617. L. M. W. BOSTON COLL.

Hymn for Baptism.

1 THIS child we dedicate to thee,
O God of grace and purity!
Shield it from sin and threatening wrong,
And let thy love its life prolong.

2 O, may thy spirit gently draw
Its willing soul to keep thy law;
May virtue, piety, and truth
Dawn even with its dawning youth.

3 Grant that, with true and faithful heart,
We, too, may act the Christian's part,
Cheered by each promise thou hast given,
And laboring for the prize in heaven.

618. C. M. JAS. NEWTON.

After Baptism.

1 LET plenteous grace descend on those,
Who, hoping in thy word,
This day have solemnly declared
That Jesus is their Lord.

2 With cheerful feet may they advance,
And run the Christian race,
And, through the troubles of the way,
Find all-sufficient grace.

3 Lord, plant us all into thy death,
That we thy life may prove, —
Partakers of thy cross beneath,
And of thy crown above.

619. L. M. COLLYER

The Baptism of a Household.

1 UNITED prayers ascend to thee,
Eternal Parent of mankind!
Smile on this waiting family;
Thy blessing let thy servants find.

2 Let the dear pledges of their love
Like tender plants around them grow:
Thy present grace, and joys above,
Upon their little ones bestow.

3 Receive, at their believing hand,
The charge which they devote as thine,
Obedient to their Lord's command,
And seal, with power, the rite divine.

4 To every member of their house
Thy grace impart, thy love extend;
Grant every good that time allows,
With heavenly joys that never end.

620. C. M. DODDRIDGE

Christians buried and risen with Christ.

1 BAPTIZED into our Saviour's death
Our souls to sin must die;
With Christ our Lord we live anew,
With Christ ascend on high.

2 There, by his Father's side, he sits,
Enthroned divinely fair,
Yet owns himself our brother still,
And our forerunner there.

3 Rise from these earthly trifles, rise
On wings of faith and love;
Above our choicest treasure lies, —
And be our hearts above.

4 But earth and sin will draw us down,
When we attempt to fly;
Lord, send thy strong, attractive power
To fix our souls on high.

621. L. M. KELL

A Welcome to Christian Fellowship.

1 COME in, thou blessèd of the Lord,
O, come in Jesus' precious name;

We welcome thee with one accord,
And trust the Saviour does the same.

2 Those joys which earth cannot afford,
We 'll seek in fellowship to prove,
Joined in one spirit to our Lord,
Together bound by mutual love.

3 And while we pass this vale of tears,
We 'll make our joys and sorrows known
We 'll share each other's hopes and fears,
And count a brother's care our own.

4 Once more our welcome we repeat;
Receive assurance of our love:
O, may we all together meet
Around the throne of God above!

622. C. M. S. F. SMITH

Christian Fellowship.

1 PLANTED in Christ, the living Vine,
This day, with one accord,
Ourselves, with humble faith and joy,
We yield to thee, O Lord.

2 Joined in one body may we be;
One inward life partake;
One be our heart; one heavenly hope
In every bosom wake.

3 In prayer, in effort, tears, and toils,
One wisdom be our guide;
Taught by one Spirit from above,
In thee may we abide.

4 Around this feeble, trusting band
Thy sheltering pinions spread,
Nor let the storms of trial beat
Too fiercely on our head.

5 Then, when, among the saints in light,
Our joyful spirits shine,

Shall anthems of immortal praise,
O Lamb of God, be thine.

623. S. M. FAWCETT.

Christian Fellowship.

1 BLEST be the tie that binds
Our hearts in Christian love;
The fellowship of kindred minds
Is like to that above.

2 Before our Father's throne
We pour our ardent prayers;
Our fears, our hopes, our aims are one,
Our comforts and our cares.

3 We share our mutual woes,
Our mutual burdens bear;
And often for each other flows
The sympathizing tear.

4 When we asunder part,
It gives us inward pain;
But we shall still be joined in heart,
And hope to meet again.

5 This glorious hope revives
Our courage by the way;
While each in expectation lives,
And longs to see the day.

6 From sorrow, toil, and pain,
And sin, we shall be free,
And perfect love and friendship reign
Through all eternity.

THE LORD'S SUPPER.

624. C. M. B. W. NOEL

Remembering Christ.

1 IF human kindness meets return,
And owns the grateful tie ; —
If tender thoughts within us burn
To feel a friend is nigh ; —

2 O, shall not warmer accents tell
The gratitude we owe
To Him who died our fears to quell,
And save from sin and woe.

3 While yet his anguished soul surveyed
Those pangs he would not flee,
What love his latest words displayed ! —
" Meet and remember me."

4 Remember thee ! thy death, thy shame,
The griefs which thou didst bear !
O memory, leave no other name
But his recorded there !

625. C. M. ANONY

Coming to the Table of the Lord.

1 LET vain pursuits and vain desires
Be banished from the heart,
The Saviour's love fill every breast,
And light and life impart.

2 He knew how frail our nature is,
Our souls how apt to stray ;
How much we need his gracious help
To keep us in the way !

3 These faithful pledges of his love
His mercy did ordain,

To bring refreshment to our souls,
And faith and hope sustain.

4 Since such his condescending grace,
Let us, with hearts sincere,
Obedient to his holy will,
His table now draw near.

5 And while we join to celebrate
The sufferings of our Lord
May we receive new grace and power,
T' obey his holy word.

626. C. M. MONTGOMERY

"This do in Remembrance of me."

1 ACCORDING to thy gracious word,
In meek humility,
This will I do, my dying Lord, —
I will remember thee.

2 Thy body, broken for my sake,
My bread from heaven shall be ;
Thy testamental cup I take,
And thus remember thee.

3 Gethsemane can I forget ?
Or there thy conflict see,
Thine agony and bloody sweat,
And not remember thee ?

4 When to the cross I turn mine eyes,
And rest on Calvary,
O Lamb of God, my sacrifice,
I must remember thee ; —

5 Remember thee, and all thy pains,
And all thy love to me ;
Yea, while a breath, a pulse remains,
Will I remember thee.

627. S. M. FURNESS

A Communion Hymn.

1 O, FOR a prophet's fire,
O, for an angel's tongue,
To speak the mighty love of Him
Who on the cross was hung!

2 In vain our hearts attempt,
In language meet, to tell
How through a thousand sorrows burned
That flame unquenchable.

3 Yet would we praise that love,
Beyond expression dear:
Come, gather round this table, then,
And celebrate it here.

4 These symbols of his death,
O, with what power they speak!
Prophetic lips and angels' lyres,
Compared with these, are weak.

5 And shall they plead in vain
With our forgetful souls?
Forbid it, God, while through our veins
The vital current rolls.

628. C. M. BIRMINGHAM COLI

For Communicants.

1 YE followers of the Prince of Peace,
Who round his table draw,
Remember what his spirit was,
What his peculiar law.

2 The love which all his bosom filled
Did all his actions guide;
Inspired by love, he lived and taught;
Inspired by love, he died.

3 Let each the sacred law fulfil;
Like his be every mind;

Be every temper formed by love,
And every action kind.

4 Let none who call themselves his friends
Disgrace the honored name,
But by a near resemblance prove
The title which they claim.

629. C. M. E. Taylor.

Christian Fellowship.

1 O, HERE, if ever, God of love,
Let strife and hatred cease,
And every heart harmonious move,
And every thought be peace.

2 Not here, where met to think on Him
Whose latest thoughts were ours,
Shall mortal passions come to dim
The prayer devotion pours.

3 No, gracious Master, not in vain
Thy life of love hath been;
The peace thou gav'st may yet remain,
Though thou no more art seen.

4 "Thy kingdom come": we watch, we wait
To hear thy cheering call,
When heaven shall ope its glorious gate,
And God be all in all.

630. S. M. English Baptist Coll

Obeying Christ.

1 HERE, Saviour, we would come,
In thine appointed way;
Obedient to thy high commands,
Our solemn vows we pay.

2 O, bless this sacred rite,
To bring us near to thee;
And may we find that as our day
Our strength shall also be.

631. L. M. WATTS.

The Memorial of our absent Lord.

1 JESUS is gone above the sky,
  Where our weak senses reach him not;
And earthly objects court our eye,
  To thrust the Saviour from our thought.

2 He knows what treacherous hearts we have,
  Prone to forget his wondrous grace;
And kindly this memorial gave,
  Till we ascend to see his face.

3 The Lord of life this table spread
  With tokens of his dying love;
And we, who on its richness feed,
  A foretaste gain of joys above.

4 Be sinful pleasures all forgot,
  And earth grow less in our esteem;
Christ and his love fill every thought,
  And faith and hope be fixed on him!

632. S. M. FURNESS

A Communion Hymn.

1 HERE, in the broken bread,
  Here, in the cup we take,
His body and his blood behold,
  Who suffered for our sake.

2 Yes, that our souls might live,
  Those sacred limbs were torn,
That blood was spilt, and pangs untold
  Were by the Saviour borne.

3 O Thou who didst allow
  Thy Son to suffer thus,
Father, what more couldst thou have done
  Than thou hast done for us?

4 We are persuaded now,
  That nothing can divide

Thy children from thy boundless love,
Displayed in him who died; —

5 Who died to make us sure
Of mercy, truth, and peace,
And from the power and pains of sin
To bring a full release.

633. C. M. GREENWOOD

The Table of the Lord.

1 NOW I approach thy table, Lord,
With reverent joy and love:
I call to mind my Saviour's word,
And will obedient prove.

2 O, shall I not remember one,
Who bled and died for me?
Nor think on all that he has done,
To make me pure and free?

3 Yea, I 'll remember him and strive
To love him more and more;
So that I may with Jesus live,
When this short life is o'er.

634. L. M. DODDRIDGE

Invitation to the Lord's Supper.

1 FATHER! and is thy table spread?
And does thy cup with love o'erflow?
Thither be these thy children led,
And let them all its sweetness know.

2 O, let thy table honored be,
And furnished well with joyful guests,
And may each soul salvation see,
That here its sacred pledges tastes.

3 Let crowds approach, with hearts prepared,
With warm desire let all attend;
Nor, when we leave our Father's board,
The pleasure or the profit end.

4 Revive thy dying churches, Lord,
And bid our drooping graces live ;
And more that energy afford
A Saviour's death alone can give.

5 Nor let thy spreading gospel rest,
Till through the world thy truth has run,
And with this bread all men be blest,
Who feel the influence of the sun !

635. 8 & 7s. M. EXETER COLL

After Communion.

1 FROM the table now retiring,
Which for us the Lord hath spread,
May our souls, refreshment finding,
Grow in all things like our Head !

2 His example by beholding,
May our lives his image bear !
Him our Lord and Master calling,
His commands may we revere !

3 Love to God and man displaying,
Walking steadfast in his way,
Joy attend us in believing,
Peace from God through endless day !

636. L. M. PIERPONT

Remembrance and Love of Christ.

1 OUR Father ! we approach thy board,
As children that would be forgiven ;
Remembering him, thy Son, who poured
His blood, to seal our hope of heaven.

2 O, listen to our fervent prayer ;
That he who hung on Calvary's hill,
And gave thee back his spirit there,
May live in our affections still.

637. S. M. WATTS.

The Love of our Saviour prompting to Christian Love.

1 JESUS, the Friend of man,
Invites us to his board;
The welcome summons we obey,
And own our gracious Lord.

2 Here we show forth his love,
Which spake in every breath,
Prompted each action of his life,
And triumphed in his death.

3 Here let our powers unite
His honored name to raise;
Let grateful joy fill every mind,
And every voice be praise.

4 One faith, one hope, one Lord,
One God alone we know;
Brethren we are; let every heart
With kind affections grow.

5 Warmed with our Master's love,
And thy unmeasured grace,
Lord! let our thankful hearts expand,
And all mankind embrace.

638. 7s. M. BOWRING.

Communion Hymn.

1 NOT with terror do we meet
At the board by Jesus spread;
Not in mystery drink and eat
Of the Saviour's wine and bread.

2 'T is his memory we record,
'T is his virtues we proclaim;
Grateful to our honored Lord,
Here we bless his sacred name.

3 See him, on the dreadful day
Of his mortal agony,

Break the bread, and hear him say,
 "Eat of this, and think of me!"

4 See him standing on the brink
 Of the tomb, and hark, he cries,
"Take the cup, and, as you drink,
 O, remember him who dies!"

5 Yes, we will remember thee,
 Friend and Saviour; and thy feast
Of all services shall be
 Holiest and welcomest.

639. C. M. S. Gilman.

Communion Hymn.

1 O GOD, accept the sacred hour
 Which we to thee have given,
And let this hallowed scene have power
 To raise our souls to heaven.

2 Still let us hold, till life departs,
 The precepts of thy Son,
Nor let our thoughtless, thankless hearts
 Forget what he has done.

3 His true disciples may we live,
 From all corruption free,
And humbly learn like him to give
 Our powers, our wills, to thee.

4 And oft along life's dangerous way,
 To smooth our passage through,
Wilt thou on this thy holy day
 For us this scene renew.

640. . M. Lutheran Coll.

Close of Communion Service.

1 PITY the nations, O our God,
 Constrain the earth to come;
Send thy victorious word abroad,
 And bring the strangers home.

2 We long to see thy churches full,
That all thy faithful race
May, with one voice, and heart, and soul,
Sing thy redeeming grace.

641. L. M. WATTS

The Lord's Supper instituted.

1 'T WAS on that dark, that awful night,
When powers of earth and hell arose
Against the Son of God's delight,
And friends betrayed him to his foes, —

2 Before the mournful scene began,
He took the bread, and blest, and brake,
What love through all his actions ran!
What wondrous words of grace he spake!

3 "This is my body, broke for sin;
Receive and eat the living food";
Then took the cup and blest, and said,
"'T is the new covenant in my blood."

4 "Do this," he cried, "till time shall end,
In memory of your dying Friend;
Meet at my table, and record
The love of your departed Lord."

5 Jesus, thy feast we celebrate;
We show thy death, we sing thy name,
Till thou return, and we shall eat
The marriage-supper of the Lamb.

642. S. M. DODDRIDGE

Communion with God and Christ.

1 OUR Heavenly Father calls,
And Christ invites us near;
With both our friendship shall be sweet,
And our communion dear.

2 God pities all my griefs;
He pardons every day;

Almighty to protect my soul,
  And wise to guide my way

3 Jesus, my living Head,
  I bless thy faithful care ;
Mine advocate before the throne,
  And my forerunner there.

4 Here fix, my roving heart,
  Here wait, my warmest love,
Till the communion be complete
  In nobler scenes above.

643. L. M. DUBLIN COLL

" This do in Remembrance of me."

1 "EAT, drink, in memory of your Friend ! "
  Such was our Master's last request ;
Who all the pangs of death endured,
  That we might live for ever blest.

2 Yes, we 'll record thy matchless love,
  Thou dearest, tenderest, best of friends ! —
Thy dying love the noblest praise
  Our hearts can offer thee transcends.

3 'T is pleasure more than earth can give
  Thy goodness through these veils to see ;
Thy table food celestial yields,
  And happy they who sit with thee.

644. 8 & 7s. M. ANONYMOU

The Eucharist.

1 AS in solemn congregation
  We attend upon thy house
For the sweet commemoration
  And renewal of our vows ;
Let thy favor, with us resting,
  Consecrate the bread and wine ,
May we, of thy goodness tasting,
  All be filled with love divine !

2 Jesus gave the sacred token
Of his passion, wine and bread,
Symbols of his body broken,
And his blood for sinners shed.
To the rite we come, confessing
Free redemption, grace unbought;
His be every name of blessing,
For his love, surpassing thought!

3 May thy counsels, King of glory!
Grateful awe and rapture move,
As we meditate the story
Of the Saviour's dying love;
Hear us, Lord, of thee entreating
Strength to walk in Jesus' ways!
God of light, shine on our meeting!
God of grace, accept our praise!

645. 7s. M. ANONYMOUS.

A Communion Hymn.

1 AT thy table, Lord of life,
May our souls find peace and rest;
On the Saviour may we lean,
Safe repose upon his breast.

2 He invites us to this feast,
He hath said, "Remember me";
May we come with trustful hearts,
Hearts devoted, Lord, to thee.

3 May thy grace our souls awake,—
Make them glow with holy love;—
While we take the bread and cup,
Set our hearts on things above.

4 Like the Saviour, may we be
Always doing, Lord, thy will;—
Let it be our chief concern
Thy good pleasure to fulfil.

646. C. M. DALE

Christ blessing the Bread.

1 BEHOLD, amid his little flock,
The Saviour stands serene,
Unawed by suffering yet to be,
Unchanged by what hath been.

2 Still beams the light of love undimmed
In that benignant eye,
Nor, save his own prophetic word,
Aught speaks him soon to die.

3 He pours within the votive cup
The rich blood of the vine,
And "Drink ye all the hallowed draught,"
He cries ; "this blood is mine."

4 He breaks the bread ; then clasps his hands,
And lifts his eyes in prayer,
"Receive ye this and view by faith
My body symbolled there.

5 "And oft your willing vows renew
Around the sacred board,
And break the bread and pour the wine
In memory of your Lord.

6 "To drink with me the grape's fresh blood
To you shall yet be given,
Fresh from the deathless Vine that blooms
In blest abodes of heaven."

647. S. M N. Y. COLL.

A Communion Hymn.

1 YES, to the last command
We will obedient prove ;
Around his table will we stand,
In memory of his love.

2 His precious blood he shed
For our unworthy race,

While uttering in th' Almighty's stead
His messages of grace.

3 O, if our senseless pride
His dying words neglect,
'T is we who pierce his sacred side,
And we who God reject!

4 Then let us ever keep
This consecrated feast,
Till memory shall have sunk to sleep,
Or life itself have ceased.

EARLY INSTRUCTION AND PIETY.

648. C. M. Episcopal Coll.

Early Piety.

1 O, IN the morn of life, when youth
With vital ardor glows,
And shines in all the fairest charms
That beauty can disclose, —

2 Deep in thy soul, before its powers
Are yet by vice enslaved,
Be thy Creator's glorious name
And character engraved; —

3 Ere yet the shades of sorrow cloud
The sunshine of thy days,
And cares and toils, in endless round,
Encompass all thy ways; —

4 Ere yet thy heart the woes of age,
With vain regret, deplore,
And sadly muse on former joys,
That now return no more.

5 True wisdom, early sought and gained,
In age will give thee rest;

O, then improve the morn of life,
To make its evening blest.

649. C. M. WATTS.

Early Piety.

1 WHEN children give their hearts to God,
'T is pleasing in his eyes;
A flower, when offered in the bud,
Is no vain sacrifice.

2 It saves us from a thousand snares
To mind religion young;
Grace will preserve our following years,
And make our virtues strong.

3 To thee, Almighty God, to thee
May we our hearts resign;
'T will please us to look back and see,
That our whole lives were thine

650. C. M. HEBER.

Early Religion.

1 BY cool Siloam's shady rill
How fair the lily grows!
How sweet the breath, beneath the hill,
Of Sharon's dewy rose!

2 Lo! such the child whose early feet
The paths of peace have trod,
Whose secret heart, with influence sweet,
Is upward drawn to God.

3 By cool Siloam's shady rill
The lily must decay;
The rose, that blooms beneath the hill,
Must shortly fade away.

4 And soon, too soon, the wintry hour
Of man's maturer age
Will shake the soul with sorrow's power
And stormy passion's rage.

5 O Thou who givest life and breath,
We seek thy grace alone,
In childhood, manhood, age, and death,
To keep us still thine own.

651. C. M. WATTS.

Importance of the Bible to the Young.

1 HOW shall the young secure their hearts,
And guard their lives, from sin?
Thy word the choicest rules imparts
To keep the conscience clean.

2 'T is, like the sun, a heavenly light,
That guides us all the day,
And, through the dangers of the night,
A lamp to lead our way.

3 Thy precepts make us truly wise;
We hate the sinner's road:
We hate our own vain thoughts that rise,
But love thy law, O God!

4 Thy word is everlasting truth;
How pure is every page!
That holy book shall guide our youth,
And well support our age.

652. C. M. SALISBURY COL.

"Remember thy Creator in the Days of thy Youth."

1 IN the soft season of thy youth,
In nature's smiling bloom,
Ere age arrive, and, trembling, wait
Its summons to the tomb, —

2 Remember thy Creator, God;
For him thy powers employ;
Make him thy fear, thy love, thy hope,
Thy confidence, thy joy.

3 He shall defend and guide thy course
Through life's uncertain sea,

Till thou art landed on the shore
Of blest eternity.

4 Then seek the Lord betimes, and choose
The path of heavenly truth ;
The earth affords no lovelier sight
Than a religious youth.

653. 7 & 6s. M. S. F. SMITH

Remember thy Creator.

1 " REMEMBER thy Creator "
While youth's fair spring is bright,
Before thy cares are greater,
Before comes age's night ;
While yet the sun shines o'er thee,
While stars the darkness cheer,
While life is all before thee,
Thy great Creator fear.

2 " Remember thy Creator "
Ere life resigns its trust,
Ere sinks dissolving nature,
And dust returns to dust ;
Before with God, who gave it,
The spirit shall appear :
He cries, who died to save it,
" Thy great Creator fear."

654. L. M. 6 L. E. TAYLOR

" Remember thy Creator, while the evil Days come not.

1 TRULY the light of morn is sweet,
And sweet it is to see the sun ;
But, cheerful though the hours may fleet,
And years pass gaily, one by one,
O, blot not, reckless, from thy mind
The thought of darker days behind.

2 Rejoice, O child of mortal birth,
In all the pride of youth rejoice ;

And let the beauteous things of earth
 Allure thine eye, invite thy choice ;
Yet know, for blessings freely given,
Thine is a large account with Heaven.

3 And, O, remember, ere the day,
 The evil day, of grief shall come,
When all the joy is passed away,
 And naught is left but gathering gloom, —
Remember, ere thy pleasures pall,
Him first, and last, who gave them all.

655. S. M. MRS. SIGOURNEY

Child's Prayer at entering Church.

1 LORD, lead my heart to learn ;
 Prepare my ears to hear ;
And let me useful knowledge seek,
 In thy most holy fear.

2 If unforgiven sin
 Within my bosom lies,
Or evil motives linger there
 T' offend thy perfect eyes, —

3 Remove them far away,
 Inspire me with thy love,
That I may please thee here below,
 And dwell with thee above.

656. S. M. ANONYMOUS.

God's Works praise him.

1 TEN thousand different flowers
 To thee sweet offerings bear ;
And cheerful birds in shady bowers
 Sing forth thy tender care.

2 The fields on every side,
 The trees on every hill,
The glorious sun, the rolling tide,
 Proclaim thy wonders still.

3 But trees, and fields, and skies,
Still praise a God unknown,
For gratitude and love can rise
From living hearts alone.

4 These living hearts of ours
Thy holy name would bless;
The blossoms of ten thousand flowers
Would please thee, Father, less.

5 While earth itself decays,
Our souls can never die;
O, tune them all to sing thy praise
In better songs on high.

657. C. M. HERBERT

The Soul's Beauty unfading.

1 SWEET day! so cool, so calm, so bright,
Bridal of earth and sky,
The dew shall weep thy fall to-night,
For thou, alas! must die.

2 Sweet rose! in air whose odors wave,
And color charms the eye,
Thy root is ever in its grave,
And thou, alas! must die.

3 Sweet spring! of days and roses made,
Whose charms for beauty vie,
Thy days depart, thy roses fade;
Thou, too, alas! must die.

4 Only a sweet and holy soul
Hath tints that never fly;
While flowers decay, and seasons roll,
This lives, and cannot die.

658. S. M. ANONYMOUS

The Young asking for Divine Guidance.

1 FROM earliest dawn of life,
Thy goodness we have shared;

And still we live to sing thy praise,
By sovereign mercy spared.

2 To learn and do thy will,
O Lord, our hearts incline;
And o'er the paths of future life
Command thy light to shine.

3 While taught thy word of truth,
May we that word receive,
And, when we hear of Jesus' name,
In that blest name believe!

4 O, let us never tread
The broad, destructive road,
But trace those holy paths which lead
To glory and to God!

659. S. M. ANONYMOU

Thoughts on Death.

1 LET children never fear
To leave this world of ours;
To close their eyes to beauty here,
And summer's fading flowers.

2 Beyond the hills that stand
In majesty alone,
There is a brighter, purer land,
And there our Father's throne.

3 No mortal step can tread
Upon a shore so fair;
No mortal voice can there be heard,
But angel harps are there.

4 And thither soars the soul,
When life's brief day is done, –
There is the destined, happy goal
For each immortal one.

5 Then shall we turn away,
When God would call us home?

No ! let us rather gladly say,
Lord ! at thy call we come.

660. C. M. DOANE

Life's little Lines.

1 LIFE'S little lines, how short, how faint,
How fast they fade away ;
Its highest hopes, its brightest joys,
Are compassed in a day.

2 Yet, though so changing and so brief
Our life's eventful page,
It has its charm for every grief,
Its joy for every age.

3 Let ours be virtue's deathless charm,
And faith's untiring flight ;
Then shall we rise from death's dark sleep
To worlds of cloudless light.

661. S. M. ANONYMOUS.

Frailty.

1 THE lilies of the field,
That quickly fade away,
May well to us a lesson yield ;
For we are frail as they.

2 Just like an early rose,
I 've seen an infant bloom ;
But death, perhaps, before it blows,
Will lay it in the tomb.

3 Then let us think on death,
Though we are young and gay ;
For God, who gave our life and breath,
Can take them both away.

4 To God, who made them all,
Let children humbly cry ;
And then, whenever death may call,
They 'll be prepared to die.

662. 8 & 7s. M. Anonymous

Opening of a Sabbath School.

1 WE have met in peace together
In this house of God again;
Constant friends have led us hither,
Here to chant the solemn strain;
Here to breathe our adoration,
Here the Saviour's praise to sing;
May the Spirit of salvation
Come with healing in his wing.

2 We have met, and time is flying;
We shall part, and still his wing,
Sweeping o'er the dead and dying,
Will the changeful seasons bring:
Let us, while our hearts are lightest,
In our fresh and early years,
Turn to Him whose smile is brightest,
And whose grace will calm our fears.

3 He will aid us, should existence
With its sorrows sting the breast;
Gleaming in the onward distance,
Faith will mark the land of rest:
There, 'midst day-beams round him playing,
We our Father's face shall see,
And shall hear him gently saying,
"Little children, come to me."

663. C. M. H. K. White.

Commencing Hymn.

1 O LORD, another week is flown,
And we, a youthful band,
Are met once more before thy throne,
To bless thy fostering hand.

2 And wilt thou lend a listening ear
To praises low as ours?

Thou wilt! for thou dost love to hear
The song which meekness pours.

3 And, Jesus, thou thy smiles wilt deign,
As in thy name we pray;
For thou didst bless the infant train,
And we are weak as they.

4 O, let thy grace perform its part,
And bid our passions cease;
And shed abroad in every heart
Thine everlasting peace.

664. 7s. M. T. Gray, Jr.

Prayer for a Blessing.

1 SUPPLIANT, lo! thy children bend,
Father, for thy blessing now;
Thou canst teach us, guide, defend;
We are weak, almighty thou.

2 With the peace thy word imparts
Be the taught and teachers blest;
In our lives, and in our hearts,
Father, be thy laws impressed.

3 Shed abroad in every mind
Light and pardon from above,
Charity for all our kind,
Trusting faith, and holy love.

665. C. M. J. Taylor

Songs of Children in Heaven.

1 THERE is a glorious world of light
Above the starry sky,
Where saints departed, clothed in white,
Adore the Lord most high.

2 And hark! — amid the sacred songs
Those heavenly voices raise,
Ten thousand thousand infant tongues
Unite in perfect praise.

3 Those are the hymns that we shall know
If Jesus we obey ;
That is the place where we shall go,
If found in wisdom's way.

4 This is the joy we ought to seek,
And make our chief concern ;
For this we come, from week to week,
To read, and hear, and learn.

5 Soon will our earthly race be run,
Our mortal frame decay ;
Children and teachers, one by one,
Must pass from earth away.

6 Great God ! impress the serious thought,
This day, on every breast ;
That both the teachers and the taught
May enter to thy rest.

666. H. M. Pratt's Coll

United Praise of Teachers and Children.

1 COME, let our voices join
In joyful songs of praise ;
To God, the God of love,
Our thankful hearts we 'll raise ;
To God alone all praise belongs, —
Our earliest and our latest songs.

2 Within these hallowed walls
Our wandering feet are brought,
Where prayer and praise ascend,
And heavenly truths are taught :
To God alone your offerings bring ;
Let young and old his praises sing.

3 Lord, let this work of love
Be crowned with full success ;
Let thousands, yet unborn,
Thy sacred name here bless :

To thee, O Lord, all praise to thee
We 'll raise, throughout eternity.

667. C. M. UNION COLL

Youthful Praise.

1 GREAT God, in whom we live and move,
Accept our feeble praise,
For all the mercy, grace, and love,
Which crown our youthful days.

2 For countless mercies, love unknown,
Lord, what can we impart?
Thou dost require one gift alone, —
The offering of the heart.

3 Incline us, Lord, to give it thee;
Preserve us by thy grace,
Till death shall bring us all to see
Thy glory face to face.

668. L. M. MONTGOMERY.

Sabbath School Anniversary.

1 FROM year to year in love we meet;
From year to year in peace we part;
The tongues of children uttering sweet
The thrilling joy of every heart.

2 But time rolls on; and, year by year,
We change, grow up, or pass away ·
Not twice the same assembly here
Have hailed the children's festal day.

3 Death, ere another year, shall strike
Some in our number marked to fall:
Be young and old prepared alike;
The warning is to each, to all.

4 Oft broke, our failing ranks renew;
Send teachers, children, in our place,
More humble, docile, faithful, true,
More like thy Son, from race to race.

669. C. M. ANONYMOUS.

Death of a Teacher.

1 FAREWELL, dear friend! a long farewell!
For we shall meet no more
Till we are raised with thee to dwell
On Zion's happy shore.

2 Our friend and *brother*, lo! is dead!
The cold and lifeless clay
Has made in dust its silent bed,
And there it must decay.

3 Farewell, dear friend, again farewell, —
Soon we shall rise to thee;
And when we meet, no tongue can tell
How great our joys shall be.

4 No more we 'll mourn thee, parted friend,
But lift our ardent prayer,
And every thought and effort bend
To rise and join thee there.

670. 8 & 7s. M. WATERSTON.

Death of a Pupil.

1 ONE sweet flower has drooped and faded,
One sweet infant voice has fled,
One fair brow the grave has shaded,
One dear school-mate now is dead.

2 But we feel no thought of sadness,
For our friend is happy now;
She has knelt in soul-felt gladness,
Where the blessèd angels bow.

3 *She* has gone to heaven before us,
But *she* turns and waves *her* hand,
Pointing to the glories o'er us,
In that happy spirit-land.

4 May our footsteps never falter
In the path that *she* has trod;

May we worship at the altar
Of the great and living God.

5 Lord, may angels watch above us,
Keep us all from error free, —
May they guard, and guide, and love us,
Till, like *her*, we go to thee.

671. C. M. HEMANS

Death of a Pupil.

1 CALM on the bosom of thy God,
Young spirit, rest thee now!
E'en while with us thy footstep trod,
His seal was on thy brow.

2 Dust, to its narrow house beneath!
Soul, to its place on high!
They that have seen thy look in death
No more may fear to die.

3 Lone are the paths, and sad the hours,
Since thy meek spirit 's gone;
But, O, a brighter home than ours,
In heaven, is now thine own!

672. C. M. BOSTON S. S. H. BOOK.

Death of a Scholar.

1 DEATH has been here, and borne away
A *brother* from our side:
Just in the morning of *his* day,
As young as we *he* died.

2 We cannot tell who next may fall
Beneath thy chastening rod;
One must be first, but let us all
Prepare to meet our God.

3 May each attend, with willing feet,
The means of knowledge here;
And wait around thy mercy-seat,
With hope as well as fear.

4 Lord, to thy wisdom and thy care
May we resign our days ;
Content to live and serve thee here,
Or die and sing thy praise.

673. 11s. M. ANONYMOUS.

The Resurrection.

1 SWEET spices they brought on their star-lighted way,
And came to the grave by the dawning of day ;
" But who will the stone from the sepulchre roll ?"
They said, as the tear from their weeping eyes stole.

2 The stone is removed, and the Saviour is gone : —
O, hail, ye disciples, this bright Sabbath morn ;
Lift, lift your glad voices in triumph on high ;
Your Master has risen, and ye shall not die.

3 May Christ now appear, as to Mary he came,
And fill every bosom with piety's flame ;
Then heaven's bright glories we soon shall obtain,
Nor Sabbaths so peaceful be useless and vain.

674. 7 & 6s. M. BOSTON S. S. H. BOOK

Anniversary of Independence.

1 WE come, with joy and gladness,
To breathe our songs of praise,
Nor let one note of sadness
Be mingled in our lays ;
For 't is a hallowed story,
This theme of freedom's birth :
Our fathers' deeds of glory
Are echoed round the earth.

2 The sound is waxing stronger,
And thrones and nations hear, —
Proud men shall rule no longer,
For God the Lord is near :

And he will crush oppression,
  And raise the humble mind,
And give the earth's possession
  Among the good and kind.

3 And then shall sink the mountains,
  Where pride and power are crowned,
And peace, like gentle fountains,
  Shall shed its pureness round.
O God! we would adore thee,
  And in thy shadow rest;
Our fathers bowed before thee,
  And trusted and were blest.

675. 7s. M. HEBER

"Consider the Lilies of the Field; — behold the Fowls of the Air."

1 LO! the lilies of the field!
How their leaves instruction yield!
Hark to nature's lesson given
By the blessèd birds of heaven!
Every bush and tufted tree
Warbles trust and piety:
Children, banish doubt and sorrow, —
God provideth for the morrow.

2 One there lives, whose guardian eye
Guides our earthly destiny;
One there lives, who, Lord of all,
Keeps his children lest they fall:
Pass we, then, in love and praise,
Trusting him, through all our days,
Free from doubt and faithless sorrow, —
God provideth for the morrow.

676. C. M. ANONYMOUS

Trust in the Lord.

1 MY soul, why sink when griefs oppress,
  Or start when fears alarm?

Trust in the Lord, in thy distress,
Thy refuge is his arm.

2 Though hope and joy have from thee flown
And left thee to despair,
Trust in the Lord, in him alone
Repose thine every care.

3 What though the floods may near thee roll,
The sky grow darker still, —
Trust in the Lord, he keeps thy soul,
And storms obey his will.

4 How oft when pressed by mighty foes
Did no escape appear:
Trust in the Lord thou didst repose,
And come off conqueror.

5 And will he now his help deny,
And leave thee to thy lot?
Trust in the Lord; he still is nigh,
His nature changes not.

6 Yes, O my soul, I yet will say,
'Midst anguish and distress,
Trust in the Lord! e'en though he slay,
My cause with him shall rest.

677. S. M. ANONYMOUS.

The Spring.

1 SWEET is the time of spring,
When nature's charms appear;
The birds with ceaseless pleasure sing,
And hail the opening year:
But sweeter far the spring
Of wisdom and of grace,
When children bless and praise their King,
Who loves the youthful race.

2 Sweet is the dawn of day,
When light just streaks the sky;

When shades and darkness pass away,
And morning's beams are nigh :
But sweeter far the dawn
Of piety in youth ;
When doubt and darkness are withdrawn,
Before the light of truth.

3 Sweet is the early dew,
Which gilds the mountain tops,
And decks each plant and flower we view
With pearly, glittering drops :
But sweeter far the scene
On Zion's holy hill,
When there the dew of youth is seen
Its freshness to distil.

678. 7 & 6s. M. MISS SIMES

Summer.

1 'T IS summer, glorious summer ; —
Behold the glad, green earth,
How from her grateful bosom
The herb and flower spring forth ;
These are her rich thanksgivings,
The incense floats above !
Father ! what may we offer ?
Thy chosen flower is love !

2 'T is summer, blessèd summer ; —
The lofty hills are bright ;
All nature's fountains sparkle, —
Shall ours have lesser light ?
No ; bid each spirit praise Him
Who hangs on every tree
A thousand living lyres,
Awak'ning harmony !

3 'T is summer in our bosoms,
When youthful snares we fly,

And strength and peace are given
  By angel ministry ; —
'T is summer in yon heaven,
  Where, teachers, ye shall know,
While time shall last, the blessedness
  Wrought by your love below.

679. 8 & 7s. M. HORNE

Autumn Warnings.

1 SEE the leaves around us falling,
  Dry and withered, to the ground ;
Thus to thoughtless mortals calling,
  In a sad and solemn sound : —

2 " Youth, on length of days presuming,
  Who the paths of pleasure tread, —
View us, late in beauty blooming,
  Numbered now among the dead.

3 " What though yet no losses grieve you,
  Gay with health and many a grace ;
Let not cloudless skies deceive you :
  Summer gives to autumn place.

4 " Yearly in our course returning,
  Messengers of shortest stay,
O, receive our kindly warning, —
  Heaven and earth shall pass away "

5 On the tree of life eternal,
  Let our highest hopes be stayed :
This alone, for ever vernal,
  Bears a leaf that shall not fade.

680. C. M. PHILLIPS'S SERV. BOOK.

Thunder-storm.

1 THE thunder bursts ! its rolling might
  Seems the firm hills to shake ;
And in terrific splendor bright,
  The gathered lightnings break.

2 Yet doth not God behold thee still,
With all-surveying eye ?
Doth not his power all nature fill,
Around, beneath, on high ?

3 Then fear not, though the angry sky
A thousand darts should cast ;
Why should we tremble e'en to die,
And be with him at last ?

681. 6 & 5s. M. MRS. S. J. HALE

The Lord's Prayer.

1 OUR Father in heaven,
We hallow thy name !
May thy kingdom holy
On earth be the same !
O, give to us daily
Our portion of bread ;
It is from thy bounty
That all must be fed.

2 Forgive our transgressions,
And teach us to know
That humble compassion
Which pardons each foe :
Keep us from temptation,
From weakness and sin,
And thine be the glory
For ever. — Amen.

682. C. M. ANONYMOUS

A Child's Prayer.

1 LORD, teach a little child to pray,
And, O, accept my prayer ;
Thou canst hear all the words I say,
For thou art everywhere.

2 A little sparrow cannot fall
Unnoticed, Lord, by thee ;

And though I am so young and small,
Thou dost take care of me.

3 Teach me to do whate'er is right,
And, when I sin, forgive;
And make it still my chief delight
To serve thee while I live.

683. L. M. ANONYMOUS.

Sunday Morning. For a Child.

1 CALLED by the Sabbath bells away
Unto thy holy temple, Lord,
I 'll go, with willing mind, to pray,
To praise thy name, and hear thy word.

2 O sacred day of peace and joy,
Thy hours are ever dear to me;
Ne'er may a sinful thought destroy
The holy calm I find in thee.

3 Dear are thy peaceful hours to me,
For God has given them in his love,
To tell how calm, how blest, shall be
The endless day of heaven above.

684. L. M. PIERPONT

Morning Hymn. For a Child.

1 O GOD, I thank thee that the night
In peace and rest hath passed away;
And that I see, in this fair light,
My Father's smile, that makes it day.

2 Be thou my Guide, and let me live
As under thine all-seeing eye:
Supply my wants, my sins forgive,
And make me happy when I die.

685. L. M. ANONYMOUS.

Sunday Evening. For a Child.

1 AGAIN we 've seen the Sabbath day,
And heard of Jesus and of heaven;

We thank thee, Father, and we pray
That this day's sins may be forgiven.

2 May all we heard and understood
Be well remembered through the week,
And help to make us wise and good,
More humble, diligent, and meek.

686. L. M. PIERPONT

Evening Hymn. For a Child.

1 ANOTHER day its course has run,
And still, O God, thy child is blest ,
For thou hast been by day my sun,
And thou wilt be by night my rest

2 Sweet sleep descends, my eyes to close ,
And now, when all the world is still,
I give my body to repose, —
My spirit to my Father's will.

687. 6s. M. FURNESS

The Want within.

1 I FEEL within a want
For ever burning there,
What I so thirst for, grant,
O Thou who hearest prayer !

2 This is the thing I crave,
A likeness to thy Son ;
This would I rather have
Than call the world my own.

3 Like him, now in my youth,
I long, O God, to be,
In tenderness and truth,
In sweet humility.

4 'T is my most fervent prayer,
Be it more fervent still,
Be it my highest care,
Be it my settled will.

688. C. M. L. G. Pray

Brotherly Love.

1 FATHER in heaven! we thank the care
That planned our lot on earth,
Made us each other's love to share,
By ties of kindred birth.

2 Brothers and sisters hand in hand
Together taught to go;
Our pleasures one, a happy band, —
Or one in scenes of woe.

3 Since God such ties has round us thrown,
To make us happy here, —
O, let no want of love be shown,
To cause a single tear.

4 Thus happy live, thus happy die,
In union sweet below,
That when to other worlds we fly,
To higher joys may go.

689. C. M. William Cutter

Youthful Example.

1 WHAT if the little rain should say,
So small a drop as I
Can ne'er refresh these thirsty fields,
I 'll tarry in the sky?

2 What if a shining beam of noon
Should in its fountain stay,
Because its feeble light alone
Cannot create a day?

3 Doth not each rain-drop help to form
The cool, refreshing shower,
And every ray of light to warm
And beautify the flower?

4 Go thou, and strive to do thy share; —
One talent, — less than thine, —

Improved with steady zeal and care,
Would gain rewards divine.

690. L. M. ANONYMOUS.

For the Close of a Sabbath School.

1 FATHER, once more let grateful praise
And humble prayer to thee ascend;
Thou Guide and Guardian of our ways,
Our early and our only Friend.

2 Since every day and hour that 's gone
Has been with mercy richly crowned,
Mercy, we know, shall still flow on,
For ever sure, as time rolls round.

3 Hear then the parting prayers we pour,
And bind our hearts in love alone;
And if we meet on earth no more,
May we at last surround thy throne.

691. 8 & 7s. M. L. G. PRAY

Anniversary Hymn.

1 LORD, we come to seek thy blessing,
Objects of thy tender care;
Every good on earth possessing,
If thy favor we but share.

2 Nature speaks, in all her beauty,
Of the hand that fashioned her;
So must we, by love and duty,
All our gifts to thee refer.

3 Here the Sunday School and temple
Throw their doors for us apart,
Trained to be both true and gentle,
Wise in mind and pure in heart.

4 On this joyful, blest occasion,
We our hearts would lift to thee;
Catch the tones of soft persuasion, —
Happy, true, and thoughtful be.

692. 8 & 7s. M. FROM THE GERMAN

Thanksgiving.

1 PRAISE the Lord, when blushing morning
Wakes the blossoms fresh with dew,
Praise him when revived creation
Beams with beauties fair and new.

2 Praise the Lord, when early breezes
Come so fragrant from the flowers,
Praise, thou willow, by the brook-side,
Praise, ye birds, among the bowers.

3 Praise the Lord, and may his blessing
Guide us in the way of truth,
Keep our feet from paths of error,
Make us holy in our youth.

4 Praise the Lord, ye hosts of heaven,
Angels, sing your sweetest lays,
All things utter forth his glory,
Sound aloud Jehovah's praise.

FAST AND THANKSGIVING.

693. L. M. DYER.

Public Humiliation.

1 GREAT Maker of unnumbered worlds,
And whom unnumbered worlds adore, —
Whose goodness all thy creatures share,
While nature trembles at thy power, —

2 Thine is the hand that moves the spheres,
That wakes the wind and lifts the sea;
And man, who moves the lord of earth,
Acts but the part assigned by thee.

3 While suppliant crowds implore thine aid,
To thee we raise the humble cry;

Thine altar is the contrite heart,
  Thine incense the repentant sigh.

4 O, may our land, in this her hour,
  Confess thy hand, and bless the rod,
By penitence make thee her Friend,
  And find in thee a guardian God.

694. C. M. S. STREETER

Humiliation and Prayer.

1 HERE, in thy temple, Lord, we meet,
  And bow before thy throne ;
Abased and guilty, at thy feet,
  We seek thy grace alone.

2 Our sins rise up in dread array,
  And fill our hearts with fear ;
Our trembling spirits melt away,
  But find no helper near.

3 O, send thy pity from on high
  With pardon all-divine ;
Bring now thy gracious spirit nigh,
  And make us wholly thine.

4 We humbly mourn our follies past,
  Each guilty path deplore ;
Resolved, while feeble life shall last,
  To tread those paths no more.

695. C. M. RIPPON'S COLL

Judgments for National Sins deprecated.

1 ALMIGHTY Lord, before thy throne
  Thy mourning people bend ;
'T is on thy pardoning grace alone
  Our dying hopes depend.

2 Dark judgments, from thy heavy hand,
  Thy dreadful power display ;
Yet mercy spares our guilty land,
  And still we live to pray.

3 How changed, alas! are truths divine,
For error, guilt, and shame!
What impious numbers, bold in sin,
Disgrace the Christian name!

4 O, turn us, turn us, mighty Lord;
Convert us by thy grace;
Then shall our hearts obey thy word,
And see again thy face.

5 Then, should oppressing foes invade,
We will not yield to fear,
Secure of all-sufficient aid,
When thou, O God, art near.

696. L. M. MONTGOMERY.

Penitence and Forgiveness.

1 HAVE mercy on me, O my God!
In loving kindness hear my prayer;
Withdraw the terror of thy rod;
Lord, in thy tender mercy, spare.

2 Offences rise where'er I look,
But I confess their guilt to thee;
Blot my transgressions from thy book;
Wash me from all iniquity.

3 Not streaming blood nor cleansing fire
Thy seeming anger can appease;
Burnt-offerings thou dost not require,
Or gladly I would render these.

4 The broken heart in sacrifice,
Alone, will thine acceptance meet;
My heart, O God, do not despise,
Abased and contrite at thy feet.

5 Thy consolations, as of old,
Now to my troubled mind restore;
By thy free spirit's might uphold,
And guide my steps to fall no more.

697. S. M. DRUMMOND

"Is it such a Fast that I have chosen?"

1 "IS this a fast for me?"—
Thus saith the Lord our God;—
"A day for man to vex his soul,
And feel affliction's rod?—

2 "Like bulrush low to bow
His sorrow-stricken head,
With sackcloth for his inner vest,
And ashes round him spread?

3 "Shall day like this have power
To stay th' avenging hand,
Efface transgression, or avert
My judgments from the land?

4 "No; is not this alone
The sacred fast I choose,—
Oppression's yoke to burst in twain,
The bands of guilt unloose?—

5 "To nakedness and want
Your food and raiment deal,
To dwell your kindred race among,
And all their sufferings heal?

6 "Then, like the morning ray,
Shall spring your health and light;
Before you, righteousness shall shine,
Behind, my glory bright!"

698. C. M. BREVIARY.

Humility under Affliction.

1 O SINNER, bring not tears alone,
Or outward form of prayer,
But let it in thy heart be known
That penitence is there.

2 To smite the breast, the clothes to rend,
God asketh not of thee:

Thy secret soul he bids thee bend
  In true humility.

3 O, let us, then, with heartfelt grief,
  Draw near unto our God,
And pray to him to grant relief,
  And stay the lifted rod.

4 O righteous Judge, if thou wilt deign
  To grant us what we need,
We pray for time to turn again,
  And grace to turn indeed.

699. L. M. Aikin

In Time of War.

1 WHILE sounds of war are heard around,
And death and ruin strow the ground,
To thee we look, on thee we call,
The Parent and the Lord of all.

2 Thou who hast stamped on human kind
The image of a heaven-born mind,
And in a Father's wide embrace
Hast cherished all the kindred race, —

3 Great God, whose powerful hand can bind
The raging waves, the furious wind,
O, bid the human tempest cease,
And hush the maddening world to peace.

4 With reverence may each hostile land
Hear and obey that high command,
Thy Son's blest errand from above, —
"My creatures, live in mutual love!"

700. C. M. Anonymous.

For a Day of Fasting and Prayer.

1 NOW let our prayers ascend to thee,
  Thou great and holy One;
Above the world raise thou our hearts;
  In us, thy will be done.

2 O, let us feel how frail we are,
How much we need thy grace;
O, strengthen, Lord, our fainting souls,
While here we seek thy face.

3 Our sins, alas! before thee rise;
Thou knowest all our guilt;
Let not our faith, our hope, our trust,
On earthly things be built.

4 Forgive our sins, thy spirit grant,
Let love our souls refine,
And heavenly peace and holy hope
Assure that we are thine.

701. C. M. TATE & BRADY

God our Deliverer.

1 O LORD, our fathers oft have told,
In our attentive ears,
Thy wonders in their days performed,
And in more ancient years.

2 'T was not their courage, nor their sword,
To them salvation gave;
'T was not their number, nor their strength,
That did their country save.

3 But thy right hand, — thy powerful arm, —
Whose succour they implored;
Thy providence protected them,
Who thy great name adored.

4 As thee their God our fathers owned,
So thou art still our King;
O, therefore, as thou didst to them,
To us deliverance bring.

5 To thee the glory we'll ascribe,
From whom salvation came;
In God, our shield, we will rejoice,
And ever bless thy name.

702. 7s. M. SACRED LYRICS.

Thanksgiving.

1 SWELL the anthem, raise the song ;
Praises to our God belong ;
Saints and angels, join to sing
Praises to the Heavenly King.

2 Blessings from his liberal hand
Flow around this happy land :
Kept by him, no foes annoy ;
Peace and freedom we enjoy.

3 Here, beneath a virtuous sway,
May we cheerfully obey, —
Never feel oppression's rod, —
Ever own and worship God.

4 Hark ! the voice of nature sings
Praises to the King of kings ;
Let us join the choral song,
And the grateful notes prolong.

703. C. M. CHRISTIAN PSALMIST

Thanks for an abundant Harvest.

1 FOUNTAIN of mercy, God of love !
How rich thy bounties are !
The rolling seasons, as they move,
Proclaim thy constant care.

2 When in the bosom of the earth
The sower hid the grain,
Thy goodness marked its secret birth,
And sent the early rain.

3 The spring's sweet influence, Lord, was thine :
The plants in beauty grew :
Thou gav'st refulgent suns to shine,
And mild, refreshing dew.

4 These various mercies from above
Matured the swelling grain ;

A kindly harvest crowns thy love,
  And plenty fills the plain.

5 We own and bless thy gracious sway;
  Thy hand all nature hails;
Seed-time nor harvest, night nor day,
  Summer nor winter, fails.

704. L. M. Campbell's Coll

The Joy in Harvest.

1 GREAT God, as seasons disappear,
And changes mark the rolling year,
Thy favor still doth crown our days,
And we would celebrate thy praise.

2 The harvest song we would repeat:
"Thou givest us the finest wheat":
"The joy of harvest" we have known:
The praise, O Lord, is all thine own.

3 Our tables spread, our garners stored,
O, give us hearts to bless thee, Lord;
Forbid it, Source of light and love,
That hearts and lives should barren prove.

4 Another harvest comes apace:
Mature our spirits by thy grace,
That we may calmly meet the blow
The sickle gives to lay us low;—

5 That so, when angel reapers come
To gather sheaves to thy blest home,
Our spirits may be borne on high
To thy safe garner in the sky.

705. 6 & 4s. M. Montgomery

Praise to the God of Harvest.

1 THE God of harvest praise;
In loud thanksgiving raise
  Hand, heart, and voice;

The valleys smile and sing,
Forests and mountains ring,
The plains their tribute bring,
The streams rejoice.

2 Yea, bless his holy name,
And purest thanks proclaim
Through all the earth;
To glory in your lot
Is duty, — but be not
God's benefits forgot,
Amidst your mirth.

3 The God of harvest praise;
Hands, hearts, and voices raise,
With sweet accord;
From field to garner throng,
Bearing your sheaves along,
And in your harvest song
Bless ye the Lord.

706. L. M. DODDRIDGE

The Year crowned with Goodness.

1 ETERNAL Source of every joy,
Thy praise may well our lips employ,
While in thy temple we appear,
Whose goodness crowns the circling year.

2 Wide as the wheels of nature roll,
Thy hand supports the steady pole;
The sun is taught by thee to rise,
And darkness when to veil the skies.

3 The flowery spring, at thy command,
Embalms the air and paints the land;
The summer suns with vigor shine,
To raise the corn and cheer the vine.

4 Thy hand in autumn richly pours
Through all our coasts abundant stores;

And winters, softened by thy care,
No more a dreary aspect wear.

5 Still be the cheerful homage paid
With morning light and evening shade;
Seasons, and months, and weeks, and days,
Demand successive songs of praise.

707. 8 & 7s. M. CROSSE

The Sacrifice of Thanksgiving.

1 LORD of heaven, and earth, and ocean,
Hear us from thy bright abode,
While our hearts, with true devotion,
Own their great and gracious God.

2 Health and every needful blessing
Are thy bounteous gifts alone;
Comforts undeserved possessing,
Here we bend before thy throne.

3 Thee, with humble adoration,
Lord, we praise for mercies past;
Still to this most favored nation
May those mercies ever last.

708. 11 & 8s. M. EPISCOPAL COLL

Thanksgiving and Praise in the Sanctuary.

1 BE joyful in God, all ye lands of the earth;
O, serve him with gladness and fear;
Exult in his presence with music and mirth;
With love and devotion draw near.

2 Jehovah is God, and Jehovah alone,
Creator and Ruler o'er all;
And we are his people; his sceptre we own;
His sheep, and we follow his call.

3 O, enter his gates with thanksgiving and song;
Your vows in his temple proclaim;
His praise in melodious accordance prolong,
And bless his adorable name.

4 For good is the Lord, inexpressibly good,
And we are the work of his hand;
His mercy and truth from eternity stood,
And shall to eternity stand.

709. L. P. M. Roscoe

Praise to the Author of National Blessings.

1 GREAT God, beneath whose piercing eye
The world's extended kingdoms lie,
We bow before thy heavenly throne;
Thy favoring smile upholds them all;
Thine anger smites them, and they fall;
Thy power we see, thy greatness own.

2 To thee, with grateful hearts, we raise
The tribute of exulting praise,
Our country's Guardian, Guide, and Friend;
Preserved by thee for ages past,
For ages let thy kindness last,
And e'er thy sheltering care extend.

710. L. M. Heginbotham.

The God of all Grace.

1 GREAT God, let all my tuneful powers
Awake, and sing thy mighty name:
Thy hand revolves my circling hours,—
Thy hand, from whence my being came.

2 Seasons and moons, still rolling round
In beauteous order, speak thy praise;
And years, with smiling mercy crowned,
To thee successive honors raise.

3 My life, my health, my friends, I owe
All to thy vast, unbounded love;
Ten thousand precious gifts below,
And hope of nobler joys above.

4 Thus will I sing till nature cease,
Till sense and language are no more,

And after death thy boundless grace,
Through everlasting years, adore.

711. L. P. M. KIPPIS.

Thanksgiving for National Prosperity.

1 HOW rich thy gifts, Almighty King!
From thee our public blessings spring;
Th' extended trade, the fruitful skies,
The treasures liberty bestows,
Th' eternal joys the gospel shows,
All from thy boundless goodness rise.

2 Here commerce spreads the wealthy store
Which pours from every foreign shore;
Science and art their charms display;
Religion teaches us to raise
Our voices to our Maker's praise,
As truth and conscience point the way

3 With grateful hearts, with joyful tongues
To God we raise united songs;
His power and mercy we proclaim;
This land through every age shall own,
Jehovah here has fixed his throne,
And triumph in his mighty name.

4 Long as the moon her course shall run,
Or man behold the circling sun,
O, still may God amidst us reign;
Crown our just counsels with success,
With peace and joy our borders bless,
And all our sacred rights maintain.

712. L. M. STEELE

Thanksgiving for National Peace.

1 GREAT Ruler of the earth and skies,
A word of thine Almighty breath
Can sink the world, or bid it rise;
Thy smile is life, thy frown is death.

2 When angry nations rush to arms,
And rage, and noise, and tumult reign,
And war resounds its dire alarms,
And slaughter dyes the hostile plain;

3 Thy sovereign eye looks calmly down,
And marks their course, and bounds their power.
Thy law the angry nations own,
And noise and war are heard no more.

4 Then peace returns with balmy wing;
Sweet peace! with her what blessings fled!
Glad plenty laughs, the valleys sing,
Reviving commerce lifts her head.

5 Thou good, and wise, and righteous Lord!
All move subservient to thy will;
Both peace and war await thy word,
And thy sublime decrees fulfil.

6 To thee we pay our grateful songs;
Thy kind protection still implore:
O, may our hearts, and lives, and tongues,
Confess thy goodness, and adore.

713. L. M. L. H. Sigourney

Harvest.

1 GOD of the year! with songs of praise
And hearts of love, we come to bless
Thy bounteous hand, for thou hast shed
Thy manna o'er our wilderness.

2 In early spring-time thou didst fling
O'er earth its robe of blossoming;
And its sweet treasures, day by day,
Rose quickening in thy blessèd ray.

3 God of the seasons! thou hast blest
The land with sunlight and with showers,
And plenty o'er its bosom smiles,
To crown the sweet autumnal hours.

4 Praise, — praise to thee ! Our hearts expand
To view these blessings of thy hand,
And on the incense-breath of love
Ascend to their bright home above.

OPENING AND CLOSING OF THE YEAR

714. 7s. M. NEWTON.

New Year's Day.

1 WHILE, with ceaseless course, the sun
Hasted through the former year,
Many souls their race have run,
Never more to meet us here ;
Fixed in an eternal state,
They have done with all below ;
We a little longer wait,
But how little none can know.

2 As the wingéd arrow flies,
Speedily the mark to find ;
As the lightning from the skies
Darts and leaves no trace behind ; —
Swiftly thus our fleeting days
Bear us down life's rapid stream :
Upward, Lord, our spirits raise ;
All below is but a dream.

3 Thanks for mercies past receive ;
Pardon of our sins renew ;
Teach us, henceforth, how to live,
With eternity in view ;
Bless thy word to old and young ;
Fill us with a Saviour's love ;
When our life's short race is run,
May we dwell with thee above.

715. L. M. DODDRIDGE

A Song for the opening Year.

1 GREAT God, we sing that mighty hand
By which supported still we stand;
The opening year thy mercy shows;
Let mercy crown it till its close.

2 By day, by night, at home, abroad,
Still we are guarded by our God;
By his incessant bounty fed,
By his unerring counsel led.

3 With grateful hearts the past we own,
The future — all to us unknown —
We to thy guardian care commit,
And peaceful leave before thy feet.

4 In scenes exalted or depressed,
Be thou our joy, and thou our rest;
Thy goodness all our hopes shall raise,
Adored through all our changing days.

5 When death shall close our earthly songs,
And seal in silence mortal tongues,
Our Helper, God, in whom we trust,
In brighter worlds our souls shall boast.

716. C. M. NEWTON

New Year. Prayer for a Blessing.

1 NOW, gracious Lord, thine arm reveal,
And make thy glory known;
Now let us all thy presence feel,
And soften hearts of stone.

2 From all the guilt of former sin
May mercy set us free;
And let the year we now begin,
Begin and end with thee.

3 Send down thy spirit from above,
That saints may love thee more

And sinners now may learn to love,
Who never loved before.

4 And when before thee we appear,
In our eternal home,
May growing numbers worship here,
And praise thee in our room.

717. C. M. HEGINBOTHAM.

New Year. Providential Goodness.

1 GOD of our lives, thy various praise
Our voices shall resound :
Thy hand directs our fleeting days,
And brings the seasons round.

2 To thee shall grateful songs arise,
Our Father and our Friend,
Whose constant mercies from the skies
In genial streams descend.

3 In every scene of life, thy care,
In every age, we see ;
And constant as thy favors are,
So let our praises be.

4 Still may thy love, in every scene,
In every age, appear ;
And let the same compassion deign
To bless the opening year.

5 If mercy smile, let mercy bring
Our wandering souls to God :
In our affliction we shall sing
If thou wilt bless the rod.

718. 5 & 12s. M. C. WESLEY.

The New Year.

1 COME, let us anew
Our journey pursue, —
Roll round with the year,
And never stand still till the Master appear ;

His adorable will
Let us gladly fulfil,
And our talents improve
By the patience of hope, and the labor of love

Our life is a dream;
Our time, as a stream,
Glides swiftly away,
And the fugitive moment refuses to stay;
The arrow is flown;
The moment is gone;
The millennial year
Rushes on to our view, and eternity 's near.

3 O, that each, in the day
Of his coming, may say,
"I have fought my way through;
I have finished the work thou didst give me to do";
O, that each from his Lord
May receive the glad word,
"Well and faithfully done;
Enter into my joy, and sit down on my throne."

719. C. M. DODDRIDGE.

Close of the Year.

1 AWAKE, ye saints, and raise your eyes,
And lift your voices high;
Awake, and praise that sovereign love
That shows salvation nigh.

2 On all the wings of time it flies;
Each moment brings it near:
Then welcome each declining day
Welcome each closing year.

3 Not many years their rounds shall run,
Nor many mornings rise,
Ere all its glories stand revealed
To our admiring eyes.

4 Ye wheels of nature, speed your course ;
   Ye mortal powers, decay ;
Fast as ye bring the night of death,
   Ye bring eternal day.

720. C. M. ANONYMOUS

Reflections at the End of the Year.

1 AND now, my soul, another year
   Of thy short life is past ;
I cannot long continue here,
   And this may be my last.

2 Much of my hasty life is gone,
   Nor will return again ;
And swift my passing moments run, —
   The few that yet remain.

3 Awake, my soul ; with utmost care
   Thy true condition learn :
What are thy hopes ? how sure ? how fair ?
   What is thy great concern ?

4 Behold another year begins ;
   Set out afresh for heaven ;
Seek pardon for thy former sins,
   In Christ so freely given.

5 Devoutly yield thyself to God,
   And on his grace depend ;
With zeal pursue the heavenly road,
   Nor doubt a happy end.

721. L. M. DODDRIDGE.

Close of the Year.

1 OUR Helper, God, we bless his name,
Whose love for ever is the same ;
The tokens of whose gracious care
Begin, and crown, and close the year.

2 Amid ten thousand snares we stand,
Supported by his guardian hand ;

And see, when we review our ways,
Ten thousand monuments of praise.

3 Thus far his arm hath led us on ;
Thus far we make his mercy known ;
And while we tread this desert land,
New mercies shall new songs demand.

4 Our grateful souls on Jordan's shore
Shall raise one sacred pillar more,
Then bear, in his bright courts above,
Inscriptions of immortal love.

722. C. M. DODDRIDGE

Close of the Year.

1 REMARK, my soul, the narrow bound
Of each revolving year ;
How swift the weeks complete their round .
How short the months appear !

2 So fast eternity comes on,
And that important day
When all that mortal life hath done
God's judgment shall survey.

3 Yet like an idle tale we pass
The swift-revolving year,
And study artful ways t' increase
The speed of its career.

4 Awake, O God, my careless heart
Its great concerns to see,
That I may act the Christian part,
And give the year to thee.

5 So shall their course more grateful roll,
If future years arise ;
Or this shall bear my waiting soul
To joy beyond the skies.

723. 10s. M. E. Taylor

The changing Year.

1 GOD of the changing year, whose arm of power
In safety leads through danger's darkest hour.
Here in thy temple bow thy creatures down,
To bless thy mercy, and thy might to own.

2 Thine are the beams that cheer us on our way.
And pour around the gladdening light of day ;
Thine is the night, and the fair orbs that shine
To cheer its hours of darkness, — all are thine

3 If round our path the thorns of sorrow grew,
And mortal friends were faithless, thou wert true,
Did sickness shake the frame, or anguish tear
The wounded spirit, thou wert present there.

4 Yet when our hearts review departed days,
How vast thy mercies ! how remiss our praise
Well may we dread thine awful eye to meet,
Bend at thy throne, and worship at thy feet.

5 O, lend thine ear, and lift our voice to thee ;
Where'er we dwell, still let thy mercy be ;
From year to year, still nearer to thy shrine
Draw our frail hearts, and make them wholly thine.

724. 7s. M. Newton

Uncertainty of Life. New Year.

1 SEE ! another year is gone !
Quickly have the seasons past !
This we enter now upon
Will to many prove their last.
Mercy hitherto has spared,
But have mercies been improved ?
Let us ask, Am I prepared
Should I be this year removed ?

2 Some we now no longer see,
Who their mortal race have run,

Seemed as fair for life as we,
When the former year begun.
Some — but who God only knows —
That are here assembled now,
Ere the present year shall close,
To the stroke of death must bow

3 If from guilt and sin set free
By the knowledge of thy grace,
Welcome, then, the call will be
To depart and see thy face.
To thy saints while here below,
With new years new mercies come
But the happiest year they know
Is the last, that leads them home.

725. S. M. BEDDOME

Purposes on Beginning a New Year.

1 MY few revolving years,
How swift they glide away!
How short the term of life appears
When past, — but as a day!

2 A dark and cloudy day,
Clouded by grief and sin;
A host of enemies without,
Distressing fears within.

3 Lord, through another year
If thou permit my stay,
With diligence may I pursue
The true and living way!

726. L. M. DODDRIDGE

The Flight of Time.

1 GOD of eternity, from thee
Did infant Time his being draw;
Moments, and days, and months, and years
Revolve by thine unvaried law.

2 Silent and swift they glide away;
Steady and strong the current flows,
Lost in eternity's wide sea, —
The boundless gulf from whence it rose.

3 With it the thoughtless sons of men
Upon the rapid stream are borne
Swift on to their eternal home,
Whence not one soul can e'er return.

4 Yet, while the shore, on either side,
Presents a gaudy, flattering show,
We gaze, in fond amazement lost,
Nor think to what a world we go.

5 Great Source of wisdom, teach my heart
To know the price of every hour,
That time may bear me on to joys
Beyond its measure and its power.

727. 10 & 11s. M. DODDRIDGE

For New Year's Day.

1 HOUSE of our God, with cheerful anthems ring,
While all our lips and hearts his graces sing;
The opening year his bounties shall proclaim,
And all its days be vocal with his name.
The Lord is good, his mercy never-ending,
His blessings in perpetual showers descending.

2 Thou earth, enlightened by his rays divine,
Pregnant with grass, and corn, and oil, and wine;
Crowned with his goodness, let the nations meet,
And lay their crowns at his paternal feet;
With grateful love that liberal hand confessing,
Which through each heart diffuseth every blessing.

3 His mercy never ends; the dawn, the shade,
Still see new beauties through new scenes displayed
Succeeding ages bless this sure abode,
And children lean upon their father's God.

The soul of man, through its immense duration,
Drinks from this source immortal consolation.

4 Burst into praise, my soul! all nature join;
Angels and men in harmony combine;
While human years are measured by the sun,
And while eternity its course shall run,
His goodness, in perpetual showers descending,
Exalt in songs and raptures never-ending.

THE SEASONS.

728. C. M. Needham.

The Providence of God in the Seasons.

1 THE rolling year, Almighty Lord!
Obeys thy powerful nod;
Each season, as it silent moves,
Declares the present God.

2 Waked by thy voice, blooms forth the spring,
In living verdure dressed;
On hills, in vales, through fields and groves,
Thy beauties stand confessed.

3 The sun calls forth the summer months,
Nor do the hours delay;
The fruits with varied colors glow
Beneath his ripening ray.

4 Thy bounty, Lord! in autumn shines,
And spreads a general feast;
In which thy creatures all partake,
The greatest and the least.

5 When winter rears her hoary head,
And shows her furrowed brow,
In storms and tempests, frosts and snows,
How awful, Lord, art thou!

6 The rolling year, Almighty Lord!
Obeys thy powerful nod;
Each season, as it silent moves,
Declares the present God.

729. L. M. ENFIELD'S SELECT

The Goodness of God in the Seasons.

1 GREAT God! at whose all-powerful call
At first arose this beauteous frame,
By thee the seasons change, and all
The changing seasons speak thy name.

2 Thy bounty bids the infant year,
From winter storms recovered, rise;
When thousand grateful scenes appear,
Fresh opening to our wondering eyes.

3 O, how delightful 't is to see
The earth in vernal beauty dressed!
While in each herb, and flower, and tree,
Thy bright perfections shine confessed!

4 Indulgent God! from every part,
Thy plenteous blessings largely flow;
We see, — we taste; — let every heart
With grateful love and duty glow.

730. C. M. WATTS

Seasons.

1 WITH songs and honors sounding loud,
Address the Lord on high;
O'er all the heavens he spreads his cloud,
And waters veil the sky.

2 He sends his showers of blessings down,
To cheer the plains below;
He makes the grass the mountains crown,
And corn in valleys grow.

3 His steady counsels change the face
Of each declining year;

He bids the sun cut short his race,
And wintry days appear.

4 On us his providence has shone,
With gentle, smiling rays;
O, may our lips and lives make known
His goodness and his praise.

731. C. M. ANONYMOUS.

Spring.

1 WHEN brighter suns and milder skies
Proclaim the opening year,
What various sounds of joy arise!
What prospects bright appear!

2 Earth and her thousand voices give
Their thousand notes of praise;
And all, that by his mercy live,
To God their offering raise.

3 The streams, all beautiful and bright,
Reflect the morning sky;
And there, with music in his flight,
The wild bird soars on high.

4 Thus, like the morning, calm and clear,
That saw the Saviour rise,
The spring of heaven's eternal year
Shall dawn on earth and skies.

5 No winter there, no shades of night,
Obscure those mansions blest,
Where, in the happy fields of light,
The weary are at rest.

732. C. M. STEELE.

Spring.

1 WHEN verdure clothes the fertile vale,
And blossoms deck the spray,
And fragrance breathes in every gale,
How sweet the vernal day!

2 Hark! how the feathered warblers sing!
'T is nature's cheerful voice;
Soft music hails the lovely spring,
And woods and fields rejoice.

3 O God of nature and of grace,
Thy heavenly gifts impart;
Then shall my meditation trace
Spring, blooming in my heart.

4 Inspired to praise, I then shall join
Glad nature's cheerful song,
And love and gratitude divine
Attune my joyful tongue.

733. S. M. ANONYMOUS.

The Seasons. Summer.

1 GREAT God, at thy command
Seasons in order rise:
Thy power and love in concert reign
Through earth, and seas, and skies.

2 How balmy is the air!
How warm the sun's bright beams!
While, to refresh the ground, the rains
Descend in gentle streams.

3 With grateful praise we own
Thy providential hand,
While grass, and herbs, and waving corn,
Adorn and bless the land.

4 But greater still the gift
Of thy belovéd Son;
By him forgiveness, peace, and joy,
Through endless ages run.

734. 7 & 6s. M. BRITISH MAGAZINE.

Autumn.

1 THE leaves around me falling
Are preaching of decay;

The hollow winds are calling,
  "Come, pilgrim, come away":
The day, in night declining,
  Says I must, too, decline;
The year its bloom resigning,
  Its lot foreshadows mine.

2 The light my path surrounding,
  The loves to which I cling,
The hopes within me bounding,
  The joys that round me wing,—
All, all, like stars at even,
  Just gleam and shoot away,
Pass on before to heaven,
  And chide at my delay.

3 The friends gone there before me
  Are calling from on high,
And happy angels o'er me
  Tempt sweetly to the sky:
"Why wait," they say, "and wither
  'Mid scenes of death and sin?
O, rise to glory, hither,
  And find true life begin."

735. C. M. ANONYMOUS

Harvest.

1 TO praise the bounteous Lord of all,
  Wake all our thankful powers;
He calls, and at his call come forth
  The smiling harvest hours.

2 His covenant with the earth he keeps;
  His goodness we will sing;
Summer and winter know their time,
  And harvest crowns the spring.

3 Teach us, O gracious God, to sow
  The seeds of righteousness;

Shine on our souls, and with thy beams
  The ripening harvest bless.

736. C. M. Steele

Winter.

1 STERN Winter throws his icy chains,
  Encircling nature round;
How bleak, how comfortless, the plains,
  Late with gay verdure crowned!

2 The sun withholds his vital beams,
  And light and warmth depart;
And drooping, lifeless nature seems
  An emblem of my heart.

3 Return, O blissful sun, and bring
  Thy soul-reviving ray;
This mental winter shall be spring,
  This darkness, cheerful day.

4 O happy state! divine abode,
  Where spring eternal reigns,
And perfect day, the smile of God,
  Fills all the heavenly plains.

5 Great Source of light, thy beams display,
  My drooping joys restore,
And guide me to the seats of day,
  Where winter frowns no more.

737. C. M. Watts

Winter.

1 THE hoary frost, the fleecy snow,
  Descend and clothe the ground;
The liquid streams forbear to flow,
  In icy fetters bound.

2 When, from his dreadful stores on high,
  God pours the sounding hail,
The man that does his power defy
  Shall find his courage fail.

3 God sends his word, and melts the snow ,
The fields no longer mourn ;
He calls the warmer gales to blow,
And bids the spring return.

4 The changing wind, the flying cloud,
Obey his mighty word ;
With songs and honors sounding loud,
Praise ye the sovereign Lord.

738. S. M. MONTGOMERY

Seed-time.

1 SOW in the morn thy seed ;
At eve hold not thy hand ;
To doubt and fear give thou no heed ;
Broadcast it o'er the land ; —

2 And duly shall appear,
In verdure, beauty, strength,
The tender blade, the stalk, the ear,
And the full corn at length.

3 Thou canst not toil in vain ;
Cold, heat, and moist, and dry
Shall foster and mature the grair
For garners in the sky.

4 Thence, when the glorious end,
The day of God, shall come,
The angel-reapers shall descend,
And heaven cry, " Harvest home ! "

739. H. M. FREEMAN

Imitation of Thompson's Hymn on the Seasons.

1 LORD of the worlds below !
On earth thy glories shine ;
The changing seasons show
Thy skill and power divine.
The rolling years
Are full of thee ;
In all we see
A God appears.

2 Forth in the flowery spring,
We see thy beauty move ;
The birds on branches sing
Thy tenderness and love ;
Wide flush the hills ; | Devotion's calm
The air is balm ; | Our bosom fills.

3 Then come, in robes of light,
The summer's flaming days ;
The sun thine image bright,
Thy majesty, displays ;
And oft thy voice | But still our souls
In thunder rolls ; | In thee rejoice.

4 In autumn, a rich feast
Thy common bounty gives
To man, and bird, and beast,
And every thing that lives.
Thy liberal care | And harvest moon,
At morn and noon, | Our lips declare.

5 In winter, awful thou !
With storms around thee cast ;
The leafless forests bow
Beneath thy northern blast.
While tempests lower | We homage bring,
To thee, dread King, | And own thy power.

740. 7s. M. BARBAULD

The Seasons.

1 PRAISE to God, immortal praise,
For the love that crowns our days !
Bounteous Source of every joy,
Let thy praise our tongues employ.

2 All that Spring, with bounteous hand,
Scatters o'er the smiling land, —
All that liberal Autumn pours
From her rich, o'erflowing stores, —

3 These to that dear Source we owe
Whence our sweetest comforts flow ,
These, through all my happy days,
Claim my cheerful songs of praise.

4 Lord, to thee my soul should raise
Grateful, never-ending praise,
And, when every blessing 's flown,
Love thee for thyself alone.

741. C. M. WATTS

The Blessing of Rain.

1 'T IS by thy strength the mountains stand,
God of eternal power ;
The sea grows calm at thy command,
And tempests cease to roar.

2 Thy morning light and evening shade
Successive comforts bring ;
Thy plenteous fruits make harvest glad,
Thy flowers adorn the spring.

3 Seasons and times, and moons and hours,
Heaven, earth, and air are thine ;
When clouds distil in fruitful showers,
The Author is divine.

4 Those wandering cisterns in the sky,
Borne by the winds around,
With watery treasures well supply
The furrows of the ground.

5 The thirsty ridges drink their fill,
And ranks of corn appear ;
Thy ways abound with blessings still,
Thy goodness crowns the year.

742. 8s. M. HAWES.

Spring.

1 THE winter is over and gone,
The thrush whistles sweet on the spray,

The turtle breathes forth her soft moan,
The lark mounts and warbles away

2 Shall every creature around
Their voices in concert unite,
And I, the most favored, be found
In praising to take less delight ?

3 Awake, then, my harp, and my lute !
Sweet organs your notes softly swell !
No longer my lips shall be mute,
The Saviour's high praises to tell.

4 His love in my heart shed abroad,
My graces shall bloom as the spring ,
This temple, his spirit's abode ;
My joy as my duty to sing.

NATIONAL HYMNS.

743. C. M. Wrefor

Prayer for our Country.

1 LORD, while for all mankind we pray,
Of every clime and coast,
O, hear us for our native land, —
The land we love the most.

2 O, guard our shores from every foe,
With peace our borders bless,
With prosperous times our cities crown,
Our fields with plenteousness.

3 Unite us in the sacred love
Of knowledge, truth, and thee ;
And let our hills and valleys shout
The songs of liberty.

4 Here may religion pure and mild
Smile on our Sabbath hours ;

And piety and virtue bless
The home of us and ours.

5 Lord of the nations, thus to thee
Our country we commend ;
Be thou her refuge and her trust,
Her everlasting friend.

744. L. M. PRESBYTERIAN COLL

God acknowledged in National Blessings.

1 GREAT God of nations, now to thee
Our hymn of gratitude we raise ;
With humble heart and bending knee,
We offer thee our song of praise.

2 Thy name we bless, Almighty God,
For all the kindness thou hast shown
To this fair land the pilgrims trod, —
This land we fondly call our own.

3 Here Freedom spreads her banner wide,
And casts her soft and hallowed ray ;
Here thou our fathers' steps didst guide
In safety through their dangerous way.

4 We praise thee that the gospel's light
Through all our land its radiance sheds,
Dispels the shades of error's night,
And heavenly blessings round us spreads.

5 Great God, preserve us in thy fear ;
In dangers still our guardian be ;
O, spread thy truth's bright precepts here ;
Let all the people worship thee.

745. L. M. FLINT

Remembrance of our Fathers.

1 IN pleasant lands have fallen the lines
That bound our goodly heritage,
And safe beneath our sheltering vines
Our youth is blest, and soothed our age.

2 What thanks, O God, to thee are due,
That thou didst plant our fathers here,
And watch and guard them as they grew, —
A vineyard to the Planter dear!

3 The toils they bore our ease have wrought,
They sowed in tears, in joy we reap;
The birthright they so dearly bought
We 'll guard till we with them shall sleep.

4 Thy kindness to our fathers shown,
In weal and woe, through all the past,
Their grateful sons, O God, shall own,
While here their name and race shall last.

746. L. M. 6 L. G. Mellen

The Pilgrims.

1 FROM stern oppression's haughty land
The pilgrims crossed the boisterous wave,
A patient, firm, and patriot band;
The God of battles made them brave:
O, make us ever blest and free,
A land of peace and liberty.

2 To thee, their steadfast, suppliant eyes
Were raised 'mid war and dread alarm;
O God of battles, from the skies
Thy mercy sent the conquering arm;
Still guard our freedom, rights, and fame,
While we exalt thy holy name.

3 Here we, the children of the free,
Now gladly chant the joyful song,
And own our boundless debt to thee,
Which time shall gladly bear along.
Be this our universal cry,
For God, for home, for liberty.

747. 6 & 4s. M. ANONYMOUS

Prayer for our Country.

1 GOD bless our native land!
Firm may she ever stand
Through storm and night!
When the wild tempests rave,
Ruler of winds and wave!
Do thou our country save,
By thy great might.

For her our prayer shall rise
To God above the skies;
On him we wait;
Thou who hast heard each sigh
Watching each weeping eye,
Be thou for ever nigh; —
God save the state!

748. C. M. ANONYMOUS

God's Kindness to our Forefathers.

1 TO Him from whom our blessings flow,
Who all our wants supplies,
This day the choral song and vow
From grateful hearts shall rise.

2 'T was he who led the pilgrim band
Across the stormy sea;
'T was he who stayed the tyrant's hand,
And set our country free,

3 When shivering on a strand unknown,
In sickness and distress,
Our fathers looked to God alone,
To save, protect, and bless.

4 Be thou our nation's strength and shield,
In manhood as in youth;
Thine arm for our protection wield,
And guide us by thy truth.

749. 6 & 4s. M. S. F. Smith.

National Hymn.

1 MY country, 't is of thee,
Sweet land of liberty,
Of thee I sing ;
Land where my fathers died,
Land of the pilgrim's pride,
From every mountain side
Let freedom ring.

2 My native country, thee —
Land of the noble, free —
Thy name — I love ;
I love thy rocks and rills,
Thy woods and templed hills ;
My heart with rapture thrills
Like that above.

3 Let music swell the breeze,
And ring from all the trees
Sweet freedom's song ;
Let mortal tongues awake ;
Let all that breathe partake ;
Let rocks their silence break, —
The sound prolong.

4 Our fathers' God, to thee,
Author of liberty,
To thee we sing :
Long may our land be bright
With freedom's holy light ;
Protect us by thy might,
Great God, our King.

750. L. M. Whittier

National Anniversary.

1 O THOU, whose presence went before
Our fathers in their weary way,

As with thy chosen moved of yore
  The fire by night, the cloud by day!

2 When from each temple of the free
  A nation's song ascends to heaven,
Most holy Father, unto thee
  Now let our humble prayer be given.

3 Sweet peace is here; and hope and love
  Are round us as a mantle thrown,
And unto thee, supreme above,
  The knee of prayer is bowed alone.

4 And grant, O Father, that the time
  Of earth's deliverance may be near,
When every land and tongue and clime
  The message of thy love shall hear, —

5 When, smitten as with fire from heaven,
  The captive's chain shall sink in dust,
And to his fettered soul be given
  The glorious freedom of the just.

751. 8 & 7s. M. PIERPONT

Anniversary Hymn.

1 GOD of mercy, do thou never
  From our offering turn away,
But command a blessing ever
  On the memory of this day.

2 Light and peace do thou ordain it;
  O'er it be no shadow flung,
Let no deadly darkness stain it,
  And no clouds be o'er it hung.

3 May the song this people raises,
  And its vows to thee addressed,
Mingle with the prayers and praises,
  That thou hearest from the blest.

4 When the lips are cold that sing thee,
  And the hearts that love thee dust,

Father, then our souls shall bring thee
Holier love and firmer trust.

752. L. M. WHITTIER

Freedom.

1 O HOLY Father, just and true
Are all thy works and words and ways,
And unto thee alone are due
Thanksgiving and eternal praise!
As children of thy gracious care,
We veil the eye, — we bend the knee, -
With broken words of praise and prayer,
Father and God, we come to thee.

2 For thou hast heard, O God of right,
The sighing of the hapless slave;
And stretched for him the arm of might,
Not shortened that it could not save.
The laborer sits beneath his vine,
The shackled soul and hand are free; -
Thanksgiving! — for the work is thine!
Praise! — for the blessing is of thee.

3 Speed on thy work, Lord God of hosts!
And when the bondsman's chain is riven,
And swells from all our country's coasts
The anthem of the free to heaven,
O, not to those whom thou hast led,
As with thy cloud and fire before,
But unto thee, in fear and dread,
Be praise and glory evermore.

753. C. M. C. SPRAGUE

The Pilgrims.

1 OUR fathers, Lord, to seek a spot
Where they might kneel to thee,
Their own fair heritage forgot,
And braved an unknown sea.

2 Here found their pilgrim souls repose
  Where long the heathen roved;
And here their humble anthems rose
  To bless the Power they loved.

3 They sleep in dust, — but where they trod,
  A feeble, fainting band,
Glad millions catch the strain, O God,
  And sound it through the land.

754. L. M. W. P. LUNT.

Our Forefathers.

1 WHEN, driven by oppression's rod,
  Our fathers fled beyond the sea,
Their care was first to honor God,
  And next to leave their children free.

2 Above the forest's gloomy shade
  The altar and the school appeared;
On that the gifts of faith were laid,
  In this their precious hopes were reared.

3 Armed with intelligence and zeal,
  Their sons shook off the tyrant's chain,
The rights of freemen quick to feel,
  And nobly daring to maintain.

4 The altar and the school still stand,
  The sacred pillars of our trust,
And freedom's sons shall fill the land
  When we are sleeping in the dust.

5 Before thine altar, Lord, we bend,
  With grateful song and fervent prayer,
For thou who wast our fathers' friend
  Wilt make our offspring still thy care.

755. L. M. 6 L. H. WARE, JR

The God of our Fathers.

1 LIKE Israel's hosts to exile driven,
  Across the flood the pilgrims fled;

Their hands bore up the ark of Heaven,
And Heaven their trusting footsteps led,
Till on these savage shores they trod,
And won the wilderness for God.

2 Then, where their weary ark found rest,
Another Zion proudly grew;
In more than Judah's glory dressed,
With light that Israel never knew.
From sea to sea her empire spread,
Her temple Heaven, and Christ her head.

3 Then let the grateful Church to-day
Its ancient rite with gladness keep;
And still our fathers' God display
His kindness, though the fathers sleep.
O, bless, as thou hast blessed the past,
While earth, and time, and heaven shall last.

756. P. M. H. WARE, JR

The Progress of Freedom.

1 OPPRESSION shall not always reign;
There comes a brighter day,
When freedom, burst from every chain,
Shall have triumphant way.
Then right shall over might prevail,
And truth, like hero armed in mail,
The hosts of tyrant wrong assail,
And hold eternal sway.

2 What voice shall bid the progress stay
Of truth's victorious car?
What arm arrest the growing day,
Or quench the solar star?
What reckless soul, though stout and strong,
Shall dare bring back the ancient wrong,
Oppression's guilty night prolong,
And freedom's morning bar?

3 The hour of triumph comes apace,
The fated, promised hour,
When earth upon a ransomed race
Her bounteous gifts shall shower.
Ring, Liberty, thy glorious bell!
Bid high thy sacred banner swell!
Let trump on trump the triumph tell
Of Heaven's redeeming power.

757. L. M. C. SPRAGUE.

For the Blessing of Schools.

1 O THOU, at whose dread name we bend,
To whom our purest vows we pay,
God over all, in love descend,
And bless the labors of this day.

2 Our fathers here, a pilgrim band,
Fixed the proud empire of the free;
Art moved in gladness o'er the land,
And Faith her altars reared to thee.

3 Here, too, to guard, through every age,
The sacred rights their valor won,
They bade instruction spread her page,
And send down truth from sire to son.

4 Here still, through all succeeding time,
Their stores may truth and learning bring,
And still the anthem-note sublime
To thee from children's children sing.

DEDICATION AND ORDINATION.

758. L. M. PIERPONT

Dedication of a House of Worship.

1 O, BOW thine ear, Eternal One !
On thee our heart adoring calls ;
To thee the followers of thy Son
Have raised and now devote these walls.

2 Here let thy holy days be kept ;
And be this place to worship given,
Like that bright spot where Jacob slept,
The house of God, the gate of heaven.

3 Here may thine honor dwell ; and here,
As incense, let thy children's prayer,
From contrite hearts and lips sincere,
Rise on the still and holy air.

4 Here be thy praise devoutly sung ;
Here let thy truth beam forth to save,
As when, of old, thy spirit hung,
On wings of light, o'er Jordan's wave.

5 And when the lips, that with thy name
Are vocal now, to dust shall turn,
On others may devotion's flame
Be kindled here, and purely burn !

759. C. M. BRYANT

Dedication Hymn.

1 O THOU, whose own vast temple stands,
Built over earth and sea,
Accept the walls that human hands
Have raised to worship thee.

2 Lord, from thine inmost glory send,
Within these courts to bide,

The peace that dwelleth, without end,
  Serenely by thy side.

3 May erring minds that worship here
  Be taught the better way,
And they who mourn, and they who fear,
  Be strengthened as they pray !

4 May faith grow firm, and love grow warm,
  And pure devotion rise,
While round these hallowed walls the storm
  Of earth-born passion dies !

760. L. M. WILLIS.

Dedication Hymn.

1 THE perfect world, by Adam trod,
Was the first temple, — built by God ;
His fiat laid the corner-stone,
And heaved its pillars, one by one.

2 He hung its starry roof on high, —
The broad, illimitable sky ;
He spread its pavement, green and bright,
And curtained it with morning light.

3 The mountains in their places stood, —
The sea, the sky, — and "all was good" ;
And, when its first pure praises rang,
The "morning stars together sang."

4 Lord ! 't is not ours to make the sea,
And earth, and sky a house for thee ;
But in thy sight our offering stands,
A humbler temple, "made with hands."

761. H. M. FRANCIS.

Prayer for God's Presence and Blessing.

1 GREAT King of glory, come,
  And with thy favor crown
This temple as thy home,
  This people as thine own :

Beneath this roof, O, deign to show
How God can dwell with men below.

2 Here may thine ears attend
Our interceding cries,
And grateful praise ascend,
Like incense to the skies :
Here may thy word melodious sound,
And spread celestial joys around.

3 Here may our unborn sons
And daughters sound thy praise,
And shine, like polished stones,
Through long-succeeding days :
Here, Lord, display thy saving power,
While temples stand and men adore.

4 Here may the listening throng
Imbibe thy truth and love ;
Here Christians join the song
Of seraphim above ;
Till all, who humbly seek thy face,
Rejoice in thy abounding grace.

762. L. M. MONTGOMERY

A blessing implored.

1 HERE, in thy name, Eternal God,
We build this earthly house for thee ;
O, choose it for thy fixed abode,
And guard it long from error free.

2 Here, when thy people seek thy face,
And dying sinners pray to live,
Hear thou, in heaven, thy dwelling-place,
And when thou hearest, Lord, forgive.

3 Here, when thy messengers proclaim
The blesséd gospel of thy Son,
Still by the power of his great name
Be mighty signs and wonders done.

4 When children's voices raise the song,
Hosanna! to their Heavenly King,
Let heaven with earth the strain prolong;
Hosanna! let the angels sing.

5 But will, indeed, Jehovah deign
Here to abide, no transient guest?
Here will our great Redeemer reign,
And here the Holy Spirit rest?

6 Thy glory never hence depart;
Yet choose not, Lord, this house alone;
Thy kingdom come to every heart;
In every bosom fix thy throne.

763. 7s. M. MONTGOMERY

The House of Prayer and Praise.

1 LORD of hosts, to thee we raise
Here a house of prayer and praise;
Thou thy people's hearts prepare
Here to meet for praise and prayer.

2 Let the living here be fed
With thy word, the heavenly bread;
Here, in hope of glory blest,
May the dead be laid to rest; —

3 Here to thee a temple stand,
While the sea shall gird the land;
Here reveal thy mercy sure,
While the sun and moon endure.

4 Hallelujah! — earth and sky
To the joyful sound reply;
Hallelujah! — hence ascend
Prayer and praise till time shall end.

764. L. M. MONTGOMERY.

A Pastor welcomed.

1 WE bid thee welcome in the name
Of Jesus, our exalted Head;

Come as a servant ; so he came,
   And we receive thee in his stead.

2 Come as an angel, hence to guide
   A band of pilgrims on their way ;
That, safely walking at thy side,
   We never fail, nor faint, nor stray.

3 Come as a teacher sent from God,
   Charged his whole council to declare ;
Lift o'er our ranks the prophet's rod,
   While we uphold thy hands with prayer

4 Come as a messenger of peace,
   Filled with the Spirit, fired with love ;
Live to behold our large increase,
   And die to meet us all above.

765. 6 & 4s. M. J. Young.

Prayer for a Minister's Success.

1 O HOLY Lord, our God!
By heavenly hosts adored,
   Hear us, we pray ;
To thee the cherubim,
Angels, and seraphim
Unceasing praises bring, —
   Their homage pay.

2 Here give thy word success,
And this thy servant bless, —
   His labors own ;
And while the sinner's Friend
His life and words commend,
Thy Holy Spirit send,
   And make him known.

3 May every passing year
More happy still appear
   Than this glad day ;

With numbers fill the place,
Adorn thy saints with grace;
Thy truth may all embrace,
O Lord! we pray.

4 O Lord, our God! arise;
And now, before our eyes,
Thy arm make bare;
Unite our hearts in love,
Till, raised to heaven above,
We all its goodness prove,
And praise thee there.

766. 8 & 6s. M. S. F. Smith.

Benefits of the Ministry.

1 BLEST is the hour when cares depart,
And earthly scenes are far, —
When tears of woe forget to start,
And gently dawns upon the heart
Devotion's holy star.

2 Blest is the place where angels bend
To hear our worship rise,
Where kindred thoughts their musings blend,
And all the soul's affections tend
Beyond the veiling skies.

3 Blest are the hallowed vows that bind
Man to his work of love, —
Bind him to cheer the humble mind,
Console the weeping, lead the blind,
And guide to joys above.

4 Sweet shall the song of glory swell,
Spirit divine, to thee,
When they whose work is finished well
In thy own courts of rest shall dwell,
Blest through eternity.

767. L. M. PIERPONT

Ordination Hymn.

1 O THOU, who art above all height!
Our God, our Father, and our Friend!
Beneath thy throne of love and light,
Let thine adoring children bend.

2 We kneel in praise, that here is set
A vine that by thy culture grew;
We kneel in prayer, that thou wouldst wet
Its opening leaves with heavenly dew.

3 Since thy young servant now hath given
Himself, his powers, his hopes, his youth
To the great cause of truth and heaven,
Be thou his guide, O God of truth!

4 Here may his doctrines drop like rain,
His speech like Hermon's dew distil,
Till green fields smile, and golden grain,
Ripe for the harvest, waits thy will.

5 And when he sinks in death, — by care,
Or pain, or toil, or years oppressed, —
O God! remember then our prayer,
And take his spirit to thy rest.

768. 7s. M. E. PEABODY

Ordination.

1 LIFT aloud the voice of praise!
God, our Father and our Friend,
Hear the prayer and song we raise,
Weak yet trusting we would bend.

2 Lo! another servant brought
To the heritage of God; —
May he teach as Christ hath taught,
Tread the path his Saviour trod.

3 To the vineyard may he come
Girded with celestial might:

Skilled to draw thy children home,
  Taught to give the darkened light.

4 Unto thee a people bend, —
  Bind us heart to heart in love ;
Flock and pastor, we would tend
  Ever toward our home above.

769. L. M. H. WARE, JR

Ordination or Installation.

1 O THOU, who on thy chosen Son
  Didst send thy spirit like a dove,
To mark the long expected one,
  And seal the messenger of love ;

2 And when the heralds of his name
  Went forth, his glorious truth to spread,
Didst send it down in tongues of flame
  To hallow each devoted head.

3 So, Lord, thy servant now inspire
  With holy unction from above ;
Give him the tongue of living fire,
  Give him the temper of the dove.

4 Lord, hear thy suppliant church to-day ;
  Accept our work, our souls possess,
'T is ours to labor, watch, and pray ;
  Be thine to cheer, sustain and bless.

CHARITABLE AND MISSIONARY MEETINGS.

770. L. M. 6 L. J. TAYLOR.

For a charitable Occasion.

1 O YE who seek Jehovah's face,
  Bow at his throne, and feel his grace,

Who ask in prayer, and own in praise,
That bounteous love which gilds your days,
Catch from above the hallowed flame,
And dignify the Christian name.

2 Where'er distress and pain appear,
Let pity's ready hand be there ;
With cheering wine and fragrant oil,
Bid languor glow and anguish smile ;
Though woe her lowliest form may wear,
Yet God has stamped his image there.

3 When he, the sovereign Judge, draws nigh,
And holds th' unerring beam on high,
Then shall sweet charity prevail,
And angels mark the sinking scale ;
Jesus shall call his followers home : —
" Ye blessèd of my Father, come ! "

771. C. M. BODEN'S COLL.

Kindness to the Afflicted.

1 BRIGHT Source of everlasting love,
To thee our souls we raise,
And to thy sovereign bounty rear
A monument of praise.

2 Thy mercy gilds the path of life
With every cheering ray,
And kindly checks the rising tear,
Or wipes that tear away.

3 What shall we render, bounteous Lord,
For all the grace we see ?
The goodness feeble man can yield
Extendeth not to thee.

4 To scenes of woe, to beds of pain,
We 'll cheerfully repair,
And, with the gifts thy hand bestows,
Relieve the sufferers there.

5 The widow's heart shall sing for joy ;
The orphan shall be glad ;
And hungering souls we 'll gladly point
To Christ, the living bread.

772. L. M. WATTS

The Rewards of Beneficence.

1 BLEST is the man, whose heart is kind,
And melts in pity to the poor ;
Who, with a sympathizing mind,
Feels what his fellow-men endure.

2 His heart contrives for their relief
More good than his own hands can do ;
He, in the time of general grief,
Shall find the Lord hath pity too.

3 This man shall live secure on earth
With secret blessings on his head,
While sword, or pestilence, or dearth
Around him multiply their dead.

4 Or if with mortal sufferings tried,
Sufferings shall all his soul refine ;
Sweet hope his refuge shall provide,
And minister a bliss divine.

773. C. M. BROWNE

For a charitable Occasion.

1 O, HOW can they look up to heaven,
And ask for mercy there,
Who never soothed the poor man's pang,
Nor dried the orphan's tear !

2 The dread Omnipotence of heaven
We every hour provoke ;
Yet still the mercy of our God
Withholds th' avenging stroke.

3 And Christ was still the healing Friend
Of poverty and pain,

And never did imploring wretch
His garment touch in vain.

4 May we with humble effort take
Example from above,
And thence the active lesson learn
Of charity and love.

5 But chiefly be the labor ours
To shade the early plant;
To guard from ignorance and guilt
The infancy of want.

774. 8 & 7s. M. PIERPONT

For a Benevolent Society.

1 MIGHTY One, whose name is Holy,
Thou wilt save thy work alive;
And the spirit of the lowly
Thou wilt visit and revive.
What thy prophets thus have spoken,
Ages witness as they roll;
Bleeding hearts and spirits broken
Touched by thee, O God, are whole

2 By thy pitying spirit guided,
Jesus sought the sufferer's door,
Comforts for the poor provided,
And the mourner's sorrows bore.
So, it was thy spirit beaming
In his face whose name we bear,
That sustained him, while redeeming
Power's pale victims from despair.

3 To the prisoner, wan and wasting
In the voiceless dungeon's night,
He thine own apostle hasting,
Led him forth, unbound, to light.
So thy mercy's angel, bending,
Heard a friendless prisoner call,

And, through night's cold vault descending,
Loosed from chains thy servant Paul.

4 Father, as thy love is endless,
Working by thy servants thus,
The forsaken and the friendless
Deign to visit, e'en by us.
So shall each, with spirit fervent
Laboring with thee here below,
Be declared thy faithful servant,
Where there 's neither want nor woe.

775. C. M. ANONYMOUS

The Orphan's Hymn.

1 WHERE shall the child of sorrow find
A place for calm repose?
Thou Father of the fatherless,
Pity the orphan's woes!

2 What friend have I in heaven or earth,
What friend to trust but thee?
My father 's dead, — my mother 's dead:
My God! "remember me."

3 Thy gracious promise now fulfil,
And bid my trouble cease;
In thee the fatherless shall find
Pure mercy, grace, and peace.

4 I 've not a secret care or pain
But he that secret knows;
Thou Father of the fatherless,
Pity the orphan's woes!

776. 7 & 6s. M. HEBER.

Missionary Hymn.

1 FROM Greenland's icy mountains,
From India's coral strand, —
Where Afric's sunny fountains
Roll down their golden sand, —

From many an ancient river,
From many a palmy plain,—
They call us to deliver
Their land from error's chain.

2 What though the spicy breezes
Blow soft o'er Ceylon's isle;
Though every prospect pleases,
And only man is vile;
In vain, with lavish kindness,
The gifts of God are strown;
The heathen, in his blindness,
Bows down to wood and stone.

3 Shall we, whose souls are lighted
By wisdom from on high,
Shall we to men benighted
The lamp of life deny?
Salvation! O, salvation!
The joyful sound proclaim,
Till each remotest nation
Has learnt Messiah's name.

777. L. M. WATTS

Universal Reign of Christ.

1 GREAT God, whose universal sway
The known and unknown worlds obey,
Now give the kingdom to thy Son,
Extend his power, exalt his throne.

2 The heathen lands, that lie beneatn
The shades of overspreading death,
Revive at his first dawning light,
And deserts blossom at the sight.

3 The saints shall flourish in his days,
Dressed in the robes of joy and praise;
Peace, like a river, from his throne,
Shall flow to nations yet unknown.

778. L. M. A. Balfour.

The Missionary charged and encouraged.

1 GO, messenger of peace and love,
To people plunged in shades of night;
Like angels sent from fields above,
Be thine to shed celestial light.

2 Go to the hungry, — food impart;
To paths of peace the wanderer guide;
And lead the thirsty, panting heart
Where streams of living water glide.

3 Go, bid the bright and morning star
From Bethlehem's plains resplendent shine.
And, piercing through the gloom afar,
Shed heavenly light and love divine.

4 O, faint not in the day of toil,
When harvest waits the reaper's hand;
Go, gather in the glorious spoil,
And joyous in his presence stand.

5 Thy love a rich reward shall find
From Him who sits enthroned on high;
For they who turn the erring mind
Shall shine like stars above the sky.

779. 8 & 9s. M. Sacred Songs

Death of a Missionary.

1 WEEP not for the saint that ascends
To partake of the joys of the sky;
Weep not for the seraph that bends
With the worshipping chorus on high;
Weep not for the spirit now crowned
With the garland to martyrdom given;
O, weep not for him; he has found
His reward and his refuge in heaven.

2 But weep fer their sorrows who stand
And lament o'er the dead by his grave;

Who sigh when they muse on the land
  Of their home far away o'er the wave ;
And weep for the nations that dwell
  Where the light of the truth never shone,
Where anthems of peace never swell,
  And the love of the Lord is unknown.

780. L. M. SHRUBSOLE.

Divine Power supplicated.

1 ARM of the Lord, awake, awake ;
Put on thy strength, the nations shake ;
Now let the world, adoring, see
Triumphs of mercy wrought by thee

2 Say to the heathen from thy throne,
"I am Jehovah, God alone":
Thy voice their idols shall confound,
And cast their altars to the ground.

3 Let Zion's time of favor come ;
O, bring the tribes of Israel home :
Soon may our wondering eyes behold
Gentiles and Jews in Jesus' fold.

4 Almighty God, thy grace proclaim
Through every clime, of every name ,
Let adverse powers before thee fall,
And crown the Saviour Lord of all.

781. 10s. M. [illegible]

Gentiles coming into the Church.

1 RISE, crowned with light, imperial Salem rise :
Exalt thy towering head, and lift thine eyes ,
See heaven its sparkling portals wide display,
And break upon thee in a flood of day.

2 See a long race thy spacious courts adorn ;
See future sons and daughters, yet unborn,
In crowding ranks on every side arise,
Demanding life, impatient for the skies.

3 See barbarous nations at thy gates attend,
Walk in thy light, and in thy temple bend ;
See thy bright altars thronged with prostrate kings,
While every land its joyous tribute brings.

4 The seas shall waste, the skies to smoke decay,
Rocks fall to dust, and mountains melt away ;
But fixed his word, his saving power remains ;
Thy realm shall last, thy own Messiah reigns.

782. C. M. W. Ward

Prayer for the Success of the Gospel.

1 GREAT God, the nations of the earth
Are by creation thine ;
And in thy works, by all beheld,
Thy radiant glories shine.

2 But, Lord, thy greater love has sent
Thy gospel to mankind,
Unveiling what rich stores of grace
Are treasured in thy mind.

3 O, when shall these glad tidings spread
The spacious earth around,
Till every tribe and every soul
Shall hear the joyful sound ?

4 Smile, Lord, on each divine attempt
To spread the gospel's rays,
And build on sin's demolished throne
The temples of thy praise.

783. 7s. M. Montgomery.

Jubilee Song.

1 HARK ! the song of jubilee,
Loud as mighty thunders roar,
Or the fulness of the sea,
When it breaks upon the shore !

2 See, Jehovah's banner furled ;
Sheathed his sword:—he speaks —'t is done

Now the kingdoms of this world
Are the kingdom of his Son.

3 He shall reign from pole to pole
With supreme, unbounded sway;
He shall reign, when, like a scroll,
Yonder heavens have passed away.

4 Hallelujah! for the Lord
God omnipotent shall reign:
Hallelujah! — let the word
Echo round the earth and main.

5 Hallelujah! hark! the sound,
From the centre to the skies,
Wakes, above, beneath, around,
All creation's harmonies.

784. C. M. NEEDHAM

Prayer for the Spread of the Gospel.

1 GREAT God of grace! arise and shine,
With beams of heavenly light:
From this dark world of sin dispel
The long and gloomy night.

2 No more may senseless idols share
The honors due to thee:
May every nation know thy name,
And thy salvation see.

3 No more may persecution dare
To lift her iron rod;
No longer shed the blood of saints,
And plead a zeal for God.

4 With its own pure and native light,
Still may thy gospel shine:
And error fly like noxious mists
Before this light divine.

5 While heaven-born truth her charms reveals,
May love each breast inspire;

Nor one base passion ever mix,
To quench this sacred fire.

785. 7 & 6s. M. Lyte.

The Salvation of Israel.

1 O, THAT the Lord's salvation
Were out of Zion come,
To heal his ancient nation,
To lead his outcasts home !

2 How long the holy city
Shall heathen feet profane ?
Return, O Lord, in pity ;
Rebuild her walls again.

3 Let fall thy rod of terror ;
Thy saving grace impart ;
Roll back the veil of error ;
Release the fettered heart.

4 Let Israel, home returning,
Her lost Messiah see ;
Give oil of joy for mourning,
And bind thy church to thee.

786. C. P. M. Episcopal Coll.

On Western Missions.

1 WHEN, Lord, to this our western land,
Led by thy providential hand,
Our wandering fathers came,
Their ancient homes, their friends in youth,
Sent forth the heralds of thy truth,
To keep them in thy name.

2 Then, through our solitary coast,
The desert features soon were lost ;
Thy temples there arose ;
Our shores, as culture made them fair,
Were hallowed by thy rites, by prayer,
And blossomed as the rose.

3 And, O, may we repay this debt
To regions solitary yet
Within our spreading land!
There brethren, from our common home,
Still westward, like our fathers, roam,
Still guided by thy hand.

4 Father, we own this debt of love;
O, shed thy spirit from above,
To move each Christian breast,
Till heralds shall thy truth proclaim,
And temples rise, to fix thy name,
Through all our boundless West!

787. C. M. S. W. LIVERMORE.

The Western Churches.

1 OUR pilgrim brethren dwelling far,—
O God of truth and love,
Light thou their path with thine own star,
Bright beaming from above.

2 Wide as their mighty rivers flow,
Let thine own truth extend;
Where prairies spread and forests grow,
O Lord, thy gospel send.

3 Then will a mighty nation own
A union firm and strong;—
The sceptre of th' eternal throne
Shall rule its councils long.

788. L. M. EPISCOPAL CO

For Laborers in God's Harvest.

1 O SPIRIT of the living God,
In all thy plenitude of grace,
Where'er the foot of man hath trod,
Descend on our degenerate race!

2 Give tongues of fire and hearts of love,
To preach the reconciling word;

Give power and unction from above,
Where'er the joyful sound is heard.

3 Be darkness, at thy coming, light;
Confusion, order, in thy path;
Souls without strength inspire with might;
Bid mercy triumph over wrath.

4 Convert the nations; far and nigh,
The triumphs of the cross record;
The name of Jesus glorify,
Till every people call him Lord.

789. L. M. VOKE.

For the Spread of the Gospel.

1 EXERT thy power, thy rights maintain,
Almighty, Everlasting King!
The influence of thy crown increase,
And strangers to thy footstool bring.

2 In one vast symphony of praise,
Gentile and Jew shall then unite;
And unbelief no longer reign,
But sink in shades of endless night.

3 Then Afric's liberated sons
Shall chant to Asia's rapturous song,
Europe resound her Saviour's fame,
And western climes the notes prolong.

4 To every land beneath the sun
Immanuel's kingdom shall extend;
And every man in every clime
Shall meet a brother and a friend.

790. L. M. WINCHELL'S SEL

Missionaries encouraged.

1 YE Christian heralds,—go, proclaim
Salvation in Immanuel's name;
To distant climes the tidings bear,
And plant the rose of Sharon there

2 He 'll shield you with a wall of fire,
With holy zeal your hearts inspire,
Bid raging winds their fury cease,
And calm the savage breast to peace.

3 And when our labors all are o'er,
Then shall we meet to part no more, —
Meet, with the ransomed throng to fall,
And crown the Saviour Lord of all.

791. 7s. M. BRYANT.

A Blessing invoked on Christian Teachers.

1 MIGHTY One, before whose face
Wisdom had her glorious seat,
When the orbs that people space
Sprang to birth beneath thy feet;

2 Source of truth, whose rays alone
Light the mighty world of mind;
God of love, who from thy throne
Kindly watchest all mankind;

3 Shed on those, who in thy name
Teach the way of truth and right,
Shed that love's undying flame,
Shed that wisdom's guiding light

SEAMEN'S HYMNS.

792. L. M. WATTS.

The Seaman's Song.

1 WOULD you behold the works of God,
His wonders in the world abroad?
With hardy mariners survey
The unknown regions of the sea.

2 They leave their native shores behind,
And seize the favor of the wind;

Till God command, and tempests rise,
That heave the ocean to the skies.

3 When land is far and death is nigh,
Bereaved of hope, to God they cry:
His mercy hears their loud address,
And sends salvation in distress.

4 He bids the winds their wrath assuage,
And stormy tempests cease to rage;
The grateful band their fears give o'er,
And hail with joy their native shore.

5 O, may the sons of men record
The wondrous goodness of the Lord;
Let them their purest offerings bring,
And in the church his glory sing.

793. C. M. ADDISON.

The Christian Mariner safe.

1 HOW are thy servants blest, O Lord!
How sure is thy defence!
Eternal Wisdom is their guide,
Their help, Omnipotence.

2 In foreign realms, and lands remote,
Supported by thy care,
Through burning climes they pass unhurt,
And breathe in tainted air.

3 When by the dreadful tempest borne
High on the broken wave,
They know thou art not slow to hear,
Nor impotent to save.

4 The storm is laid; the winds retire,
Obedient to thy will;
The sea, that roars at thy command,
At thy command is still.

5 In midst of dangers, fears, and deaths,
Thy goodness we 'll adore;

We 'll praise thee for thy mercies past,
And humbly hope for more.

794. L. M. L. H. Sigourney

Prayer at Sea.

1 PRAYER may be sweet in cottage homes,
Where sire and child devoutly kneel,
While through the open casement nigh
The vernal blossoms fragrant steal.

2 Prayer may be sweet in stately halls,
Where heart with kindred heart is blent,
And upward to th' eternal throne
The hymn of praise melodious sent.

3 But he who fain would know how warm
The soul's appeal to God may be,
From friends and native land should turn,
A wanderer on the faithless sea ; —

4 Should hear its deep, imploring tone
Rise heavenward o'er the foaming surge,
When billows toss the fragile bark,
And fearful blasts the conflict urge.

5 Naught, naught appears but sea and sky ;
No refuge where the foot may flee :
How will he cast, O Rock divine,
The anchor of his soul on thee !

795. C. M. Madan's Coll.

Thanksgiving for Deliverance in a Storm.

1 OUR little bark, on boisterous seas,
By cruel tempests tossed,
Without one cheerful beam of hope,
Expecting to be lost, —

2 We to the Lord, in humble prayer,
Breathed out our sad distress ;
Though feeble, yet with contrite hearts,
We begged return of peace.

3 Then ceased the stormy winds to blow ,
The surges ceased to roll ;
And soon again a placid sea
Spoke comfort to the soul.

4 O, may our grateful, trembling hearts
Their hallelujahs sing
To him who hath our lives preserved, —
Our Father and our King.

796. L. M. C. Wesley.

The Mariner's Hymn.

1 GLORY to thee, whose powerful word
Bids the tempestuous wind arise ;
Glory to thee, the sovereign Lord
Of air, and earth, and seas, and skies !

2 Let air, and earth, and skies obey,
And seas thine awful will perform ;
From them we learn to own thy sway,
And shout to meet the gathering storm.

3 What though the floods lift up their voice,
Thou hearest, Lord, our louder cry ;
They cannot damp thy children's joys,
Or shake the soul when God is nigh.

4 Roar on, ye waves ! our souls defy
Your roaring to disturb our rest ;
In vain t' impair the calm ye try,
The calm in a believer's breast.

797. C. M. Hemans.

The Seaman's Hymn of Praise.

1 O GOD, thy name they well may praise,
Who to the deep go down,
And trace the wonders of thy ways,
When rocks and billows frown.

2 If glorious be that awful deep,
No human power can bind,

What then art thou, who bidst it keep
Within its bounds confined.

3 Let heaven and earth in praise unite,
Eternal praise to thee,
Whose word can rouse the tempest's might,
Or still the raging sea.

798. C. M. ANONYMOUS

The Sailor's Grave.

1 NOT in the church-yard shall he sleep,
Amid the silent gloom, —
His home was on the mighty deep,
And there shall be his tomb.

2 He loved his own bright, deep blue sea,
O'er it he loved to roam;
And now his winding sheet shall be
That same bright ocean's foam.

3 No village bell shall toll for him
Its mournful, solemn dirge;
The winds shall chant a requiem
To him beneath the surge.

4 For him, break not the grassy turf,
Nor turn the dewy sod;
His dust shall rest beneath the surf,
His spirit with its God.

799. L. M. 6 L. ANONYMOUS

The Mariner's Hymn.

1 LORD of the Sea! — thy potent sway
Old Ocean's wildest waves obey;
The gale that whistles through the shrouds,
The storm that drives the frighted clouds, —
If but thy whisper order peace,
How soon their rude commotions cease!

2 Lord of the Sea! — the silent hour,
And deep, dull calm, confess thy power:

The sun that pours his welcome light,
The moon that makes the dark scene bright,
The guiding star, the favoring wind,
Display a good and sovereign mind.

3 Lord of the Sea! — the seaman keep
From all the dangers of the deep!
When high the white-capped billows rise,
When tempests roar along the skies,
When foes or shoals awaken fear, —
O, in thy mercy be thou near!

4 Lord of the Sea! — when, safe from harm,
The sailor rests in slumbers calm,
May dreams of home his spirit cheer, —
Dreams that shall never false appear;
May thoughts of friends, and peace, and thee,
His solid consolation be!

5 Lord of the Sea! — a sea is life
Of care and sorrow, woe and strife!
With watchful pains we steer along,
To keep the right path, shun the wrong:
God grant, that, after every roam,
We gain an everlasting home!

800. L. M. B. W. Noe

Night at Sea.

1 WHEN restless on my bed I lie,
Still courting sleep, which still will fly,
Then shall reflection's brighter power
Illume the lone and midnight hour.

2 If hushed the breeze, and calm the tide,
Soft will the stream of memory glide;
And all the past, a gentle train,
Waked by remembrance, live again.

3 If loud the wind, the tempest high,
And darkness wraps the sullen sky,

I muse on life's tempestuous sea,
And sigh, O Lord, to come to thee.

4 Tossed on the deep and swelling wave,
O, mark my trembling soul, and save;
Give to my mind that harbour near,
Where thou wilt chase each grief and fear.

801. 8s. M. H. F. GOULD

Hymn at Sea.

1 O THOU who hast spread out the skies,
And measured the depths of the sea,
'Twixt heavens and ocean shall rise
Our incense of praises to thee.

2 We know that thy presence is near
While heaves our bark far from the land;-
We ride o'er the deep without fear;—
The waters are held in thy hand.

3 Eternity comes in the sound
Of billows that never can sleep!
There 's Deity circling us round,—
Omnipotence walks o'er the deep!

4 O Father, our eye is to thee,
As on for the haven we roll;
And faith in our Pilot shall be
An anchor to steady the soul.

802. S. M. S. GRAHAM

A Home everywhere.

1 HEAVE, mighty ocean, heave,
And blow thou boisterous wind,
Onward we swiftly glide, and leave
Our home and friends behind.

2 Away, away, we steer,
Upon the ocean's breast;
And dim the distant heights appear,
Like clouds along the west.

3 There is a loneliness
Upon the mighty deep;
And hurried thoughts upon us press,
As onwardly we sweep.

4 But there is hope and joy,
Wherever we may be;
Danger nor death can e'er destroy
Our trust, O God, in thee.

5 Then wherefore should we grieve,
Or what have we to fear?
Though home and friends and life we leave,
Our God is ever near.

6 Sweep, mighty ocean, sweep;
Ye winds, blow foul or fair;
Our God is with us on the deep,
Our home is everywhere.

SOCIAL AND DOMESTIC WORSHIP.

803. L. M. NEWTON

Meeting of Christian Friends.

1 KINDRED in Christ, for his dear sake,
A hearty welcome here receive;
May we together now partake
The joys which only he can give.

2 May he by whose kind care we meet,
Send his good Spirit from above,
Make our communications sweet,
And cause our hearts to burn with love.

3 Forgotten be each worldly theme,
When Christians meet together thus;
We only wish to speak of him
Who lived, and died, and reigns, for us

4 We 'll talk of all he did, and said,
And suffered, for us here below,
The path he marked for us to tread,
And what he 's doing for us now.

804. C. M. Ancient Hymns

The Joy of social Devotion.

1 O, IT is joy in one to meet
Whom one communion blends,
Council to hold in converse sweet,
And talk as Christian friends.

2 'T is joy to think the angel train,
Who 'mid heaven's temple shine,
To seek our earthly temples deign,
And in our anthems join.

3 But chief 't is joy to think that He,
To whom his church is dear,
Delights her gathered flock to see,
Her joint devotions hear.

4 Then who would choose to walk abroad,
While here such joys are given?
"This is indeed the house of God,
And this the gate of heaven!"

805. 7s. M. Wesleyan.

Call to social Worship.

1 LET us join, as God commands,
Let us join our hearts and hands;
Help to gain our calling's hope;
Help to build each other up;
Carry on the Christian's strife;
Walk in holiness of life;
Faithfully our gifts improve
For the sake of him we love; —

2 Still forget the things behind;
Follow Christ in heart and mind;

Toward the mark unwearied press
Seize the crown of righteousness.
While we walk with God in light,
God our hearts will still unite;
Dearest fellowship we prove, —
Fellowship in Jesus' love.

3 Hence may all our actions flow,
Love the proof that Christ we know;
Mutual love the token be,
Lord, that we belong to thee;
Love, thine image, love impart;
Stamp it on our face and heart;
Only love to us be given;
Lord, we ask no other heaven.

806. C. M. ANCIENT HYMN

Call to Social Worship.

1 O, COME, and let th' assembly all
To serve our God unite,
And, mindful of the social call,
Partake the social rite.

2 In token of the common vow,
Be ours, with one consent,
The worship of the lowly brow,
And knees devoutly bent!

3 But chief, inflamed with heavenly fire,
Devotion's better part,
Be ours instinct with one desire,
The worship of the heart!

4 Let each, let all, their prayers above
In one oblation blend,
And God, the God of peace and love,
On all, on each descend!

807. 7s. M. NEWTON.

Love of social Worship.

1 AS the sun's enlivening eye
Shines on every place the same ;
So the Lord is always nigh
To the souls that love his name.

2 When they move at duty's call,
He is with them by the way ;
He is ever with them all,
Those who go and those who stay.

3 From his holy mercy-seat
Nothing can their souls confine ;
Still in spirit they may meet,
And in sweet communion join.

808. S. M. WESLEYAN.

Call to Labor in God's Vineyard.

1 THE vineyard of the Lord
Before his laborers lies ;
And, lo ! we see the vast reward
Which waits us in the skies.

2 O, let us then proceed
In God's great work below,
And, following our triumphant Head,
To further conquests go.

3 The church of the first-born,
We shall with them be blest,
And, crowned with endless joy, return
To our eternal rest.

4 Then spend our days beneath,
Toiling in cheerful hope ;
And fearless pass the vale of death,
And gain the mountain-top.

5 To gather home his own,
God shall his angels send,

And bid our bliss, on earth begun,
In deathless triumphs end.

809. C. M. REED.

Gratitude for Preservation.

1 COME, let us strike our harps afresh
To great Jehovah's name;
Sweet be the accents of our tongues
When we his love proclaim.

2 'T was by his bidding we were called
In pain a while to part;
'T is by his care we meet again,
And gladness fills our heart.

3 Blest be the hand that has preserved
Our feet from every snare,
And blest the goodness of the Lord,
Which to this hour we share.

4 O, may thy spirit's quickening power
Now sanctify our joy,
And warm our zeal in works of love
Our talents to employ.

5 Fast, fast our minutes fly away;
Soon shall our wanderings cease:
Then with our Father we shall dwell,
A family of peace.

810. 8 & 7s. M. (Peculiar.) PARTING GIFT

Hope of Meeting.

1 WHEN forced to part from those we love,
Though sure to meet to-morrow,
We still a painful anguish prove,—
We feel a pang of sorrow.

2 But who can e'er describe the tears
We shed when thus we sever,
If doomed to part for months, for years,—
To part perhaps for ever?

3 Yet, if our aims are fixed aright,
A sacred hope is given
Though here our prospects end in night,
We 'll meet again in heaven.

4 Then let us form those bonds above
Which time can ne'er dissever,
Since, parting in a Saviour's love,
We part to meet for ever.

811. 6 & 5s. M. (Peculiar.) SELECT HYMNS.

Reunion in Heaven.

1 WHEN shall we meet again ? —
Meet ne'er to sever ?
When will Peace wreath her chain
Round us for ever ?
Our hearts will ne'er repose
Safe from each blast that blows
In this dark vale of woes, —
Never, — no, never !

2 When shall love freely flow
Pure as life's river ?
When shall sweet friendship glow
Changeless for ever ?
Where joys celestial thrill,
Where bliss each heart shall fill,
And fears of parting chill
Never, — no, never !

3 Up to that world of light
Take us, dear Saviour ;
May we all there unite,
Happy for ever :
Where kindred spirits dwell,
There may our music swell,
And time our joys dispel
Never, — no, never !

4 Soon shall we meet again,
  Meet ne'er to sever;
Soon shall Peace wreath her chain
  Round us for ever:
Our hearts will then repose
Secure from worldly woes;
Our songs of praise shall close
  Never, — no, never!

812. C. M. WESLEY'S COLL

For mutual Edification.

1 HELP us to help each other, Lord,
  Each other's cross to bear;
Let each his friendly aid afford,
  And feel his brother's care.

2 Help us to build each other up;
  Our little stock improve;
Increase our faith, confirm our hope,
  And perfect us in love.

3 Up into thee, our living Head,
  Let us in all things grow,
Till thou hast made us free indeed,
  And spotless here below.

813. L. M. DODDRIDGE.

The Christian Farewell.

1 THY presence, everlasting God!
Wide o'er all nature spreads abroad;
Thy watchful eyes, which cannot sleep,
In every place thy children keep.

2 While near each other we remain,
Thou dost our lives and souls sustain;
When sep'rate, happy if we share
Thy smiles, thy counsels, and thy care.

3 To thee we all our ways commit,
And seek our comforts near thy feet;

Still on our souls vouchsafe to shine,
And guard and guide us still as thine.

4 Give us, in thy belovéd house,
Again to pay our grateful vows ;
Or, if that joy no more be known,
Give us to meet around thy throne.

814. L. M. HEBER.

" Why stand ye idle here ?"

1 THE God of glory walks his round,
From day to day, from year to year,
And warns us each, with awful sound,
" No longer stand ye idle here !

2 " Ye, whose young cheeks are rosy-bright,
Whose hands are strong, whose hearts are clear,
Waste not of hope the morning light !
Ah, fools ! why stand ye idle here ?

3 " O, if the griefs ye would assuage
That wait on life's declining year,
Secure a blessing for your age,
And work your Master's business here !

4 " And ye, whose locks of scanty gray
Foretell your latest travail near,
How swiftly fades your worthless day !
And stand ye yet so idle here ? "

5 O Thou, by all thy works adored,
To whom the sinner's soul is dear,
Recall us to thy vineyard, Lord,
And grant us grace to please thee here !

815. C. M. MILTON

The Blessedness of the Devout.

1 HOW lovely are thy dwellings, Lord,
From noise and trouble free ;
How beautiful the sweet accord
Of souls that pray to thee.

2 Lord God of hosts, that reign'st on high,
  They are the truly blest,
Who only will on thee rely,
  In thee alone will rest.

3 They pass refreshed the thirsty vale,
  The dry and barren ground,
As through a fruitful, watery dale,
  Where springs and showers abound.

4 They journey on from strength to strength,
  With joy and gladsome cheer,
Till all before our God at length
  In Zion do appear.

5 For God, the Lord, both sun and shield,
  Gives grace and glory bright;
No good from him shall be withheld
  Whose ways are just and right.

816. C. M. WATTS.

Effects of the Mission of Christ.

1 JOY to the world! the Lord is come!
  Let earth receive her King;
Let every heart prepare him room,
  And heaven and nature sing.

2 Joy to the earth! the Saviour reigns!
  Let men their songs employ;
While fields, and floods, rocks, hills, and plains
  Repeat the sounding joy.

3 No more let sins and sorrows grow,
  Nor thorns infest the ground;
He comes to make his blessings flow
  As far as sin is found.

4 He rules the world with truth and grace,
  And makes the nations prove
The glories of his righteousness,
  And wonders of his love.

817. 7s. M. ANONYMOUS.

For a Prayer Meeting.

1 FATHER, hear us when we pray,
Look in mercy from above;
Turn not, Lord, thy face away,
Hear, and grant thy pardoning love.

2 In the name of Christ we come,
Asking grace and seeking peace,
Raise our hearts to heaven, our home,
And from worldly cares release.

3 Pure and holy may we be,
Far removed all vain desire;
From all hate and envy free,
Let our souls to thee aspire.

4 While we love the Saviour's name,
And his words with zeal obey,
His sweet promise we may claim;—
"He will meet us when we pray."

818. S. M. SACRED LYRICS

Morning Prayer Meeting.

1 HOW sweet the melting lay,
Which breaks upon the ear,
When, at the hour of rising day,
Christians unite in prayer!

2 The breezes waft their cries
Up to Jehovah's throne;
He listens to their humble sighs,
And sends his blessings down.

3 So Jesus rose to pray
Before the morning light,—
Once on the chilling mount did stay,
And wrestle all the night.

4 Glory to God on high,
Who sends his blessings down

To rescue souls condemned to die,
And make his people one.

819. 7s. M. 6 L. SPIRITUAL SONGS

Close of a Prayer Meeting.

1 O, 'T IS sweet to mingle where
Christians meet for social prayer;
O, 't is sweet for them to raise
Songs of holy joy and praise;
Then how blest that state must be,
When they meet eternally.

2 Father, let these meetings prove
Scenes of fervent Christian love;
While we worship in this place
May we go from grace to grace,
Till we each, in his degree,
Fit for endless glory be.

820. 7s. M. WILLARD'S COLL.

Peacemakers are Children of God.

1 LO! they come from east and west;
Come t' enjoy the heavenly rest:
North and south, in bliss complete,
Round th' eternal altar meet.

2 Countless host! how great! how blest!
Wondrous joy, and peace, and rest!
What shall fit us, Lord, for this?
Fit our souls for heavenly bliss?

3 Peace on earth, and peace alone;
Peace, which makes all churches one;
Peace, the fruit of Christian love,
Fits the soul for peace above.

821. 8 & 7s. M. C. WESLEY

Domestic Worship.

1 PEACE be to this habitation;
Peace to all that dwell therein,

Peace, the earnest of salvation ;
  Peace, the fruit of pardoned sin ;
Peace, that speaks the heavenly Giver ;
  Peace to worldly minds unknown ;
Peace divine, that lasts for ever ;
  Peace, that comes from God alone.

2 Jesus, Prince of Peace, be near us ;
  Fix in all our hearts thy home ;
With thy gracious presence cheer us ;
  Let thy sacred kingdom come ;
Raise to heaven our expectation,
  Give our favored souls to prove
Glorious and complete salvation,
  In the realms of bliss above.

822. C. M. ANCIENT HYMNS

Social Evening Worship.

1 O, 'T IS a scene the heart to move,
  When, at the close of day,
Whom God unites in Christian love
  Unite their thanks to pay.

2 What though the number be but small ;
  Whenever two or three
Join on the Saviour's name to call,
  There in the midst is he.

3 When faithful and repentant hearts
  His heavenly grace ensue,
His grace, entreated, he imparts
  To many or to few.

4 O, come, then, and with joint accord
  In social worship meet ;
And, mindful of the Saviour's word,
  The Saviour's boon entreat.

823. 7s. M. 6 L. ANCIENT HYMNS

Commendatory of social Worship.

1 EVER sounds with holy hymns
The abode of saints on high,
Echoing to the seraphim's
Holy, holy, holy cry:
Joining that great psalm of praise,
We our humbler voices raise.

2 O'er our temple, Lord of all,
Thy benignant light extend;
Here be present at our call;
Here thy people's vows attend;
And our fainting souls imbue,
Father, with thy heavenly dew.

3 Here may still the meek request
Of the faithful heart obtain
Foretaste of those mansions blest,
Visions bright of glory gain,
Till, from bonds corporeal free,
We those blissful mansions see.

824. L. M. COWPER

For social Worship.

1 OUR God, where'er thy people meet,
There they behold thy mercy-seat;
Where'er they seek thee, thou art found,
And every place is hallowed ground.

2 For thou, within no walls confined,
Inhabitest the humble mind;
Such ever bring thee where they come,
And, going, take thee to their home.

3 Here may we prove the power of prayer
To strengthen faith, and sweeten care;
To teach our faint desires to rise,
And bring all heaven before our eyes.

4 Lord, we are few but thou art near;
Nor short thine arm, nor deaf thine ear:
O, rend the heavens, come quickly down,
And make a thousand hearts thine own!

825. L. M. S. S. Cutting

Family Hymn. Evening.

1 FATHER, we bless the gentle care
That watches o'er us day by day,
That guards us from the tempter's snare,
And guides us in the heavenward way: —
We bless thee for the tender love,
That mingles all our hearts in one, —
The music of the soul; — above
'T is purer spirits' unison.

2 Father, 't is evening's solemn hour,
And cast we now our cares on thee;
Darkly the storm may round us lower, —
Peace is within, — Christ makes us free, —
And when life's toil and joy are o'er,
And evening gathers on its sky,
Our circle broke, – we sing no more, —
O, may we meet and sing on high.

826. L. M. 6 L. Methodist Col.

Religion at Home.

1 WHEN quiet in my house I sit,
Thy book be my companion still;
My joy thy sayings to repeat,
Talk o'er the records of thy will,
And search the oracles divine,
Till every heart-felt word be mine.

2 O, may the gracious words divine
Subject of all my converse be;
So will the Lord his follower join,
And walk and talk himself with me;

So shall my heart his presence prove,
And burn with everlasting love.

3 Oft as I lay me down to rest,
O, may the reconciling word
Sweetly compose my weary breast,
While, trusting in my gracious Lord,
I sink in peaceful dreams away,
And visions of eternal day !

4 Rising to sing my Father's praise,
Thee may I publish all day long ;
And let thy precious word of grace
Flow from my heart and fill my tongue ;
Fill all my life with purest love,
And join me to the church above.

827. C. M. WATTS.

Christian Union.

1 LO ! what an entertaining sight
Those friendly brethren prove,
Whose cheerful hearts in bands unite
Of harmony and love !

2 Where streams of bliss from Christ, the spring,
Descend to every soul,
And heavenly peace, with balmy wing,
Shades and bedews the whole.

3 'T is pleasant as the morning dews
That fall on Zion's hill,
Where God his mildest glory shows,
And makes his grace distil.

828. C. M. ANONYMOUS.

The Love of the Brethren.

1 A HOLY air is breathing round,
A savor from above ;
Be every soul from sense unbound,
Be every spirit love.

2 O God, unite us heart to heart,
In sympathy divine,
That we be never drawn apart,
And love nor thee nor thine.

3 But, by the cross of Jesus taught,
And all thy gracious word,
Be nearer to each other brought,
And nearer to our Lord.

829. H. M. Wesley's Coll

Parting to meet again.

1 NOW, Lord, we part a while;
But, still in spirit joined,
Embrace the happy toil
Thou hast to each assigned;
And while we do thy blessèd will,
We bear our heaven about us still.

2 O, let us then go on
In all thy pleasant ways;
And, armed with patience, run
With joy th' appointed race:
Keep us, and every seeking soul,
Till all attain the heavenly goal.

3 There we shall meet again,
When all our toils are o'er,
And death, and grief, and pain,
And parting are no more, —
In the new earth and heaven above,
The world of righteousness and love,

830. L. M. R. Palmer.

Self-Consecration. *Altered, See Appendix*

1 O, SWEETLY breathe the lyres above,
When angels touch the quivering string,
And wake, to chant the Father's love,
Such strains as angel lips can sing.

2 And sweet, on earth, the choral swell,
From mortal tongues, of gladsome lays;
When pardoned souls their raptures tell,
And, grateful, hymn the Saviour's praise.

3 Great God, thy name our souls adore;
We own the bond that makes us thine;
And earthly joys, that charmed before,
For Christ, our Saviour, we resign.

4 Our hearts, by dying love subdued,
Accept thine offered grace to-day;
Beneath the cross, with souls renewed,
We bow, and own thy gracious sway.

5 In thee we trust, — on thee rely;
Though we are feeble, thou art strong;
O, keep us till our spirits fly
To join the bright, immortal throng.

831. C. M. MONTGOMERY

Resignation.

1 ONE prayer I have, — all prayers in one, —
When I am wholly thine;
Thy will, my God, thy will be done,
And let that will be mine.

2 All-wise, almighty, and all-good,
In thee I firmly trust;
Thy ways, unknown or understood,
Are merciful and just.

3 May I remember that to thee
Whate'er I have I owe;
And back, in gratitude, from me
May all thy bounties flow.

4 Thy gifts are only then enjoyed,
When used as talents lent;
Those talents only well employed
When in thy service spent.

5 And though thy wisdom takes away,
Shall I arraign thy will?
No, let me bless thy name, and say,
"The Lord is gracious still."

6 A pilgrim through the earth I roam,
Of nothing long possessed,
And all must fail when I go home,
For this is not my rest.

832. L. M. ANONYMOUS

"With his stripes we are healed."

1 A VOICE upon the midnight air,
Where Kedron's moonlit waters stray,
Weeps forth in agony and prayer,
"O Father, take this cup away!"

2 Ah! thou who sorrow'st unto death,
We conquer in thy mortal fray;
And earth for all her children saith,
"O God, take not this cup away!"

3 O Lord of sorrow, meekly die;
Thou 'lt heal or hallow all our woe;
Thy name refresh the mourner's sigh;
Thy peace revive the faint and low.

4 Great Chief of faithful souls, arise;
None else can lead the martyr band,
Who teach the brave how peril flies,
When faith, unarmed, uplifts the hand

5 O King of earth, the cross ascend;
O'er climes and ages, 't is thy throne
Where'er thy fading eye may bend,
The desert blooms and is thine own.

6 Thy parting blessing, Lord, we pray;
Make but one fold below, above;
And when we go the last, lone way,
O, give the welcome of thy love!

833. C. M. T. Moore.

Divine Consolations.

1 O THOU who driest the mourner's tear,
How dark this world would be,
If, when deceived and wounded here,
We could not fly to thee!

2 But thou wilt heal that broken heart,
Which like the plants that throw
Their fragrance from the wounded part,
Breathes sweetness out of woe.

3 When joy no longer soothes or cheers,
And e'en the hope that threw
A moment's sparkle o'er our tears
Is dimmed and vanished too;

4 O, who would bear life's stormy doom,
Did not thy wing of love
Come, brightly wafting through the gloom
Our peace-branch from above?

5 Then sorrow, touched by thee, grows bright
With more than rapture's ray;
The darkness shows us worlds of light
We never saw by day.

MORNING AND EVENING.

834. 7s. M. Episcopal Coll

Morning Hymn.

1 NOW the shades of night are gone,
Now the morning light is come;
Lord, may we be thine to-day,
Drive the shades of sin away.

2 Fill our souls with heavenly light,
Banish doubt, and clear our sight;

In thy service, Lord, to-day,
May we stand, and watch and pray.

3 Keep our haughty passions bound;
Save us from our foes around;
Going out and coming in,
Keep us safe from every sin.

4 When our work of life is past,
O, receive us then at last;
Night and sin will be no more,
When we reach the heavenly shore.

835. S. M. DWIGHT

Morning Thanksgiving.

1 SERENE I laid me down,
Beneath his guardian care:
I slept, — and I awoke, and found
My kind Preserver near.

2 Thus does thine arm support
This weak, defenceless frame;
But whence these favors, Lord, to me,
All worthless as I am?

3 O, how shall I repay
The bounties of my God?
This feeble spirit pants beneath
The pleasing, painful load.

4 My life I would anew
Devote, O Lord, to thee;
And in thy service I would spend
A long eternity.

836. L. M. WATTS

A Morning Hymn.

1 GOD of the morning, at thy voice
The cheerful sun makes haste to rise,
And like a giant doth rejoice
To run his journey through the skies.

2 O, like the sun may I fulfil
Th' appointed duties of the day ,
With ready mind and active will
March on, and keep my heavenly way.

3 Lord, thy commands are clean and pure,
Enlightening our beclouded eyes ;
Thy threatenings just, thy promise sure;
Thy gospel makes the simple wise.

4 Give me thy counsels for my guide,
And then receive me to thy bliss ;
All my desires and hopes beside
Are faint and cold compared with this.

837. C. M. SACRED OFFERING.

Grateful Acknowledgment.

1 AGAIN, from calm and sweet repose,
I rise to hail the dawn ;
Again my waking eyes unclose,
To view the smiling morn.

2 Great God of love, thy praise I'll sing ;
For thou hast safely kept
My soul beneath thy guardian wing,
And watched me while I slept.

3 Glory to thee, Eternal Lord !
O, teach my heart to pray,
And thy blest Spirit's help afford,
To guide me through the day.

4 Let every thought and word accord
With thy most holy will ;
Each deed the precepts of thy word
With pious aim fulfil.

5 From danger, sin, and every ill,
My constant guardian prove ;
O, sanctify my heart, and fill
With thoughts of holy love.

838. L. M. KENN

A Morning Invocation.

1 AWAKE, my soul, and with the sun
Thy daily stage of duty run;
Shake off dull sloth, and joyful rise
To pay thy morning sacrifice.

2 Wake, and lift up thyself, my heart,
And with the angels bear thy part,
Who all night long unwearied sing
High praises to th' Eternal King.

3 Glory to thee, who safe hast kept,
And hast refreshed me while I slept:
Grant, Lord, when I from death shall wake,
I may of endless life partake.

4 Lord, I to thee my vows renew;
Dispel my sins as morning dew;
Guard my first springs of thought and will,
And with thyself my spirit fill.

5 Direct, control, suggest, this day,
All I design, or do, or say,
That all my powers, with true delight,
In thy sole glory may unite.

839. C. M. STEELE

Gratitude and Supplication.

1 GOD of my life, my morning song
To thee I cheerful raise:
Thine acts of love 't is good to sing,
And pleasant 't is to praise.

2 Preserved by thy almighty arm,
I passed the shades of night,
Serene, and safe from every harm,
To see the morning light.

3 While numbers spent the night in sighs,
And restless pains and woes,

In gentle sleep I closed my eyes,
And woke from sweet repose.

4 O, let the same almighty care
Through all this day attend ;
From every danger, every snare,
My heedless steps defend.

5 Smile on my minutes as they roll,
And guide my future days ;
And let thy goodness fill my soul
With gratitude and praise.

840. 8 & 7s. M. CARMINA SACRA

Sabbath Morning.

1 WHILE this day its light is shedding,
Worldly thoughts and cares forbidding,
Let us give our souls to rest ;
Let us now in supplication
Look to him whose great salvation
All the world has freely blest.

2 God above, we bow before thee ;
Humbly will we now adore thee ;
Glad we 'll haste to Zion's gate ;
Glad we 'll join those holy praises
Zion's temple ever raises
High to thee, so good and great.

3 Hail ! thou place of light and glory,
Where resounds salvation's story,
Fraught with peace to sinful man :
O, how soon earth's night retreated,
O, how soon sweet hope we greeted,
When thy word its course began !

841. L. M. HAWKESWORTH.

Morning Gratitude.

1 IN sleep's serene oblivion laid,
I safely passed the silent night ;

Again I see the breaking shade, —
I drink again the morning light.

2 New-born, I bless the waking hour,
Once more, with awe, rejoice to be ;
My conscious soul resumes her power,
And springs, my guardian God ! to thee

3 O, guide me through the various maze,
My doubtful feet may this day tread ;
And spread thy shield's protecting blaze,
Where dangers press around my head.

4 A deeper shade will soon impend, —
A deeper sleep mine eyes oppress ;
Yet then thy strength shall still defend, —
Thy goodness still delight to bless.

5 That deeper shade shall break away,
That deeper sleep shall leave mine eyes,
Thy light shall give eternal day,
Thy love the rapture of the skies.

842. C. M. Spirit of the Psalms

Goodness of God. Morning.

1 DELIGHTFUL is the task to sing,
On each returning day,
The praises of our Heavenly King,
And grateful homage pay.

2 The countless worlds, which, bathed in light,
Through fields of azure move,
Proclaim his wisdom and his might,
But, O, how great his love !

3 He deigns each broken, contrite heart
With tender care to bind ;
And comfort, hope, and grace impart
To heal the wounded mind.

4 All creatures with instinctive cry,
From God implore their food ;

His bounty grants a rich supply,
And fills the earth with good.

5 Delightful is the task, O Lord!
With each returning day
Thy countless mercies to record,
And grateful homage pay.

843. C. M. MONTGOMERY.

Acknowledging God's Hand. Morning.

1 WHAT secret hand, at morning light,
Softly unseals mine eye,
Draws back the curtain of the night,
And opens earth and sky;

2 'T is thine, my God,—the same that kept
My resting hours from harm;
No ill came nigh me, for I slept
Beneath th' Almighty's arm.

3 'T is thine, my daily bread that brings,
Like manna scattered round,
And clothes me, as the lily springs
In beauty from the ground.

4 In death's dark valley though I stray,
'T would there my steps attend,
Guide with the staff my lonely way,
And with the rod defend.

5 May that sure hand uphold me still
Through life's uncertain race,
To bring me to thy holy hill,
And to thy dwelling-place.

844. L. M. 6 L. CHRISTIAN PSALMIST.

Morning or Evening Hymn.

1 WHEN, streaming from the eastern skies,
The morning light salutes mine eyes,
O Sun of righteousness divine,
On me with beams of mercy shine;

Chase the dark clouds of sin away,
And turn my darkness into day.

2 As every day thy mercy spares
Will bring its trials or its cares,
O Father, till my life shall end,
Be thou my counsellor and friend ;
Teach me thy statutes all divine,
And let thy will be always mine.

3 When each day's scenes and labors close,
And wearied nature seeks repose,
With pardoning mercy, richly blest,
Guard me, my Father, while I rest ;
And as each morning sun shall rise,
O, lead me onward to the skies !

4 And at my life's last setting sun, —
My conflicts o'er, my labors done, —
Father, thine heavenly radiance shed,
To cheer and bless my dying bed ;
And from death's gloom my spirit raise,
To see thy face, and sing thy praise.

845. C. M. KIPPIS

Morning and Evening Praise.

1 ON thee, each morning, O my God,
My waking thoughts attend,
In whom are founded all my hopes,
In whom my wishes end.

2 My soul, in pleasing wonder lost,
Thy boundless love surveys,
And, fired with grateful zeal, prepares
The sacrifice of praise.

3 When evening slumbers press my eyes,
With thy protection blest,
In peace and safety I commit
My weary limbs to rest.

4 My spirit, in thy hands secure,
Fears no approaching ill;
For, whether waking or asleep,
Thou, Lord, art with me still.

5 Then will I daily to the world
Thy wondrous acts proclaim,
Whilst all with me shall praise and sing,
And bless thy sacred name.

6 At morn, at noon, at night, I 'll still
The pleasing work pursue,
And thee alone will praise, to whom
All praise is ever due.

846. P. M. H. WARE, JR

Prayer at Morning and Evening.

1 TO prayer, to prayer! for the morning breaks,
And earth in her Maker's smile awakes;
His light is on all below and above, —
The light of gladness, and life, and love.
O, then, on the breath of this early air,
Send upward the incense of grateful prayer.

2 To prayer! for the glorious sun is gone,
And the gathering darkness of night comes on;
Like a curtain from God's kind hand it flows,
To shade the couch where his children repose.
Then kneel, while the watching stars are bright,
And give your last thoughts to the Guardian of night.

847. L. M. WATTS.

Morning or Evening Song.

1 MY God, how endless is thy love!
Thy gifts are every evening new;
And morning mercies, from above,
Gently distil like early dew.

2 Thou spread'st the curtains of the night,
Great Guardian of my sleeping hours;
Thy sovereign word restores the light,
And quickens all my drowsy powers.

3 I yield my powers to thy command;
To thee I consecrate my days;
Perpetual blessings from thine hand
Demand perpetual songs of praise.

848. 7s. M. BOWRING

All from God. Morning or Evening.

1 FATHER! thy paternal care
Has my guardian been, my guide!
Every hallowed wish and prayer
Has thy hand of love supplied;
Thine is every thought of bliss,
Left by hours and days gone by;
Every hope thy offspring is,
Beaming from futurity.

2 Every sun of splendid ray;
Every moon that shines serene;
Every morn that welcomes day;
Every evening's twilight scene;
Every hour which wisdom brings;
Every incense at thy shrine;
These, — and all life's holiest things,
And its fairest, — all are thine.

3 And for all, my hymns shall rise
Daily to thy gracious throne:
Thither let my asking eyes
Turn unwearied, righteous One!
Through life's strange vicissitude
There reposing all my care,
Trusting still through ill and good,
Fixed, and cheered, and counselled the

849. L. M. KENN

Trusting God. Evening Hymn.

1 GLORY to thee, my God, this night,
For all the blessings of the light:
Keep me, O, keep me, King of kings,
Beneath the shadow of thy wings.

2 Forgive me, Lord, through thy dear Son,
The ills which I this day have done;
That with the world, myself, and thee,
I, ere I sleep, at peace may be.

3 Teach me to live that I may dread
The grave as little as my bed;
Teach me to die that so I may
With joy behold the judgment-day.

4 Be thou my guardian while I sleep;
Thy watchful station near me keep;
My heart with love celestial fill,
And guard me from th' approach of ill.

5 Lord, let my heart for ever share
The bliss of thy paternal care:
'T is heaven on earth, 't is heaven above,
To see thy face and sing thy love.

850. C. M. ANONYMOU

"I will be glad in the Lord."

1 WHEN morning's first and hallowed ray
Breaks with its trembling light,
To chase the pearly dews away, —
Bright tear-drops of the night, —

2 My heart, O Lord, forgets to rove
But rises, gladly free,
On wings of everlasting love,
And finds its home in thee.

3 When evening's silent shades descend,
And nature sinks to rest,

Still to my Father and my Friend
  My wishes are addressed.

4 And e'en when midnight's solemn gloom
  Above, around, is spread,
Sweet dreams of everlasting bloom
  Are hovering o'er my head.

5 I dream of that fair land, O Lord,
  Where all thy saints shall be;
I wake to lean upon thy word,
  And still delight in thee.

851. 8 & 7s. M. EDMESTON

Confidence in God's Protection.

1 FATHER, breathe an evening blessing
  Ere repose our spirits seal;
Sin and want we come confessing;
  Thou canst save and thou canst heal.

2 Though destruction walk around us,
  Though the arrows past us fly,
Angel guards from thee surround us;
  We are safe, if thou art nigh.

3 Though the night be dark and dreary,
  Darkness cannot hide from thee;
Thou art he who, never weary,
  Watchest where thy people be.

4 Should swift death this night o'ertake us,
  And command us to the tomb,
May the morn in heaven awake us,
  Clad in bright, eternal bloom.

852. 8 & 7s. M. FLINT

Evening Hymn.

1 ON the dewy breath of even
  Thousand odors mingling rise,
Borne like incense up to heaven, —
  Nature's evening sacrifice.

2 With her balmy offerings blending,
Let our glad thanksgivings be
To thy throne, O Lord, ascending, —
Incense of our hearts to thee.

3 Thou, whose favors without number
All our days with gladness bless!
Let thine eye, that knows not slumber,
Guard our hours of helplessness.

4 Then, though conscious we are sleeping
In the outer courts of death,
Safe beneath a Father's keeping,
Calm we rest in placid faith.

5 Lord! when life is closing round us,
Dark with anguish, faint with fear,
Let thy beams of love surround us,
Let us know thee, feel thee, near!

853. C. M. Bowring.

Nature's Evening Hymn.

1 THE heavenly spheres to thee, O God,
Attune their evening hymn:
All wise, all holy, thou art praised
In song of seraphim!
Unnumbered systems, suns, and worlds
Unite to worship thee,
While thy majestic greatness fills
Space, time, eternity.

2 Nature, — a temple worthy thee,
That beams with light and love;
Whose flowers so sweetly bloom below,
Whose stars rejoice above,
Whose altars are the mountain cliffs
That rise along the shore;
Whose anthems, the sublime accord
Of storm and ocean roar;

3 Her song of gratitude is sung
By spring's awakening hours;
Her summer offers at thy shrine
Its earliest, loveliest flowers;
Her autumn brings its ripened fruits,
In glorious luxury given;
While winter's silver heights reflect
Thy brightness back to heaven.

4 On all thou smil'st; and what is man
Before thy presence, God?
A breath but yesterday inspired,
To-morrow but a clod.
That clod shall mingle in the vale,
But, kindled, Lord, by thee,
The spirit to thy arms shall spring,
To life, to liberty.

854. 7s. M. Episcopal Coll

Communion with God.

1 SOFTLY now the light of day
Fades upon our sight away;
Free from care, from labor free,
Lord, we would commune with thee.

2 Soon for us the light of day
Shall for ever pass away;
Then, from sin and sorrow free,
Take us, Lord, to dwell with thee.

855. S. M. Curtis's Coll

Flight of Time.

1 ANOTHER day is past,
The hours for ever fled,
And time is bearing us away
To mingle with the dead.

2 Our minds in perfect peace
Our Father's care shall keep;

We yield to gentle slumber now,
For thou canst never sleep.

3 How blessèd, Lord, are they
On thee securely stayed!
Nor shall they be in life alarmed,
Nor be in death dismayed.

856. 7 & 6s. M. SACRED SONGS.

Reflections at Sunset.

1 THE mellow eve is gliding
Serenely down the west;
So, every care subsiding,
My soul would sink to rest.

2 The woodland hum is ringing
The daylight's gentle close;
May angels round me singing
Thus hymn my last repose.

3 The evening star has lighted
Her crystal lamp on high;
So, when in death benighted,
May hope illume the sky.

4 In golden splendor dawning,
The morrow's light shall break;
O, on the last bright morning
May I in glory wake.

857. 7s. M. 6 L HASTINGS

Repose and Devotion.

1 NOW from labor and from care
Evening-shades have set me free;
In the work of praise and prayer,
Lord! I would converse with thee:
O, behold me from above,
Fill me with a Saviour's love!

2 Sin and sorrow, guilt and woe,
Wither all my earthly joys;

Naught can charm me here below,
But my Saviour's melting voice :
Lord ! forgive, — thy grace restore,
Make me thine for evermore.

3 For the blessings of this day,
For the mercies of this hour,
For the gospel's cheering ray,
For thy Spirit's quickening power, —
Grateful notes to thee I raise ;
O, accept my song of praise !

858 S. M. CONDER.

Saturday Evening.

1 THE hours of evening close ;
Its lengthened shadows, drawn
O'er scenes of earth, invite repose,
And wait the Sabbath-dawn.

2 So let its calm prevail
O'er forms of outward care ;
Nor thought for "many things" assail
The still retreat of prayer.

3 Our guardian Shepherd near
His watchful eye will keep ;
And, safe from violence and fear,
Will fold his flock to sleep.

4 So may a holier light
Than earth's our spirits rouse,
And call us, strengthened by his might,
To pay the Lord our vows.

859. L. M. 6 L. PRATT'S COLL

Saturday Evening.

1 SWEET is the last, the parting ray,
Which ushers placid evening in ;
When, with the still, expiring day,
The Sabbath's peaceful hours begin :

How grateful to the anxious breast
The sacred hours of holy rest!

2 Hushed is the tumult of the day,
And worldly cares and business cease,
While soft the vesper-breezes play,
To hymn the glad return of peace:
Delightful season! kindly given
To turn the wandering thoughts to heaven.

3 Oft as this peaceful hour shall come,
Lord! raise my thoughts from earthly things
And bear them to my heavenly home,
On faith and hope's celestial wings;
Till the last gleam of life decay,
In one eternal Sabbath day.

860. 8 & 7s. M. 6 L. KELLY

An Evening Offering.

1 THROUGH the day thy love has spared us.
Now we lay us down to rest;
Through the silent watches guard us,
Let no foe our peace molest;
Father, thou our guardian be;
Sweet it is to trust in thee.

2 Pilgrims here on earth and strangers,
Dwelling in the midst of foes, —
Us and ours preserve from dangers,
In thine arms let us repose,
And, when life's short day is past,
Rest with thee in heaven at last.

861. L. M. W. H. BURLEIGH.

A Psalm of Night.

1 DAY unto day doth utter speech,
And night to night thy voice makes known;
Through all the earth, where thought may reach,
Is heard the glad and solemn tone;

And worlds beyond the farthest star
  Whose light hath reached the human eye,
Catch the high anthem from afar,
  That rolls along immensity.

2 O Holy Father, 'mid the calm
  And stillness of the evening hour,
We, too, would lift our solemn psalm
  To praise thy goodness and thy power;
For over us, as over all,
  Thy tender mercies still extend,
Nor vainly shall the contrite call
  On thee, their Father and their Friend

862. L. M. BOWRI

The Blessing of Sleep.

1 REVIVING sleep! thy sheltering wing
  Is o'er the couch of labor spread;
Sweet minister, unearthly thing,
  That hovers round the tired one's head.

2 As calm and cold as mortal clay
  When life is fled, earth soundly sleeps,
When evening veils the eye of day,
  And darkness rules the ocean deeps.

3 O, then, thy spirit, Lord, anew
  Enkindles strength in sleeping men;
It falls as falls the evening dew,
  And life's sad waste repairs again.

4 Be nature's gentle slumbers mine;
  And lead me gently to the last,
Until I hear thy voice divine,
  "Awake! for death's dark night is passed."

863. L. M. KENN

Midnight.

1 MY God, I now from sleep awake;
  The sole possession of me take;

From midnight terrors me secure,
And guard my heart from thoughts impure.

2 Blest angels, while we silent lie,
You hallelujahs sing on high;
You joyful hymn the Ever-blest,
Before the throne, and never rest.

3 I with your choir celestial join,
In offering up a hymn divine;
With you in heaven I hope to dwell,
And bid the night and world farewell.

4 O, may I always ready stand,
With my lamp burning in my hand;
May I in sight of heaven rejoice,
Whene'er I hear the Bridegroom's voice

5 Blest Jesus, thou, on heaven intent,
Whole nights hast in devotion spent;
But I, frail creature, soon am tired,
And all my zeal is soon expired.

6 Shine on me, Lord, new life impart,
Fresh ardors kindle in my heart;
One ray of thy all-quickening light
Dispels the sloth and clouds of night

864. L. M.

Evening Hymn.

1 THUS far the Lord has led me on,
Thus far his power prolongs my days!
And every evening shall make known
Some fresh memorial of his grace.

2 Much of my time has run to waste,
And I, perhaps, am near my home;
But he forgives my follies past,
He gives me strength for days to come.

3 I lay my body down to sleep;
Peace is the pillow for my head:

While well appointed angels keep
  Their watchful stations round my bed.

4 Faith in his name forbids my fear :
  O, may thy presence ne'er depart !
And in the morning make me hear
  Thy love and kindness in my heart.

5 And when the night of death shall come,
  Still may I trust almighty love, —
The love which triumphs o'er the tomb,
  And leads to perfect bliss above.

MISCELLANEOUS.

865. C. M. West Boston Coll

The Christian encouraged in Sickness.

1 O, THERE 'S a better world on high ;
  Hope on, thou pious breast ;
Faint not, thou traveller ; on the sky
  Thy weary feet shall rest.

2 Anguish may rend each vital part ;
  Poor man, thy strength how frail !
Yet Heaven's own strength shall shield thy heart,
  When flesh and heart shall fail.

3 Through death's dark vale, of deepest shade,
  Thy feet must surely go ;
Yet there, e'en there, walk undismayed ;
  'T is thy last scene of woe.

4 Thy God — and with the tenderest hand —
  Shall guard the traveller through ;
" Hail ! " shalt thou cry ; " hail ! promised land !
  And, wilderness, adieu ! "

5 O Father, make our souls thy care,
  And bring us safe to thee ;

Where'er thou art, — we ask not where, —
But there t' is heaven to be.

866. C. M. ANONYMOUS

The Widow's Prayer.

1 THOUGH faint and sick, and worn away
With poverty and woe,
My widowed feet are doomed to stray
'Mid thorny paths below, —

2 Be thou, O Lord, my Father still,
My confidence and guide ;
I know that perfect is thy will,
Whate'er that will decide.

3 I know the soul that trusts in thee
Thou never wilt forsake ;
And though a bruiséd reed I be,
That reed thou wilt not break.

4 Then keep me, Lord, where'er I go,
Support me on my way,
Though, worn with poverty and woe,
My widowed footsteps stray.

5 To give my weakness strength, O God,
Thy staff shall yet avail ;
And, though thou chasten with thy rod,
That staff shall never fail.

867. C. M. HEBER

In Times of Distress and Danger.

1 O GOD, that mad'st the earth and sky,
The darkness and the day,
Give ear to this thy family,
And help us when we pray !
For wide the waves of bitterness
Around our vessel roar,
And heavy grows the pilot's heart,
To view the rocky shore.

2 The cross our Master bore for us,
For him we fain would bear;
But mortal strength to weakness turns,
And courage to despair!
Then mercy on our failings, Lord!
Our sinking faith renew!
And, when his sorrows visit us,
O, send his patience too!

868. L. M. Rippon's Coll

On the dangerous Sickness of a Minister.

1 O THOU, before whose gracious throne
We bow our suppliant spirits down,
Thou know'st the anxious cares we feel,
And all our trembling lips would tell.

2 Thou only canst assuage our grief,
And give our sorrowing hearts relief:
In mercy, then, thy servant spare,
Nor turn aside thy people's prayer.

3 Avert thy desolating stroke,
Nor smite the shepherd of the flock;
Restore him, sinking to the grave,
Stretch out thine arm, make haste to save.

4 Bound to each soul by tender ties,
In every heart his image lies;
Thy pitying aid, O God, impart,
Nor rend him from each bleeding heart.

5 But if our supplications fail,
And prayers and tears cannot prevail,
Be thou his strength and thou his stay,
Through death's dark vale to endless day.

869. C. M. M. W. Hale

The Pure Heart.

1 WHATEVER dims thy sense of truth,
Or stains thy purity,

Though light as breath of summer air,
  Count it as sin to thee.

2 Preserve the tablet of thy thoughts
  From every blemish free,
While the Redeemer's lowly faith
  Its temple makes with thee.

3 And pray of God, that grace be given
  To tread time's narrow way :—
How dark soever it may be,
  It leads to cloudless day.

870. L. M. PEABODY.

The Religious Influences of Nature.

1 GOD of the rolling orbs above,
  Thy name is written clearly bright
In the warm day's unvarying blaze,
  Or evening's golden shower of light:
For every fire that fronts the sun,
  And every spark that walks alone
Around the utmost verge of heaven,
  Were kindled at thy burning throne.

2 God of the world, the hour must come,
  And nature's self to dust return;
Her crumbling altars must decay;
  Her incense-fires shall cease to burn:
But still her grand and lovely scenes
  Have made man's warmest praises flow,
For hearts grow holier as they trace
  The beauty of the world below.

871. C. M. R. NICOLL.

The Protestant Reformation.

1 AN offering at the shrine of power
  Our hands shall never bring;
A garland on the car of pomp
  Our hands shall never fling;

Applauding in the conqueror's path
Our voices ne'er shall be ;
But we have hearts to honor those
Who bade the world go free.

2 Praise to the good, the pure, the great,
Who made us what we are !
Who lit the flame, which yet shall glow
With radiance brighter far.
Glory to them in coming time,
And through eternity,
Who burst the captive's galling chains,
And bade the world go free.

872. 6s. M. LUTHER.

The Death of Martyrs.

1 FLUNG to the heedless winds,
Or on the waters cast,
Their ashes shall be watched,
And gathered at the last ;
And from that scattered dust,
Around us and abroad,
Shall spring a plenteous seed
Of witnesses for God.

2 The Father hath received
Their latest living breath ;
Yet vain is Satan's boast
Of victory in their death :
Still, still, though dead, they speak,
And, trumpet-tongued, proclaim
To many a wakening land
The one availing name.

873. 7s. M. BULFINCH.

"The Dayspring from on High."

1 TOILING through the livelong night,
Faint, uncertain of his way,

How the traveller hails the light,
Herald of the coming day.

2 Thus, when fraud and rapine threw
O'er the world their cloud afar,
On the good man's raptured view
Broke the dawn of Judah's star.

3 Tears of joy and gratitude
Hailed the Baptist's natal morn,
For the heavenly light renewed,
For another prophet born.

4 Born to go before the face
Of Judea's Saviour-king;
Tidings of celestial grace
To the mourning land to bring.

5 Thus began the song of praise
For the dayspring's earliest ray;
How should we the anthem raise
For the gospel's perfect day!

874. C. M. CARTER

In a Thunder-storm.

1 LET coward guilt, with pallid fear,
To sheltering caverns fly,
And justly dread the vengeful fate,
That thunders through the sky.

2 Protected by that hand whose law
The threatening storms obey,
Intrepid virtue smiles secure
As in the blaze of day.

3 In the thick cloud's tremendous gloom,
The lightning's lurid glare,
It views the same all-gracious Power,
That breathes the vernal air.

4 When through creation's vast expanse
The last dread thunders roll,

Untune the concord of the spheres,
And shake the guilty soul ;
5 Unmoved may we the final storm
Of jarring worlds survey,
That ushers in the tranquil morn
Of life's eternal day.

875. L. M. H. M. Williams.

God seen in All.

1 MY God ! all nature owns thy sway ;
Thou giv'st the night and thou the day :
When all thy loved creation wakes,
When morning, rich in lustre, breaks,
And bathes in dew the opening flower,
To thee we owe her fragrant hour ;
And when she pours her choral song,
Her melodies to thee belong.
2 Or when, in paler tints arrayed,
The evening slowly spreads her shade,
That soothing shade, that grateful gloom,
Can, more than day's enlivening bloom,
Still every fond and vain desire,
And calmer, purer thoughts inspire ;
From earth the pensive spirit free,
And lead the softened heart to thee.
3 In every scene thy hands have dressed,
In every form by thee impressed,
Upon the mountain's awful head,
Or where the sheltering woods are spread ;
In every note that swells the gale,
Or tuneful stream that cheers the vale,
The cavern's depth, or echoing grove, —
A voice is heard of praise and love.
4 As o'er thy work the seasons roll,
And soothe, with change of bliss, the soul,

O, never may their smiling train
Pass o'er the human sense in vain !
But oft, as on their charms we gaze,
Attune the wandering soul to praise ;
And be the joys that most we prize
Those joys that from thy favor rise !

876. L. M. SIR HENRY WOTTON

A happy Life.

1 HOW happy is he born and taught,
Who serveth not another's will ;
Whose armor is his honest thought,
And simple truth his utmost skill !

2 Whose passions not his masters are,
Whose soul is still prepared for death,
Untied to this vain world by care
Of public fame or private breath ;

3 Who hath his life from rumors freed,
Whose conscience is his strong retreat ,
Whose state can neither flatterers feed,
Nor ruin make oppressors great ;

4 Who God doth late and early pray
More of his grace than gifts to lend ;
To crave for less and more obey,
Nor dare with Heaven's high will contend.

5 This man is freed from servile bands
Of hope to rise or fear to fall ;
Lord of himself, though not of lands,
And, having nothing, yet hath all.

877. 11s. M. MARIE DE FLEURY.

Kedron.

1 THOU sweet-gliding Kedron, by thy silver stream
Our Saviour would linger in moonlight's soft beam :
And by thy bright waters would oftentimes stray,
And lose in thy murmurs the toils of the day.

2 How damp were the vapors that fell on his head
How hard was his pillow, how humble his bed!
The angels, astonished, grew sad at the sight,
And followed their Master with solemn delight

3 O garden of Olivet! dear, honored spot!
The fame of thy wonders shall ne'er be forgot;
The theme most transporting to seraphs above,
The triumph of sorrow, the triumph of love.

878. C. M. H. Martineau

All Men are equal.

1 ALL men are equal in their birth,
Heirs of the earth and skies;
All men are equal when that earth
Fades from their dying eyes.

2 God meets the throngs who pay their vows
In courts that hands have made;
And hears the worshipper who bows
Beneath the plantain shade.

3 'T is man alone who difference sees,
And speaks of high and low,
And worships those, and tramples these,
While the same path they go.

4 O, let man hasten to restore
To all their rights of love;
In power and wealth exult no more;
In wisdom lowly move.

5 Ye great, renounce your earth-born pride,
Ye low, your shame and fear:
Live, as ye worship, side by side;
Your brotherhood revere.

879. L. M. Anonymous

Memory of the Past.

1 HOW blest is he whose tranquil mind,
When life declines, recalls again

The years that time has cast behind,
And reaps delight from toil and pain.

2 So, when the transient storm is past,
The sudden gloom and driving shower,
The sweetest sunshine is the last;
The loveliest is the evening hour.

880. 7 & 6s. M. (Peculiar.) METH. COLL.

Quiet Religion.

1 OPEN, Lord, my inward ear,
And bid my heart rejoice;
Bid my quiet spirit hear
The comfort of thy voice;
Never in the whirlwind found,
Or where earthquakes rock the place,
Still and silent is the sound,
The whisper of thy grace.

2 From the world of sin, and noise,
And hurry, I withdraw;
For the small and inward voice
I wait with humble awe;
Silent I am now and still,
Dare not in thy presence move;
To my waiting soul reveal
The secret of thy love.

881. C. M. J. J. GURNEY

Silent Worship.

1 LET deepest silence all around
Its peaceful shelter spread;
So shall the living word abound,
The word that wakes the dead.

2 How sweet to wait upon the Lord
In stillness and in prayer!
What though no preacher speak the word,
A minister is there.

3 He knows to bend the heart of steel,
He bows the loftiest soul ;
O'er all we think and all we feel,
How matchless his control !

4 And, O, how precious is his love,
In tender mercy given ;
It whispers of the blest above,
And stays the soul on heaven.

5 From mind to mind, in streams of joy,
The holy influence spreads ;
'T is peace, 't is praise without alloy,
For God that influence sheds.

6 To thee, O God, we still will pray,
And praise thee as before ;
For this thy glorious gospel-day,
Teach us to praise thee more.

882. 7 & 6s. M. HEBER

Marriage Hymn.

1 WHEN on her Maker's bosom
The new-born earth was laid,
And nature's opening blossom
Its fairest bloom displayed ;
When all with fruits and flowers
The laughing soil was dressed,
And Eden's fragrant bowers
Received their human guest, —

2 No sin his face defiling,
The heir of nature stood,
And God, benignly smiling,
Beheld that all was good.
Yet in that hour of blessing
A single want was known, —
A wish the heart distressing, —
For Adam was alone.

3 O God of pure affection,
By men and saints adored,
O, give us thy protection
Around this nuptial board;
May thy rich bounties ever
To wedded love be shown,
And no rude hand dissever
Whom thou hast linked in one.

883. C. M. L. H. Sigourney.

Marriage Hymn.

1 NOT for the summer's hour alone,
When skies resplendent shine,
And youth and pleasure fill the throne,
Our hearts and hands we join;

2 But for those stern and wintry days
Of sorrow, pain, and fear,
When Heaven's wise discipline doth make
Our earthly journey drear; —

3 Not for this span of life alone,
Which like a blast doth fly,
And as the transient flowers of grass
Just blossom, droop, and die; —

4 But for a being without end
This vow of love we take;
Grant us, O God, one home at last,
For thy great mercy's sake.

884. C. M. Anonymous.

For a Birthday

1 SWIFT as the wingéd arrow flies,
My time is hastening on;
Quick as the lightning from the skies,
My wasting moments run.

2 O, let thy spirit lead me still,
Along the happy road;

Conform me to thy holy will,
My Father and my God.

3 Another year of life is past ;
My heart to thee incline,
That if this year should be my last,
It may be wholly thine.

885. L. M. ANONYMOUS

Temperance Hymn.

1 GOD of our fathers, 't is thy hand
Hath turned the tide of death away,
That rolled in madness o'er the land,
And filled thy people with dismay.

2 Thy voice awaked us from our dream ;
Thy spirit taught our hearts to feel ;
'T was thy own light whose radiant beam
Came down our duty to reveal.

3 Almighty Parent, still in thee
Our spirits trust for strength divine ;
Gird us with heaven's own energy,
And o'er our paths let wisdom shine.

4 The work of man's destruction stay ;
The tide of fire still backward press ;
Drive each delusive mist away,
And every humble effort bless.

886. 6 & 4s. M. PIERPONT

Temperance Hymn.

1 LET the still air rejoice, —
Be every youthful voice
Blended in one :
While we renew our strain
To Him, with joy, again,
Who sends the evening rain,
And morning sun.

2 His hand in beauty gives
Each flower and plant that lives,
Each sunny rill ;
Springs ! which our footsteps meet, —
Fountains ! our lips to greet, —
Waters ! whose taste is sweet,
On rock and hill.

3 Each summer bird that sings
Drinks from dear Nature's springs
Her early dew ;
And the refreshing shower
Falls on each herb and flower,
Giving it life and power,
Fragrant and new.

4 So let each faithful child
Drink of this fountain mild,
From early youth ;
Then shall the song we raise
Be heard in future days, —
Ours be the pleasant ways
Of peace and truth.

5 Now let each heart and hand,
Of all this youthful band,
United, move !
Till on the mountain's brow,
And in the vale below,
Our land may ever glow
With peace and love.

887. S. M. M. W Hale

Temperance Anniversary.

1 PRAISE for the glorious light
Which crowns this joyous day ;
Whose beams dispel the shades of night,
And wake our grateful lay !

2 Praise for the mighty band,
Redeemed from error's chain,
Whose echoing voices, through our land,
Join our triumphant strain!

3 Ours is no conquest gained
Upon the tented field;
Nor hath the flowing life-blood stained
The victor's helm and shield.

4 But the strong might of love,
And truth's all-pleading voice,
As angels bending from above,
Have made our hearts rejoice.

5 Lord! upward to thy throne
Th' imploring voice we raise;
The might, the strength, are thine alone!
Thine be our loftiest praise.

888. 8, 7, & 4s. M. ANONYMOUS.

"It is finished!"

1 HARK! the voice of love and mercy
Sounds aloud from Calvary!
See! it rends the rocks asunder, —
Shakes the earth, — and veils the sky!
"It is finished!"
Hear the dying Saviour cry!

2 "It is finished!" — O, what pleasure
Do these sacred words afford!
Heavenly blessings, without measure,
Flow to us through Christ the Lord!
"It is finished!"
Saints, the dying words record!

3 Tune your harps anew, ye seraphs!
Join to sing the pleasing theme;

All in earth and heaven uniting,
  Join to praise Immanuel's name :
    Hallelujah !
  Glory to the bleeding Lamb !

889. P. M. NORTON.

He has gone to his God.

1 HE has gone to his God ; he has gone to his home
No more amid peril and error to roam ;
  His eyes are no longer dim ;
    His feet will no more falter ;
  No grief can follow him ;
    No pang his cheek can alter.

2 There are paleness and weeping and sighs below ;
For our faith is faint and our tears will flow ;
  But the harps of heaven are ringing ;
    Glad angels come to greet him,
  And hymns of joy are singing ;
    While old friends pass to meet him.

3 O, honored, belovéd, to earth unconfined,
Thou hast soared on high, thou 'st left us behind ;
  But our parting is not for ever,
    We will follow thee by heaven's light,
  Where the grave cannot dissever
    The souls whom God will unite.

890. 11s. M. CUNNINGHAM

"Are they not all ministering Spirits?"

1 HOW cheering the thought, that the spirits in bliss
Will bow their bright wings to a world such as this :
Will leave the sweet joys of the mansions above,
To breathe o'er our bosoms some message of love.

2 They come,—on the wings of the morning they come,—
Impatient to lead some poor wanderer home,
Some pilgrim to snatch from this stormy abode,
And lay him to rest in the arms of his God.

891. 11 & 10s. M. HEBER

Star of the East.

1 BRIGHTEST and best of the sons of the morning,
Dawn on our darkness and lend us thine aid;
Star of the East, — the horizon adorning, —
Guide where the infant Redeemer is laid.

2 Cold on his cradle the dew-drops are shining;
Low lies his head with the beasts of the stall;
Angels bend o'er him, in slumber reclining, —
Saviour, Redeemer, Restorer of all.

3 Say, shall we yield him, in costly devotion,
Odors of Edom, and offerings divine?
Gems of the mountain, and pearls of the ocean,
Myrrh from the forest, or gold from the mine?

4 Vainly we offer each ample oblation,
Vainly with gold would his favor secure;
Richer by far is the heart's adoration,
Dearer to God are the prayers of the poor.

5 Brightest and best of the sons of the morning,
Dawn on our darkness and lend us thine aid;
Star of the East, — the horizon adorning, —
Guide where the infant Redeemer is laid.

892. 6 & 10s. M. MILTON, GARDNER, AND DWIGHT

Peace.

1 NO war nor battle's sound
Was heard the earth around, —
No hostile chiefs to furious combat ran;
But peaceful was the night
In which the Prince of Light
His reign of peace upon the earth began.

2 No conqueror's sword he bore,
Nor warlike armor wore,
Nor haughty passions roused to contest wild;

In peace and love he came,
And gentle was the reign,
Which o'er the earth he spread by influence mild.
3 Unwilling kings obeyed,
And sheathed the battle blade,
And called their bloody legions from the field;
In silent awe they wait,
And close the warrior's gate,
Nor know to whom their homage thus they yield
4 The peaceful conqueror goes,
And triumphs o'er his foes,
His weapons drawn from armories above;
Behold the vanquished sit
Submissive at his feet,
And strife and hate are changed to peace and love.

893. P. M. HEMANS.

The Pilgrim Fathers.

1 THE breaking waves dashed high
On a stern and rock-bound coast,
And the woods against a stormy sky
Their giant branches tossed;
And the heavy night hung dark,
The hills and waters o'er,
When a band of exiles moored their bark
On the wild New England shore.

2 Not as the conqueror comes,
They, the true-hearted, came;
Not with the roll of the stirring drums,
And the trumpet that sings of fame;
Not as the flying come,
In silence and in fear;—
They shook the depths of the desert gloom
With their hymns of lofty cheer.

3 Amidst the storm they sang,
And the stars heard, and the sea!

And the sounding aisles of the dim woods rang
To the anthem of the free.
The ocean eagle soared
From his nest by the white wave's foam,
And the rocking pines of the forest roared, —
This was their welcome home.

4 What sought they thus afar ?
Bright jewels of the mine ?
The wealth of seas, the spoils of war ? —
They sought a faith's pure shrine !
Ay, call it holy ground,
The soil where first they trod !
They have left unstained what there they found, —
Freedom to worship God.

894. L. M. 6 L. MONTGOMERY.

Humility.

1 THE bird that soars on highest wing
Builds on the ground her lowly nest ;
And she that doth most sweetly sing
Sings in the shade when all things rest :-
In lark and nightingale we see
What honor hath humility.

2 When Mary chose the better part,
She meekly sat at Jesus' feet ;
And Lydia's gently opened heart
Was made for God's own temple meet :-
Fairest and best adorned is she
Whose clothing is humility.

3 The saint that wears heaven's brightest crown
In deepest adoration bends ;
The weight of glory bows him down
Then most when most his soul ascends : —
Nearest the throne itself must be
The footstool of humility.

895. C. M. H. Ware, Jr.

Praise to God.

1 ALL nature's works his praise declare
To whom they all belong;
There is a voice in every star,
In every breeze a song.

2 Sweet music fills the world abroad
With strains of love and power;
The stormy sea sings praise to God, —
The thunder and the shower.

3 To God the tribes of ocean cry,
And birds upon the wing;
To God the powers that dwell on high
Their tuneful tribute bring.

4 Like them let man the throne surround,
With them loud chorus raise,
While instruments of loftiest sound
Assist his feeble praise.

5 Great God, to thee we consecrate
Our voices and our skill;
We bid the pealing organ wait
To speak alone thy will.

6 O, teach its rich and swelling notes
To lift our souls on high;
And while the music round us floats,
Let earth-born passion die.

896. C. M. Newton

True and False Zeal.

1 ZEAL is that pure and heavenly flame
The fire of love supplies;
While that which often bears the name
Is self, in a disguise.

2 True zeal is merciful and mild,
Can pity and forbear;

The false is headstrong, fierce, and wild,
And breathes revenge and war.

3 While zeal for truth the Christian warms,
He knows the worth of peace ;
But self contends for names and forms,
Its party to increase.

4 Self may its poor reward obtain,
And be applauded here ;
But zeal the best applause will gain,
When Jesus shall appear.

5 O God, the idol self dethrone,
And from our hearts remove ;
And let no zeal by us be shown,
But that which springs from love.

897. C. M. NEWTON

" Unto you who believe he is precious."

1 HOW sweet the name of Jesus sounds
In a believer's ear !
It soothes his sorrows, heals his wounds,
And drives away his fear.

2 It makes the wounded spirit whole,
It calms the troubled breast ;
'T is manna to the hungry soul,
And, to the weary, rest.

3 Weak is the effort of my heart,
And cold my warmest thought,
But when I see thee as thou art,
I 'll praise thee as I ought.

4 Till then I would thy love proclaim
With every fleeting breath ;
And may the music of thy name
Refresh my soul in death.

898. L. M. STEELE.

Entire Consecration.

1 NOW I resolve with all my heart,
With all my powers, to serve the Lord:
Nor from his ways will I depart,
Whose service is a rich reward.

2 O, be his service all my joy!—
Around let my example shine,
Till others love the blest employ,
And join in labors so divine.

3 Be this the purpose of my soul,
My solemn, my decided choice,
To yield to his supreme control,
And in his kind commands rejoice.

4 O, may I never faint nor tire,
Nor, wandering, leave his sacred ways;
Great God, accept my soul's desire,
And give me strength to live thy praise.

899. L. M. DODDRIDGE

On joining the Church.

1 O HAPPY day, that fixed my choice
On thee, my Saviour and my Lord!
Well may this glowing heart rejoice,
And tell its raptures all abroad!

2 O happy bond, that seals my vows
To Him who merits all my love!
Let cheerful anthems fill the house,
While to his altar now I move.

3 Now rest, my long-divided heart;
Fixed on this blissful centre, rest;
Here have I found a nobler part;
Here heavenly pleasures fill my breast.

4 High Heaven, that hears the solemn vow,
That vow renewed shall daily hear;

Till in life's latest hour I bow,
And bless in death a bond so dear.

900. C. H. M. SACRED LYRICS.

The everlasting Bliss of Heaven.

1 HEAVEN is the land where troubles cease,
Where toils and tears are o'er ; —
The blissful clime of rest and peace,
Where cares distract no more ;
And not the shadow of distress
Dims its unsullied blessedness.

2 Heaven is the dwelling-place of joy,
The home of light and love,
Where faith and hope in rapture die,
And ransomed souls above
Enjoy, before th' eternal throne,
Bliss everlasting and unknown.

901. C. M. MONTGOMERY

Earth's broken Ties.

1 THE broken ties of happier days,
How often do they seem
To come before the mental gaze,
Like a remembered dream ;
Around us each dissevered chain
In sparkling ruin lies,
And earthly hand can ne'er again
Unite these broken ties.

2 O, who, in such a world as this,
Could bear their lot of pain,
Did not one radiant hope of bliss
Unclouded yet remain ?
That hope the sovereign Lord has given,
Who reigns above the skies ;
Hope that unites our souls to heaven,
By faith's endearing ties.

3 Each care, each ill of mortal birth,
Is sent in pitying love
To lift the lingering heart from earth,
And speed its flight above.
And every pang that wrings the breast,
And every joy that dies,
Tells us to seek a purer rest,
And trust to holier ties.

902. 7s. M. C. Wesley

The Christian's Death.

1 LO! the prisoner is released,
Lightened of his fleshly load;
Where the weary are at rest,
He is gathered unto God:
Lo! the pain of life is past,
And his warfare now is o'er;
Death and hell behind are cast,
Grief and suffering are no more.

2 Yes! the Christian's course is run,
Ended is the glorious strife;
Fought the fight, the crown is won,
Death is swallowed up of life;
Borne by angels on their wings,
Far from earth his spirit flies
To the Lord he loved, and sings
Triumphing in paradise.

3 Join we then with one accord
In the new and joyful song;
Absent from our glorious Lord
We shall not continue long;
We shall quit the house of clay,
Better joys with him to share;
We shall see the realms of day,
We shall meet our brethren there.

903. C. M. DODDRIDGE

Christian Ambition.

1 NOW let a true ambition rise,
And ardor fire our breast,
To reign in worlds above the skies,
In heavenly glories dressed.

2 Behold Jehovah's royal hand
A radiant crown display,
Whose gems with vivid lustre shine,
While suns and stars decay.

3 Ye hearts, with youthful vigor warm,
The glorious prize pursue ;
Nor shall ye want the goods of earth,
While heaven is kept in view.

904. L. M. HENRY MOORE

For Steadiness of Principle.

1 AMIDST a world of hopes and fears,
A wild of cares, and toils, and tears,
Where foes alarm, and dangers threat,
And pleasures kill, and glories cheat :

2 Shed down, O Lord ! a heavenly ray
To guide me in the doubtful way ;
And o'er me hold thy shield of power,
To guard me in the dangerous hour.

3 Teach me the flattering paths to shun,
In which the thoughtless many run,
Who for a shade the substance miss,
And grasp their ruin in their bliss.

4 May never pleasure, wealth, or pride
Allure my wandering soul aside ;
But, through this maze of mortal ill,
Safe lead me to thy heavenly hill.

905. C. M. KNOWLES

The Mourner comforted.

1 O, WEEP not for the joys that fade
Like evening lights away,
For hopes that, like the stars decayed,
Have left thy mortal day ;
The clouds of sorrow will depart,
And brilliant skies be given ;
For bliss awaits the holy heart,
Amid the bowers of heaven.

2 O, weep not for the friends that pass
Into the lonely grave,
As breezes sweep the withered grass
Along the restless wave ;
For though thy pleasures may depart,
And mournful days be given ;
Yet bliss awaits the holy heart,
When friends rejoin in heaven.

906. 8 & 7s. M. COWPER

Future Peace and Glory of the Church.

1 HEAR what God, the Lord, hath spoken :
O my people, faint and few,
Comfortless, afflicted, broken,
Fair abodes I build for you ;
Scenes of heartfelt tribulation
Shall no more perplex your ways ;
You shall name your walls salvation,
And your gates shall all be praise.

2 There, like streams that feed the garden,
Pleasures without end shall flow ;
For the Lord, your faith rewarding,
All his bounty shall bestow ;
Still in undisturbed possession
Peace and righteousness shall reign ;

Never shall you feel oppression,
Hear the voice of war again.

3 Ye, no more your suns descending,
Waning moons no more shall see;
But, your griefs for ever ending,
Find eternal noon in me;
God shall rise, and, shining o'er you,
Change to day the gloom of night;
He, the Lord, shall be your glory,
God your everlasting light.

907. C. M. S. F. Smith

The Departed.

1 WHEN spirits from their cumbering clay
Ascend to heaven's bright shore,
Our hoping hearts with triumph say, —
"Not lost, but gone before."

2 Then calmly may our spirits bow
Beneath affliction's rod;
Who, who would murmur that his friend
Is safe in joy and God?

908. H. M. Anonymous

Close of Service.

BY us the seed is sown, —
Thy blessing, Lord, bestow;
The power is thine alone
To make it spring and grow:
Do thou the gracious harvest raise,
And thou alone shalt have the praise.

APPENDIX.

The following hymns are here inserted as originally written bv the author, Rev. R. Palmer.

382. *Self-consecration.* 6. 4.

1 MY faith looks up to thee,
Thou Lamb of Calvary,
Saviour divine:
Now hear me while I pray;
Take all my guilt away;
O, let me from this day
Be wholly thine.

2 May thy rich grace impart
Strength to my fainting heart,
My zeal inspire;
As thou hast died for me,
O, may my love to thee
Pure, warm, and changeless be —
A living fire.

3 While life's dark maze I tread,
And griefs around me spread,
Be thou my guide;
Bid darkness turn to day,
Wipe sorrow's tears away,
Nor let me ever stray
From thee aside.

4 When ends life's transient dream,
When death's cold, sullen stream
Shall o'er me roll;
Bless'd Saviour, then, in love,
Fear and distress remove;
O, bear me safe above, —
A ransomed soul.

602. *Heavenly Rest.* S. M.

1 AND is there, Lord, a rest
For weary souls designed,
Where not a care shall stir the breast,
Or sorrow entrance find.

2 Is there a blissful home,
Where kindred minds shall meet,
And live, and love, nor ever roam
From that serene retreat?

3 Are there bright, happy fields,
Where nought that blooms shall die;
Where each new scene fresh pleasure yields,
And healthful breezes sigh?

4 Are there celestial streams,
Where living waters glide,
With murmurs sweet as angel dreams,
And flowery banks beside?

5 For ever blessed they,
Whose joyful feet shall stand,
While endless ages waste away,
Amid that glorious land.

6 My soul would thither tend,
While toilsome years are given;
Then let me, gracious God, ascend
To sweet repose in heaven.

830. *Self-consecration.* L. M.

1 O, sweetly breathe the lyres above,
When angels touch the quivering string,
And wake, to chant Immanuel's love,
Such strains as angel lips can sing

2 And sweet, on earth, the choral swell
From mortal tongues, of gladsome lays;
When pardoned souls their raptures tell,
And, grateful, hymn Immanuel's praise.

3 Jesus, — thy name our souls adore;
We own the bond that makes us thine;
And carnal joys, that charmed before,
For thy dear sake we now resign.

4 Our hearts, by dying love subdued,
Accept thine offered grace to-day;
Beneath the cross, with blood bedewed,
We bow, and give ourselves away.

5 In thee we trust, — on thee rely;
Though we are feeble, thou art strong
O, keep us till our spirits fly
To join the bright, immortal throng

www.ingramcontent.com/pod-product-compliance
Lightning Source LLC
LaVergne TN
LVHW021238110826
845150LV00002B/349